Stuarts' Field Guide
NATIONAL
NATURE R
of South Africa

Published in 2018 by Struik Nature
(an imprint of Penguin Random House South Africa (Pty) Ltd)
Company Reg. No. 1953/000441/07
The Estuaries No. 4, Oxbow Crescent, Century Avenue, Century City 7441
PO Box 1144, Cape Town 8000, South Africa

Visit **www.penguinrandomhouse.co.za** and join the Struik Nature Club
for updates, news, events and special offers.
Visit Chris & Mathilde Stuart on **www.stuartonnature.com**

First published by Struik Travel & Heritage 2012
Second edition 2018

10 9 8 7 6 5 4 3 2

Copyright © in text and maps, 2012, 2018: Chris Stuart, Mathilde Stuart
Copyright © in photographs, 2012, 2018: Chris Stuart, Mathilde Stuart and individual
photographers as listed on page 316
Copyright © in published edition, 2012, 2018: Penguin Random House South Africa (Pty) Ltd

Publisher: Pippa Parker
Managing editor: Helen de Villiers
Editors: Charles de Villiers, Colette Alves, Roelien Theron
Designers: Dominic Robson, Catherine Coetzer
Cover designers: Janice Evans, Neil Bester
Cartographers: Chris Stuart, Mathilde Stuart, Catherine Coetzer
Picture researcher: Colette Stott
Indexer: Anna Tanneberger
Proofreader: Roxanne Reid

Reproduction by Hirt & Carter Cape (Pty) Ltd
Printed and bound in China by RR Donnelley Asia Printing Solutions Ltd.

All rights reserved. No part of this publication may be reproduced, stored in a retrieval system
or transmitted, in any form or by any means, electronic, mechanical, photocopying, recording or
otherwise, without the prior written permission of the publishers and the copyright holder(s).

ISBN 978 1 77584 611 6 (Print)
ISBN 978 1 77584 612 3 (ePub)

While every effort has been made to ensure that the information in this book was correct at
the time of going to press, some details might since have changed. The authors and publishers
accept no responsibility for any consequences, loss, injury, damage or inconvenience sustained
by any person using this book.

Penguin Random House is committed to a sustainable future for
our business, our readers and our planet. This book is made from
Forest Stewardship Council ® certified paper.

Front cover: Game-viewing drive, Hluhluwe-iMfolozi Park
Half-title: Leopard
Title pages: Impala at waterhole, Kruger National Park

Acknowledgements

To compile a book of this nature, many information sources have to be consulted. In addition, we received help at different levels from many individuals and organisations while gathering information. We list these kind folk below and sincerely hope we have not overlooked anybody; should we have done so please accept our apologies.

We are grateful to the &Beyond team (**www.andbeyond.com**) – especially Valeri Mouton, Duncan Butchart, Charlene Bisset, Tim Vuyk, Paul Warner, Graham Vercueil, Kevin Pretorius, Marc Lindsay-Rae and Claire Lacey – for going out of their way to help us better understand the natural history of Phinda, Kwandwe and Madikwe, and for their hospitality.

We also want to thank Wayne Erlank (Baviaanskloof Wilderness Area, Eastern Cape Parks), Brad Fike, Ric Bernard, Dan Parker (Great Fish River Nature Reserve, Eastern Cape Parks), Warwick Tarboton (Nylsvley Nature Reserve), Wessel Pretorius (Oorlogskloof Nature Reserve, Northern Cape Nature Conservation), Jeanene Jessnitz (Witsand Nature Reserve, Northern Cape Tourism), Ian and Retha Gaigher (Western Soutpansberg Biosphere Reserve), Johan van Wyk (Blouberg Nature Reserve, Limpopo Tourism & Parks), Peter Burdett (Camdeboo National Park, SANParks), Annelise le Roux (Goegap Nature Reserve, Namaqua National Park, SANParks) and Deon Joubert (Mokala National Park, SANParks).

Guy Palmer of CapeNature helped with information on reserves within that organisation's control, and Arne Purves supplied mapping material for the Western Cape. Dr Helen de Klerk is thanked for facilitating contact with Arne.

Thanks to Dr Hugo Bezuidenhout and Peter Bradshaw (SANParks) for the use of their vegetation map of Mokala National Park; Conrad Strauss (Tankwa Karoo National Park, SANParks) for supplying additional information on the vegetation of the Tankwa Karoo National Park; and Sediqa Khatieb (Biodiversity GIS Project Manager, South African National Botanical Institute, Kirstenbosch) for assisting with the vegetation maps of the West Coast and the Tankwa Karoo national parks.

Our thanks are also due to Paul Skelton of the South African Institute for Aquatic Biodiversity in Grahamstown.

Finally, we would like to thank the staff at Penguin Random House, particularly Pippa Parker and Colette Alves who steered the book through its early phases, Claudia Dos Santos and Pippa Parker for ensuring the completion of the respective editions, Catherine Coetzer and Dominic Robson for their fine page design, and freelance editor Charles de Villiers for his meticulous editing. A special word of thanks goes to Roelien Theron who has gone out of her way to ensure that no errors or mistakes slipped through the cracks – a job well done.

Chris and Mathilde Stuart
www.stuartonnature.com

CONTENTS

Buffalo

Southern red-billed hornbill

Snouted cobra

Map	8
Introduction	10
How to use this book	12

Limpopo — 14
Kruger National Park	16
Mapungubwe National Park	26
Marakele National Park	33
Western Soutpansberg & Blouberg Nature Reserve	39
Nylsvley Nature Reserve	45

North West — 50
Pilanesberg Game Reserve	52
Madikwe Game Reserve	57

KwaZulu-Natal — 62
uKhahlamba-Drakensberg Park	64
Royal Natal Park	71
Weenen Game Reserve	75
Oribi Gorge Nature Reserve	80
Ithala Game Reserve	84
Hluhluwe-iMfolozi Park	89
iSimangaliso Wetland Park	95
uMkhuze Game Reserve	103
Phinda Private Game Reserve	108
Tembe Elephant Park	112
Ndumo Game Reserve	116

Free State — 122
Golden Gate Highlands National Park	124
Willem Pretorius Game Reserve	130

Eastern Cape — 134
Garden Route National Park	136
Addo Elephant National Park	146
Camdeboo National Park	155
Mountain Zebra National Park	161

Baviaanskloof Wilderness Area	167
Great Fish River Nature Reserve	173
Kwandwe Private Game Reserve	178

Western Cape   182
Table Mountain National Park	184
Bontebok National Park	193
Agulhas National Park	198
Karoo National Park	205
West Coast National Park	212
Cederberg Wilderness Area	219
De Hoop Nature Reserve	226

Northern Cape   234
Tankwa Karoo National Park	236
Namaqua National Park	240
|Ai-|Ais/Richtersveld Transfrontier Park	244
Augrabies Falls National Park	251
Kgalagadi Transfrontier Park	258
Mokala National Park	264
Goegap Nature Reserve	268
Witsand Nature Reserve	272
Oorlogskloof Nature Reserve	277

Identification Guide   282
Birds	283
Mammals	296
Amphibians	301
Reptiles	302
Flowers	305
Trees	308

Suggested further reading	314
Useful contacts	315
Photographic credits	316
Index	317

Klipspringer

Golden orchid

Karoo toad

Legend:
South Africa map

	National boundary
·······	Provincial boundary
●	City/town
▬▬	National road
N7	Route number
	River
Swartberg	Mountain
	Coastal plain
	Lowveld
	Low hill ranges and plateaux
	Inland plateaux
	Highveld and Nuweveld range
	Drakensberg range

Legend:
Province, park and reserve maps

	National/provincial boundary
NAMIBIA	Country
LIMPOPO	Province
Durban	City/town
▬▬	National road
▬▬	Tar road
▬▬	Gravel road
N2 R62	Route number
	Park/reserve
▬▬	Park/reserve boundary
·······	Section boundary
▬▬	Marine protected area
	River
	Dam
○	Waterhole/spring/fountain
	Swamp/wetland
	Waterfall
	Mountain range
·····	4x4 trail (at least high-clearance vehicles)
·····	Hiking trail
✉	Gate
⌂	Accommodation
▲	Campsite/campground
	Office/information centre
	Hide
开	Picnic site
	Viewing point
▲	Mountain peak

8

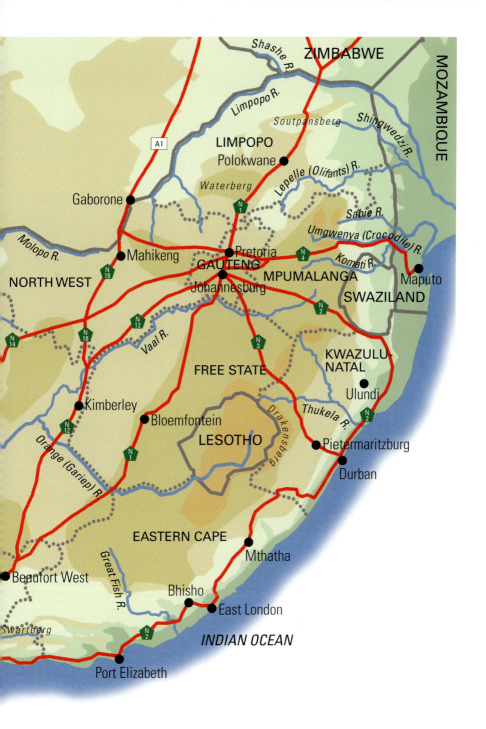

INTRODUCTION

Many South African parks and reserves offer guided tours, a particular advantage to those with limited time.

This field guide has two main aims: to outline the natural history of the best conservation areas that South Africa has to offer, and to assist the reader in identifying the more common mammals, birds, reptiles, amphibians and plants that occur in its national parks and reserves.

The first of this field guide's two sections, and by far the bigger of the two, deals with the natural history of the conservation areas. The second constitutes an extensive selection of images for easy identification of the mammals, birds, amphibians, reptiles, trees and flowers that you may encounter there.

The plains, uplands and deserts of South Africa were once the domain of great herds of game, which were closely attended by predators both large and small. The Khoekhoen peoples and the Bantu migrants hunted the game and burned the vegetation, and their domestic animals competed for grazing; but the wholesale slaughter began with the arrival of the first settlers of European origin, and the surviving game was pushed ever northwards and eastwards as more land was fenced for grazing cattle and sheep. Within 300 years the thundering herds were no more, victims of humankind's hunger for land and the insatiable demand for game meat, hides and ivory.

South Africa has been at the forefront of conservation efforts from the very beginning. At the end of the 19th century Paul Kruger, president of the *Zuid-Afrikaansche Republiek*, realized that the great game concentrations he had hunted in his youth were fast disappearing. He was far-sighted enough to proclaim Africa's first formal conservation area, the Pongola Game Reserve, in 1884. The British colonial authorities in Natal proclaimed Umfolozi (now iMfolozi), Hluhluwe and St Lucia as game reserves in 1895. This was followed in 1898 by the establishment of the Sabie Game Reserve, forerunner of the flagship park that was later to carry Kruger's name. Through political expediency, or stupidity, Pongola was deproclaimed in 1921; conservation areas increased very slowly during the first half of the 20th century. In recent decades a growing conservation awareness has resulted in the proclamation of new areas and a great expansion of existing national parks.

The conservation areas of South Africa fall into several categories: national parks, game reserves and nature reserves controlled at provincial level, and those that are privately owned. The national parks enjoy the highest level of legal protection, although one (Vaalbos) has been deproclaimed in recent times; human activities are fairly strictly controlled and exploitation of natural resources is greatly limited. Provincial reserves are more vulnerable, partly because of limited resources, funds and staff levels. In recent years many privately owned reserves and even some provincial reserves, such as Songimvelo Game Reserve in Mpumalanga, have been lost to conservation through land claims. Privately owned land can also be sold and lose its conservation status. Hence we have emphasized national and, to a lesser extent, provincial reserves.

A number of extremely important marine sanctuaries, known as marine protected areas, around South Africa's coastline are associated with the land reserves. These sanctuaries protect a vast diversity of oceanic and littoral organisms, including many important in the human food chain.

As well as protecting the natural environment and the many organisms that rely on them, conservation areas promote an understanding of the natural ecological processes and an awareness of the need for conservation.

GUIDELINES

- Do not feed any animal, no matter how appealing it may seem; by doing so you are signing its death warrant. Such an animal comes to rely on hand-outs and, more seriously, becomes a nuisance or even a threat to other visitors.
- In conservation areas where visitors are requested to stay in the car, do so, both for your own safety and to avoid disturbance.
- Drive only on public roads or designated tracks. Taking shortcuts damages the vegetation and soil, and driving too close to animals disturbs them and can create dangerous situations.
- Build fires only in designated areas, and take care to extinguish the coals properly after you are done.
- Malaria is an issue in conservation areas to the east and north of the country, including Kruger National Park.

How to use this book

This guide encompasses the most prominent features of 43 national parks, reserves and wilderness areas in South Africa. The parks and reserves are divided into chapters which in turn are sequenced into sections corresponding to the provinces in which they are located. Each chapter opens with a description of the position and physical aspects of the park or reserve. This is followed by a brief review of the sanctuary's history, from its ancient past to modern times, and an overview of the geological features, including where in the park or reserve some of its more striking formations can be seen. There is also an account of the vegetation, with an emphasis on the diversity of vegetation types, and scientific names for trees and flowers are provided to eliminate misidentification of species. Commonly encountered as well as more reclusive wildlife species – from mammals, birds, reptiles and amphibians to, on occasion, fish and invertebrates – are covered, as well as their habitats. Scattered throughout each chapter are several information and fact panels that highlight additional attractions of the park or reserve.

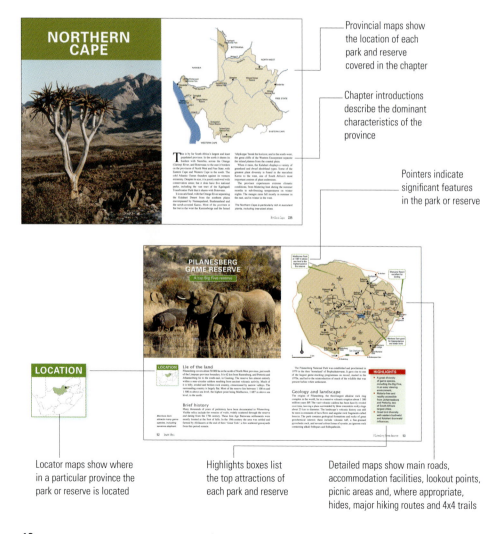

Provincial maps show the location of each park and reserve covered in the chapter

Chapter introductions describe the dominant characteristics of the province

Pointers indicate significant features in the park or reserve

Locator maps show where in a particular province the park or reserve is located

Highlights boxes list the top attractions of each park and reserve

Detailed maps show main roads, accommodation facilities, lookout points, picnic areas and, where appropriate, hides, major hiking routes and 4x4 trails

Maps of vegetation types are handy for game-watchers and bird and flower enthusiasts

Facilities and activities panels describe the amenities and help you plan what to see and do during your stay

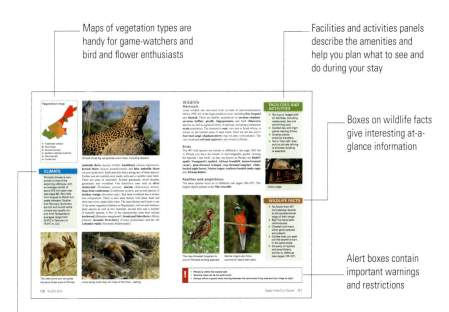

Boxes on wildlife facts give interesting at-a-glance information

Alert boxes contain important warnings and restrictions

Climate panels provide information on seasonal weather and winter and summer temperatures

The photographic identification guide features clear, close-up images as well as common names of birds, mammals, amphibians, reptiles, flowers and trees commonly seen in the parks and reserves described in the book

13

LIMPOPO

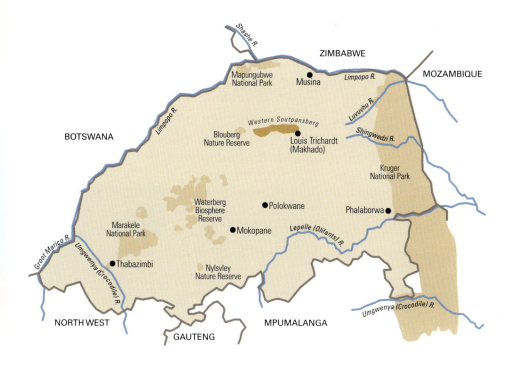

Limpopo is flanked by Botswana in the west, Zimbabwe in the north and Mozambique in the east. It shares its southern border with North West, Gauteng and Mpumalanga provinces. Kruger National Park is Limpopo's flagship, but two developing parks elsewhere in the province, Marakele and Mapungubwe, are both extremely rich in habitats and biodiversity. These two parks are very different in character, with Marakele being dominated by towering cliffs, and Mapungubwe centred on the floodplain of the Limpopo River.

The two great mountain massifs, Waterberg in the west and Soutpansberg/Blouberg in the north, are important biodiversity hotspots despite having relatively small areas under formal conservation protection. The outer edges of the province – Kruger, Limpopo River basin and the Kalahari fringe – lie considerably lower than the central plateau. The vegetation can be broadly classified into three regions: the Lowveld in the east is tropical, encompassing vast areas of savanna grassland and varying densities of woodland; the central plateau has a drier and less diverse mix of grassland and woodland; and in the west, towards the Botswana border, there are strong influences from the Kalahari, with a mix of grassland and varying densities of acacia-dominated woodland and thicket. Along the Eastern Escarpment and within the Soutpansberg there are significant pockets of montane and inland forest, diverse in both plant and animal species. The Soutpansberg is in many ways an 'island' surrounded by an 'ocean' of dry bushed savanna plains, with several species found here in total isolation.

Summers are hot, and most rain falls between October and March. Winters are mild and dry, though nights can be bitterly cold on the central plateau and in the Kalahari.

Besides the national parks and provincial conservation areas, Limpopo has vast tracts of land managed as game farms.

Gudzani Dam near Satara is one of many scattered throughout the Kruger National Park.

Limpopo 15

KRUGER NATIONAL PARK

The most diverse of South Africa's Big Five parks

LOCATION

The viewing deck at Olifants Rest Camp provides stunning views across the Lepelle (Olifants) River, a drawcard for a variety of wildlife.

Lie of the land

The Kruger National Park spans the Limpopo and Mpumalanga provinces in the north-east of the country and covers 19 455 km^2, excluding the privately owned game reserve properties (Greater Kruger) along its 'dropped fence' western boundary. It covers about 350 km north to south and 60 km east to west and shares its entire eastern boundary with Mozambique, while its northern border fronts the Limpopo River and Zimbabwe.

The Kruger's plains are broken by the low Leboeng (Lebombo) mountain range extending north and south along the Mozambique border. Rocky outcrops occur in the north and north-west, and several major rivers cut through the park. From north to south these include the Limpopo, Luvuvhu, Letaba, Lepelle (Olifants), Sabie, and the Umgwenya (Crocodile) along the southern border. Many of the smaller rivers, such as the Shisa, Shingwedzi and Timbavati, only flow after heavy rains in the catchment area. In recent years the period of flow has been reducing as more water is drawn off before reaching the western boundary. Most of the park lies between 260 m and 440 m above sea level; the lowest point is at 122 m in the Sabie Gorge and the highest is 839 m at Khandizwe, near Malelane.

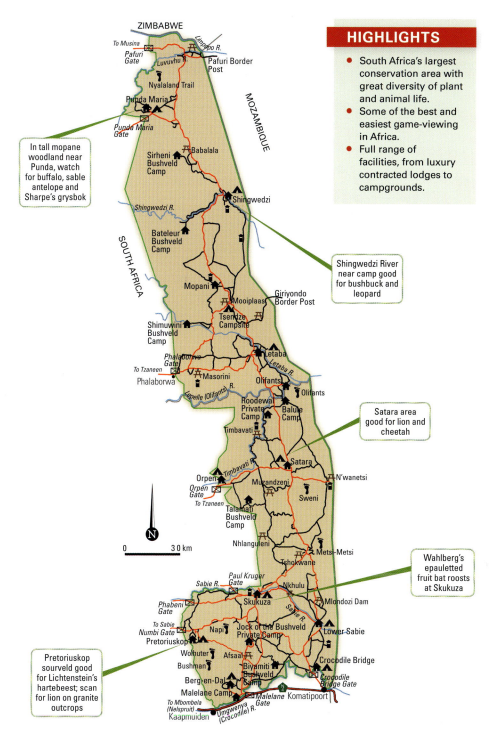

Army ants, or siafu, march in columns seeking out prey.

Brief history

The Kruger National Park contains sites from the Earlier, Middle and Later Stone Ages, some dating as far back as 1.5–1.25 million years BP. Most contain loose scatterings of stone tools and tool workings. Several Later Stone Age sites have been located under overhangs; these were occupied by San peoples from about 20 000 years BP right up to 150 years BP. Most of the stone tool scatter sites are associated with river floodplains and pans, and would have been only seasonally or temporarily occupied. *Homo sapiens* arrived in the area around 70 000 years BP. Later Stone Age occupation, associated with rock overhangs and rock paintings, was most common in the western granitic areas and in the sandstone outcrops around Punda Maria.

Invasions by southward-migrating Bantu groups, the Mutlumuvi, Shingwedzi, Shirimantanga, Mahlambamadube, Ngwenya, Tsende and Balule started in the Iron Age about 200–500 AD and lasted into the 19th century. The most celebrated site, north of Punda Maria, is Thulamela dating from the Late Iron Age, 15th to early 17th centuries. This site can be visited with a guide and consists of extensive stone walls on a hill top, with evidence of iron- and gold-smelting. Other stone-walled settlements are at Matjigwili and Makahane.

The first Europeans known to have entered the area travelled from Delagoa Bay in Mozambique in 1725 in search of trade opportunities. At Gomondwane, north of the Umgwenya (Crocodile) River, they clashed with indigenous warriors and were forced to retreat. More than a hundred years later, the first group of Voortrekkers, who left the Cape Colony in 1836, arrived in the area. The settlers, hampered by malaria and other problems, were forced to establish themselves on the escarpment, whence they descended in winter to graze their stock and, inevitably, to hunt the abundant game.

In 1898 the Sabie Game Reserve and Shingwedzi Reserve, future core components of the Kruger National Park, were proclaimed. Major James Stevenson-Hamilton, appointed warden after the 2nd Anglo-Boer War, initiated the first real efforts to control hunting in the park; he retired in 1946. The park was expanded to its present-day boundaries in 1926.

Vegetation map

- Pretoriuskop bushveld
- Mopaneveld
- Granite lowveld
- Tshokwane-Hlane basalt lowveld
- Makuleke sandy bushveld
- Malelane mountain bushveld
- Mopane basalt shrubland
- Delagoa lowveld
- Northern Lebombo bushveld
- Limpopo ridge bushveld
- Nwambyia-Pumbe sandy bushveld
- Lowveld riverine forest

White-backed vultures feeding on an elephant carcass.

Geology and landscape

The plain is divided by several major and many minor rivers. The low range of the Lebombo Mountains, consisting of rocks of volcanic origin belonging to the Letaba and Jozini Formations, lies along its eastern border. There are dramatic granite outcrops in the south-west and rugged hills to the north-west. A narrow north-south belt of shale and sandstone divides the park into mainly granite formations, producing light-coloured sandy soils, to the west, and volcanic basaltic rocks, producing dark, very fine soils, to the east. The Soutpansberg range, consisting of sandstones and volcanic rocks of the Soutpansberg Supergroup and the Karoo Sequence, extends eastwards into the north of the park in the vicinity of Punda Maria.

CLIMATE

Kruger has summer rainfall, brought by thunderstorms from late September to late March. Very little rain falls outside this period. At Pretoriuskop in the south the annual average is around 760 mm but this decreases towards the north. Average daily temperatures range from 18°C–30°C in January and 8°C–23°C in July; frost may occur in low-lying areas.

Although the mighty baobab occurs mainly in the northern section of the park, a few specimens may be seen in the central areas.

Vegetation

The numerous vegetation types are determined by the type and depth of the soils, and the local rainfall. In the north is riverine forest and woodland, taller and richer than elsewhere and containing such species as the huge, pale-barked **common cluster fig** (*Ficus sycomorus*), **jackal berry** (*Diospyros mespiliformis*), **ana tree** (*Faidherbia albida*) and **nyala tree** (*Xanthocercis zambesiaca*). The undergrowth in these linear forests is usually quite dense and may present several strata. North of the Lepelle (Olifants) River most of the area is dominated by the 'butterfly-leaved' **mopane tree** (*Colophospermum mopane*). In some areas, such as near Punda Maria, it forms tall woodland, called cathedral mopane bushveld because of its unusual height. In other areas it forms dense, low thicket and in still others, scattered bushes in extensive grassland. West of the north-west road is a scattering of bushwillows (*Combretum* spp.). In the far north, the giant-girthed **baobab** (*Adansonia digitata*) is prominent. South of the Lepelle River the vegetation becomes more diverse and complex. From the south-eastern sector to the park's southern border is open savanna grassland

A liana found along the short walking trail at Punda Maria.

Bushbuck live in several of Kruger's camps but are particularly easy to observe at Letaba.

with tall trees, although there is a large area of dense thorny thicket immediately south of Olifants Camp. You will see such species as **knob thorn** (*Senegalia nigrescens*) and **marula** (*Sclerocarya birrea*). A narrow belt of dense thorny bushveld running from west of Satara to Crocodile Bridge, known as Delagoa thorn thicket, is dominated by the **Delagoa thorn** (*Senegalia welwitschii*), and several other acacia species. To the west of this belt between Orpen and Skukuza, and extending to the southern boundary, is a large area where bushwillow species are common, including **red bushwillow** (*C. apiculatum*) and **large-fruited bushwillow** (*C. zeyheri*), with **silver cluster-leaf** (*Terminalia sericea*) and **marula**. The hill country in the south-west of the park, around Pretoriuskop and Berg-en-Dal, is open tree savanna with abundant grass growth, and **silver cluster-leaf** and **sickle bush** (*Dichrostachys cinerea*) are common. The lower areas are dominated by **scented thorn** (*Vachellia nilotica*), **red**

FACILITIES AND ACTIVITIES

- Some of the 24 SANParks rest camps (including Boulders, Jock of the Bushveld, Malelane, Roodewal and Maroela) can be hired for exclusive use (12–19 people). Privately run lodges include Imbali, Hamilton's, Hoyo Hoyo Tsonga, Shishangeni, Shawu and Shonga within the park, and Ngala, Sabi Sabi and Mala Mala in the Greater Kruger. Skukuza, where the park headquarters are, has huts and self-contained cottages, and a caravan/camping site that can accommodate hundreds. Other camps include the small Balule near Olifants Camp, Berg-en-Dal, Crocodile Bridge, Letaba, Lower Sabie, Mopani, Orpen, Pretoriuskop, Punda Maria, Satara and Shingwedzi. Most rest camps also have caravan/camping facilities. Shipandani overnight hide, near Mopani Rest Camp, and Sable overnight hide, near Phalaborwa Gate, can be hired fully equipped for exclusive use.
- All of the larger camps in Kruger have fuel and supplies. The small bushveld camps at Bateleur, Biyamiti, Shimuwini, Sirheni, Talamati and Tsendze have no fuel, shops or restaurants.
- Towns near the park boundaries, such as Mbombela (Nelspruit), Komatipoort and Phalaborwa, have a full range of services.
- Extensive network of tarred and gravel game-viewing roads. Numerous waterholes and dams attract game and birds.
- Seven 2-day, 3-night guided wilderness trails (Wolhuter, Bushman, Olifants, Nyalaland, Metsi-Metsi, Sweni and Napi); each with daily walks from a base camp. Advance booking required.
- Guided visit to Thulamela archaeological site (arranged from Punda Maria).
- Guided 4x4 group trail.
- Guided night- and day-drives from several of the larger camps.
- Private camps are usually fully catered but most of the larger SANParks rest camps have restaurants.

Satara is the second largest camp in the Kruger National Park.

thorn (*Senegalia gerrardii*) and **umbrella thorn** (*Vachellia tortilis*). The Berg-en-Dal area harbours the tall **wild teak** (*Pterocarpus angolensis*) with its large circular seed pods. The south-west of the park is diverse and of particular botanical interest.

Wildlife
Mammals

With 147 mammal species, Kruger has the greatest diversity of any national park or nature reserve in South Africa. Some species show a strong preference for certain vegetation types. Many sightings of **savanna elephant**, **roan antelope**, **tsessebe** and **common eland** are made in the mopane regions north of the Lepelle River, whereas **plains zebra**, **blue wildebeest**, **impala**, **southern giraffe** and **hook-lipped rhinoceros** prefer the central and southern grasslands and wooded savannas and hills. **Savanna buffalo** favour the northern and central parts. **Bushbuck** and **nyala** stick to the riverine woodlands while **greater kudu** occur throughout, though favouring wooded hill country. **Hippopotamus** are present in all the perennial rivers (especially the Lepelle), in annual rivers where there are large pools throughout the year, and in all the major dams. Numbers of **sable** and **roan antelope**, both favouring open and well-grassed woodlands, have declined dramatically in recent years. There are two small populations of **Lichtenstein's hartebeest**, one in the Pretoriuskop area and the other centred south of Punda Maria. Apart from **steenbok**

An elephant bull shakes a marula tree to dislodge the ripe fruit.

WILDLIFE FACTS

- The 147 mammal species recorded include all of South Africa's large carnivores.
- The park is home to South Africa's largest populations of savanna elephant, square-lipped and hook-lipped rhinoceros, savanna buffalo, plains zebra and many other plant-eaters.
- Habitat changes and predation have reduced the populations of roan and sable antelope to near-catastrophic levels.
- The 508 species of bird include rare vagrants and seasonal migrants.
- Reptile species total 114, including healthy populations of Nile crocodile and southern African python.
- At least 34 different amphibians are present, producing impressive male choruses during the rains.
- The 49 fish species include several endemics.
- Among the more than 2 000 plants are 336 trees and bushes, and 235 grasses.
- The invertebrates in Kruger have been more intensively surveyed than in any other South African national park or reserve.

Lions occur throughout the park but sightings are more frequent in the central areas.

and **common duiker**, most of the other small antelope have either localized or habitat-restricted ranges. **Suni** are restricted to two separate populations in sand thicket woodland in the far north, while **red duiker** is found only in the south-west, such as near Skukuza, in dense bush and woodland. Large carnivores such as **lion**, **leopard**, **cheetah**, **spotted hyaena** and **wild dog** occur throughout the park, but are more numerous near game concentrations. Of the smaller dogs, the **black-backed jackal** is more frequently seen than the more strictly nocturnal **side-striped jackal**, and **bat-eared fox** is only known to occur in open country north of the Letaba River. All five of South Africa's primate species occur, of which the most commonly seen is the **Chacma baboon**, though **vervet monkeys** frequently

Cheetah prefer more open and lightly bushed country.

22 Limpopo

show themselves. In the park **Sykes's monkey** only occurs in the woodland along the Luvuvhu River at Pafuri, where its 'jack' call is frequently heard. There are three elusive species of sengi, or elephant shrew, in the park, including the large **four-toed sengi**, restricted to sand thicket in the far north. An amazing 42 bat species, including the large, fox-faced **Wahlberg's epauletted fruit bat** have been recorded. The **Egyptian slit-faced bat** leaves moth wings, beetle elytra and droppings on the ground under the verandahs.

Birds

The checklist of 508 species is unequalled in South Africa, though some, such as **silvery-cheeked hornbill**, are very rare vagrants. Bird-watching at the rest camps or near a waterhole or dam can be very productive. Although each area of the park offers good birding we have consistently found the most productive camps to be Pretoriuskop, Lower Sabie, Shingwedzi and Punda Maria. About 220 species occur throughout the year, supplemented by summer migrants, including over 100 regular nomads. Some migrant species proliferate after heavy rains, such as **white stork**, **Abdim's stork**, **red-backed shrike** and **red-billed quelea**. There are several species that are more populous in Kruger than in any other South African conservation area, or make up a substantial proportion of the country's numbers. These include **saddle-billed stork**, four species of vulture, **martial eagle**, **bateleur**, **kori bustard**, **southern ground hornbill**, **yellow-billed oxpecker**, Meves's starling, **bearded scrub robin** and **brown-headed parrot**. Some **marabou stork** are resident breeders, but numbers are boosted by non-breeding migrants in summer. The raptors are very well represented, including six species of vulture, the most common being the **white-backed**, **lappet-faced** and **hooded**. **Wahlberg's eagle** is common in summer but there are also frequent sightings of **tawny** and **martial eagles**. The park contains 11 species of owl, with several species roosting in

The grey go-away-bird has a distinctive call.

Hamerkop feed on fish and invertebrates in the shallows.

A little swift in flight.

Kruger National Park 23

Speke's hinged tortoise is one of three species in the Kruger National Park.

different rest camps. A night drive is good for a number of nocturnal mammals, as well as a selection of owls and nightjars. All five local species of roller appear in Kruger; the **European roller** is ubiquitous in summer but the **racquet-tailed roller** is known only from Punda Maria northwards. A few more 'specials' include **thick-billed cuckoo**, **black coucal**, **grey-headed parrot**, **mottled spinetail**, **Böhm's spinetail**, **pennant-winged nightjar**, **blue-spotted wood dove**, **white-crowned lapwing**, **collared pratincole**, **Stierling's wren-warbler**, **bearded scrub robin** and **Arnot's chat**.

Reptiles and amphibians

At least 114 reptile species and 34 amphibians are known in the park. The substantial population of **Nile crocodile** is frequently seen along perennial rivers, large pools and in the dams, sharing these waters with **marsh**, **serrated hinged** and **black-bellied hinged terrapins**. Their land-based cousins are the **leopard tortoise**, **Bell's hinged** and **Speke's hinged tortoises**; the **Natal hinged tortoise** probably occurs in the south.

There are 51 snake species recorded, and another four are likely to occur. About 12 carry venom dangerous to humans, with **black mamba**, **Mozambique spitting cobra**, **snouted cobra**, **boomslang** and **puff adder** top of the list. **Southern African python** occur throughout the park but show a preference for rocky and wetland areas. More than 50 lizard species occur, many in inaccessible areas, but several appear in the camps and can be observed with patience. The two largest lizards are the **rock** and **water monitors**, the latter often seen patrolling river banks and swimming in pools and rivers in search of frogs and other prey. Some lizard species are widespread but others are very localized, including several, such as the **blue-tailed sandveld lizard**, that are known to occur only in the sand thicket country east of Punda Maria. Several species may be seen hunting insects around lights in the camp: **Moreau's tropical house**

This Nile crocodile forms an unusual obstacle on the Shingwedzi causeway.

24   Limpopo

gecko has its natural environment in the hollows of baobabs, under tree bark and in rock crevices; **Bibron's thick-toed gecko** is a much larger species up to 20 cm in length; and the **striped skink** is commonly seen hunting on the ground or clinging to tree trunks. The diminutive **Cape dwarf gecko**, another common sight in rest camps, unusually is day-active and unafraid of humans. The **giant plated rock lizard**, reaching 68 cm in length, may be seen sunning itself in areas with rocky outcrops. The males of many of the 34 amphibian species may be heard calling at the onset of the rains. Several toads frequent the camps at night, foraging for insects under the lights. Over the years at least 16 species have been recorded in camps, including **guttural toad**, **flat-backed toad**, **red toad**, **painted reed frog**, **red-legged kassina** and **banded rubber frog**.

Fish
At least 49 species of fish have been recorded in the waters of Kruger, most as residents but a few, such as the **bull shark**, as occasional visitors. Several species are of special interest, including the short-lived **spotted** and **rainbow killifish**, 6–10 cm in length, that live in temporary rain pans or pools, laying eggs in the bottom sediments. The adults die when the water dries up, and egg development and hatching are suspended until the arrival of the next rains and the refilling of the pool. Growth is then rapid and the fish reach adulthood in just a few weeks.

Bat boxes in Letaba camp serve as important refuges and should not be disturbed.

Invertebrates
The invertebrates of the park are probably better documented than in any other conservation area in the country, from roundworms to beetles, butterflies to grasshoppers. The best illustration of this diversity is during the summer rains when vast numbers of different insects are attracted to the camp lights. There are 18 species of sun-spiders (solifugids), more than in any other park in South Africa.

- The park is a high-risk malaria zone, especially during the rainy season. Precautions are strongly advised.
- Dangerous game is present. Only alight from your vehicle, at your own risk, where this is specifically allowed. Most of the camps are fenced but be aware that predators may still enter them occasionally.
- Keep strictly to the speed limit and always remain alert.
- Kruger is extremely popular and camps may be full, especially during school vacations.

A female golden orb spider and her diminutive mate.

Kruger National Park **25**

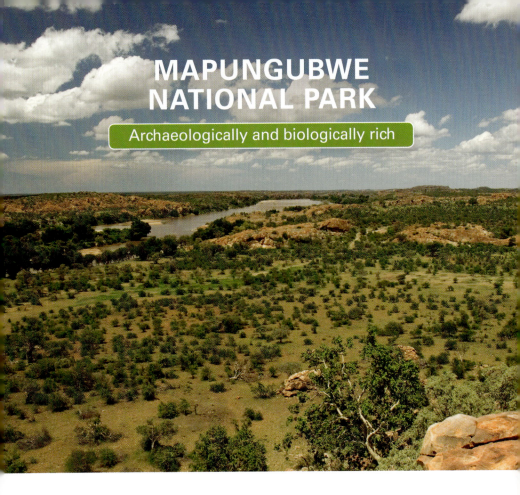

MAPUNGUBWE NATIONAL PARK

Archaeologically and biologically rich

LOCATION

The Limpopo River and its extensive floodplains form the northern boundary of Mapungubwe.

Lie of the land

Mapungubwe occupies 28 000 ha in the extreme north-west of Limpopo province at the confluence of the Limpopo and Shashe rivers. The closest towns are Musina, 90 km to the east, and Alldays, 58 km to the south. Botswana lies north-west of the park and Zimbabwe north-east. The northern boundary of the park is formed by the south bank of the Limpopo, which reaches confluence with the Shashe River in the east of the park. Western and eastern park sectors are currently separated by private land. Several privately owned nature and game reserves abut the park, including Venetia Limpopo and Vhembe.

The east of the park, including the archaeological sites, is rugged ridge and hill country with interlacing valleys and gorges, whereas the west is flatter and more wooded. Altitude ranges from 300 m to 780 m above sea level.

Mapungubwe is part of the Greater Mapungubwe Transfrontier Conservation Area currently being developed by the Peace Parks Foundation (see map on page 29). It is hoped to consolidate the area, including private game reserves from the Limpopo valley in the east and several conservation areas in Zimbabwe and Botswana, into a transfrontier park of some 800 000 ha.

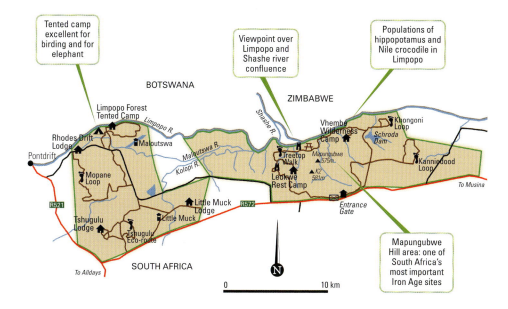

Brief history

Mapungubwe, which means 'Place of the Jackals', is an area of outstanding archaeological interest. More than 400 sites, some dating from one million years BP, span the Earlier, Middle and Later Stone Ages as well as the Iron Ages. Many sites are concentrated around the Limpopo-Shashe confluence, an area spanning the borders of all three countries. Important archaeological sites include Zhizo (AD 900–1020), Mapungubwe Hill (AD 1220–1290), K2 (Leopard's Koppie, AD 1020–1220) and Bambandyanalo (AD 1100–1250).

HIGHLIGHTS

- Interesting scenery and excellent vista of Limpopo River.
- Mapungubwe Cultural Landscape – a World Heritage Site – is one of South Africa's most important archaeological locations.
- Excellent bird-watching areas.
- Big Five as well as a great diversity of other mammal species.

There are many important rock art sites in the Limpopo River basin.

Mapungubwe National Park 27

CLIMATE

This is a semi-arid area with an average annual rainfall of 350–400 mm, nearly all of which falls in summer. Autumn and winter, from May into September, are very dry, and the area is subject to extended periods of drought. The mean summer maximum temperature is around 40°C; winters are mild with a mean minimum of 1°C and few frost nights.

Mapungubwe, the most important Iron Age site in South Africa, was the first powerful kingdom in southern Africa and held sway from about AD 900–1300, when climate change and crop failures probably brought about its demise. Mapungubwe Hill was the 'royal quarters' and the subjects lived and worked in the valleys below. The Mapungubwe culture, rooted in the Limpopo valley, created a complex of social and political groupings based on gold and ivory trading on the east coast of Africa. From AD 1290–1450 it spread north-eastwards into today's Zimbabwe and evolved into the Zimbabwe Culture.

Mapungubwe has many San rock painting sites, some dating back to 15 000 years BP. The area also contains later, and more stylized, Khoekhoen and black pastoralist rock paintings.

The arrival of white ivory hunters in the late 18th century was followed some decades later, in the late 1830s, by the settlement of Dutch-speaking farmers from the south. This led to much conflict with local Sotho and Venda communities, which had already been established in the 18th century.

Part of this area became a botanical reserve in 1922. After many vicissitudes, an expanded area was proclaimed as a national park in 1995. In 2003, the area centred on Mapungubwe Hill received World Heritage Site status.

Baobab trees are scattered throughout the park.

Geology and landscape

This is a mix of undulating to very broken hill country and deeply incised plateaux, with extensive floodplains, especially along the Limpopo River as well as several feeder-streams. The hills are mainly sandstones belonging to the Beit Bridge Complex and the Clarens Formation, though more recent sandstones and conglomerates occur in places throughout the park. There are scattered outcroppings of basalt and granite. Silts dominate the floodplains. Kimberlites of about 100 million years BP yield diamonds at the Venetia mine about 50 km south of the park boundary.

Vegetation

The flat alluvial river terraces have some of the largest trees, but riparian woodland is somewhat fragmented. Characteristic trees here include the yellowish-green barked **fever tree** (*Vachellia xanthophloea*), the large, whitish-barked **common cluster fig** (*Ficus sycomorus*) and **broom cluster fig** (*Ficus sur*), the huge **nyala tree** (*Xanthocercis zambesiaca*) and a scattering of massive **baobabs** (*Adansonia digitata*), though these are more

Vegetation map

- Mopane dominated closed woodland
- Corkwood species and sesame-bush closed shrubland
- Shakama-plum open shrubland
- Three-hook thorn (*Senegalia senegal*) closed woodland
- Ana tree (*Faidherbia albida*) closed woodland
- Narrow-leaved mustard tree and *Vachellia stuhlmannii* open shrubland
- Large fever-berry (*Croton megalobotrys*) and flame creeper (*Combretum paniculatum*) closed woodland

Left: The mopane moth is common during the rains. Its larvae, known as mopane worms, soon strip the leaves of the tree that carries their name.
Above: Most flowers, such as those of Sesamum alatum, appear at the onset of the rains.

common on higher ground and in rocky areas. The **mopane** (*Colophospermum mopane*) dominates much of the park, although its growth is bushy in some areas. Other tree species grow alongside the mopane, especially in rocky areas, such as **red bushwillow** (*Combretum apiculatum*), **knob thorn** (*Senegalia nigrescens*) and **shepherd's tree** (*Boscia albitrunca*). On the rocky ridges there tends to be a greater diversity of plants. This Limpopo ridge bushveld, particularly well preserved in Mapungubwe, includes among other trees **white seringa** (*Kirkia acuminata*), knob thorn, **tall common corkwood** (*Commiphora glandulosa*) and **large-leaved rock fig** (*Ficus abutifolia*).

Wildlife
Mammals
The 94 mammal species, including the Big Five, make this a particularly rich area. A growing **savanna elephant** population roams freely across the national borders. Other large species will also benefit from the growth of the transfrontier park and the removal of

Greater Mapungubwe Transfrontier Conservation Area

- Mapungubwe National Park
- Private game reserve
- Conservancy
- Zimbabwe public hunting area
- Communal land
- Private farm

Mapungubwe National Park   29

FACILITIES AND ACTIVITIES

- Leokwe Rest Camp in the eastern sector has 18 accommodation units, with kitchen and ablution facilities. In the north-western sector, Limpopo Forest Tented Camp has eight fully equipped safari tents on wooden platforms, and a campground near the tented camp. More accommodation is planned.
- Vhembe Wilderness Camp provides rustic accommodation.
- Organized and paid Mapungubwe Heritage Site tours; no unaccompanied access.
- Guided morning, sunset and night drives.
- Guided walks, 3+ hours.
- Extensive road network; 4x4 vehicle may be required after rain.
- No fuel available in the park; fuel and basic supplies can be obtained in Musina and Alldays.
- Several viewing platforms overlooking Limpopo River; Maloutswa bird hide near the forest camp is also excellent for game-viewing.

This viewing platform overlooks the confluence of the Shashe and Limpopo rivers.

fences. This is the only location in South Africa where four species of sengi, or elephant shrew, occur in close proximity, though separated by specific habitat requirements. It is also a bat hotspot, and 17 species have been recorded. The fig trees along the river attract fruit bats, including the tree roosting **Wahlberg's epauletted fruit bat** and the cave dwelling **Egyptian fruit bat**, whose closest known roosts are 70 km distant in the Soutpansberg, though they may have temporary roosting sites nearby. Four of South Africa's five primate species occur, including **Chacma baboon** and **vervet monkey**. Of the 14 rodent species, only the **tree squirrel** is commonly seen. The greater park area contains a full complement of carnivores, including the three big cats and the two hyaenas, but the most commonly seen are the solitary **slender mongoose**, the troop living **banded mongoose** and **dwarf mongoose**. This is also one of the few conservation areas

Troops of vervet monkey are encountered throughout the national park.

The sable antelope is one of 15 antelope species that can be found in Mapungubwe.

Common waterbuck occur throughout but tend to favour the floodplains.

in South Africa where **rock hyrax** (with a brown coat and black dorsal spot) and **yellow-spotted rock hyrax** (with a greyer coat and a pale dorsal spot) live side by side. Both **rhinoceros** species have been reintroduced, as well many antelope totalling 15 species. All four of the indigenous South African spiral-horned antelope – **common eland**, **greater kudu**, **nyala** and **bushbuck** – are present.

Birds

This is one of South Africa's best bird-watching destinations with 467 species on record, excluding rare vagrants, and a number of species are close to their southern range limit. The diversity of habitats and the presence of the Limpopo River and the Den Staat wetlands ensure a year-round parade that includes many seasonal migrants. No fewer than 10 species of owl occur, including the resident **Pel's fishing owl**, and a knowledge of calls is a distinct advantage. Some 46 species of raptor include **African fish eagle**, common along the river, and **crowned eagle** in denser riparian forest. **Verreaux's eagle** hunts hyrax along the hill and ridge country. Other species to watch for include the rare **thick-billed cuckoo**, **Meyer's parrot**, **tropical boubou**, **white-breasted cuckoo-shrike**, **three-banded courser**, both **yellow-** and **red-billed oxpeckers**, **Meves's starling** and **boulder chat**. The Limpopo Forest Tented Camp and the nearby Maloutswa bird hide are excellent viewing locations. Along the Limpopo and the wetlands, **saddle-billed**, **yellow-billed** and **open-billed storks** are regulars, as are many smaller species.

Reptiles and amphibians

The herpetofauna of the area is extremely rich. Just 15 of a probable 32 snake species have so far been confirmed. These include the **southern African python**, **black mamba**, **snouted cobra**, both **horned** and **puff adders**, and at least three species of whip, or sand, snakes (*Psammophis* spp.). Several of the 22 species of lizard are

Many bird species, such as the yellow-billed stork, are attracted to the Limpopo and its associated wetlands.

WILDLIFE FACTS

- Proposed transfrontier park offers 94 mammal species, including the Big Five, wild dog and cheetah.
- Lion population exceeds 20 individuals.
- A top birding destination with 467 species; some rare, and many at the limit of their southern range.
- Amphibian species include 17 already listed and a further 19 known to occur in the area.
- There are 43 known reptile species and a further 32 species are expected to be added to this count.
- The upper reaches of the Limpopo contain 34 fish species but not all may find suitable habitats in the river along the park frontage.
- Great tree diversity, including the baobab.

Watch for giant plated lizards sunning themselves among the boulders on rocky outcrops.

readily seen in suitable conditions. Around the Limpopo viewing platforms, the rocks may reveal the **common flat lizard**, especially the colourful males, the **rainbow skink** (younger animals have distinctive electric-blue tails) and the large **giant plated lizard**, though these favour higher boulder clusters. **Water** and **rock monitor lizards** are common. There is a healthy **Nile crocodile** population in the Limpopo River. Of the amphibians, 17 species have been confirmed but a further 19, present on neighbouring properties, will surely be found. During the dry season many species, such as the **African bullfrog**, **banded rubber frog**, **knocking sand frog** and the **mottled shovel-nosed frog**, bury themselves underground to await the next rains. Probably nine species of toad occur in the area. During the rains, a confusing chorus of calls announces the various amphibians taking the opportunity to breed in waterhole, riverside and rain puddles.

Fish

Up to 34 species of fish may occur in the Limpopo River along the park frontage, but suitable habitat might not be available for all. Unfortunately, several alien species have also found their way into the system. That top freshwater fighter the **tigerfish**, recorded as far west as Musina, may have reached park waters.

Red-billed hornbills are commonly seen.

- This is a malaria zone and precautions must be taken.
- Beware of dangerous game at hides or viewing areas. Camps are only 'proofed' against elephant, not large predators.
- Summer can be very hot, and very humid following rain.
- After heavy rain, some roads may be closed or accessible to 4x4 vehicles only.

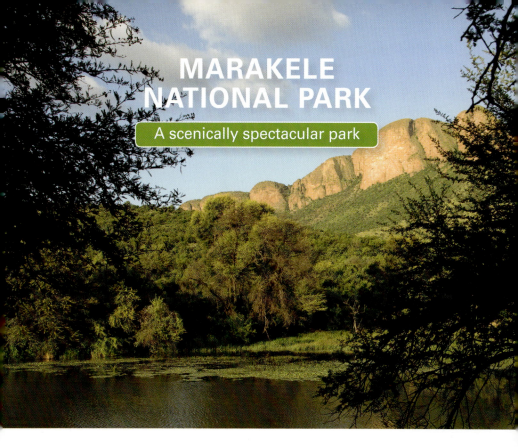

MARAKELE NATIONAL PARK
A scenically spectacular park

Lie of the land
The 67 909 ha Marakele National Park is situated in the south-western corner of Limpopo province, 15 km north-east of Thabazimbi and 250 km north-west of Johannesburg. Part of the Waterberg Biosphere Reserve, Marakele encompasses the south-western peaks and ridges of the Waterberg massif. It also incorporates a number of privately owned conservation areas. From the surrounding plains, about 1 050 m above sea level, it rises to 2 088 m and incorporates narrow valleys between steep cliffs and peaks.

LOCATION

Brief history
Although there is some evidence of Stone Age occupation in the area now constituting the Marakele National Park in the Waterberg, it seems that it was only intermittently occupied in the Later Stone Age, perhaps because of long periods of drought and famine. There are also several Iron Age sites in the park.

Pastoral Northern Ndebele and Sotho-Tswana settled here from the 16th century onwards, followed by Dutch-speaking white farmers, brought by the Great Trek of the 1830s.

The park was initially established as the Kransberg National Park in 1994 but was later expanded and renamed Marakele.

Marakele offers some of the finest scenery in Limpopo.

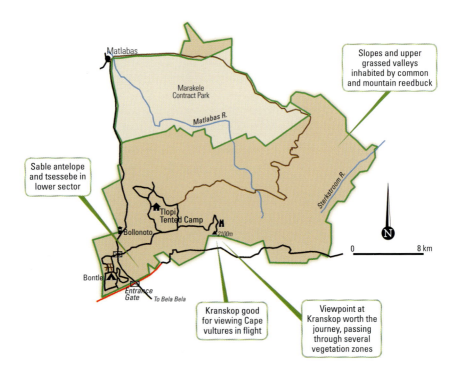

Geology and landscape

The mountains are largely sandstone of the Waterberg Group, Kransberg Subgroup, forming a mix of steep slopes and high cliffs. Other rock types from the group include conglomerates, siltstones and shale; elements of conglomerates, coarse-grained sandstone, lava and quartz porphyry from the Mokolian Waterberg Group are

HIGHLIGHTS

- Spectacular and varied mountain scenery.
- Great diversity of mammals, birds, reptiles and plants.
- South Africa's second-largest breeding colony of Cape vultures situated on Kranskop in the park.
- Excellent for viewing klipspringer, mountain reedbuck and common reedbuck.
- Malaria-free zone.

Views are spectacular from the higher reaches of the park.

34   Limpopo

The fruits of the Transvaal milkplum are eaten by baboons and many bird species.

Vegetation map

○ Western sandy bushveld
● Waterberg mountain bushveld
● Waterberg-Magaliesberg summit sourveld

also present. The rock underlying the sandy plains is similar, with outcroppings of granite and gneiss of the bushveld igneous complex. Many streams rise in the Waterberg, most notably the Matlabas River, along with the Sunday, Mamba and Sand rivers and many smaller feeder streams.

Vegetation

The vegetation can be classified into four groups: fine-leaved thornveld dominated by acacia species, broad-leaved woodland, grassland and small forest pockets in sheltered gullies. The highest ridges and peaks are Waterberg-Magaliesberg summit sourveld dominated by wiry tussock grasses such as **perennial tufted grass** (*Aristida transvaalensis*), **wether love grass** (*Eragrostis nindensis*), **stab grass** (*Andropogon schirensis*) and the highly palatable **red grass** (*Themeda triandra*). A scattering of small trees includes the **Transvaal milkplum/stamvrug** (*Englerophytum magalismontanum*) which from late spring into summer bears masses of red berries, much prized by baboons and frugivorous birds. Two proteas also grow here, **common sugarbush** (*Protea caffra*) and **silver sugarbush** (*Protea roupelliae*). Much of the remaining hilly and mountainous country is covered by Waterberg mountain bushveld with good grass cover throughout; one finds **common sugarbush** and **Transvaal beech** (*Faurea saligna*) on the higher slopes, deciduous trees dominated by **hornpod tree** (*Diplorhynchus condylocarpon*) in the middle reaches, and **silver cluster-leaf** (*Terminalia sericea*) and **wild seringa** (*Burkea africana*) at lower altitudes. On the surrounding plains of western sandy bushveld, there is a mix of small-leaved species such as **blue thorn** (*Senegalia erubescens*) and **knob thorn** (*S. nigrescens*), with broad-leaved species including **silver cluster-leaf** and **red bushwillow** (*Combretum apiculatum*). Species composition is determined by factors such as soil type and depth.

The common sugarbush occurs on higher slopes in the park.

CLIMATE

This warm, temperate region receives nearly all its rain between October and April. The annual average rainfall of 485 mm on the plains reaches 720 mm on higher ground, and is supplemented by low cloud and seasonal fog. Mean summer daily maximum temperature ranges from 26°C on the peaks to 36°C on the plains, while mean winter minima vary from 1°C to 6°C, with frequent frost at lower altitudes.

FACILITIES AND ACTIVITIES

- Tlopi Tented Camp has fully equipped safari tents on platforms.
- Campground near entrance gate.
- 38 km road network, in need of upgrading in parts.
- 4x4 route.
- Guided game drives and walks planned.
- No fuel or supplies available in the park; range of services available in Thabazimbi.

Tlopi Tented Camp has fully equipped safari tents.

WILDLIFE FACTS

- The 91 mammal species include the Big Five and wild dog.
- The 363 bird species include 44 raptors, and the park has the second-largest Cape vulture breeding colony.
- Reptile species are believed to number at least 62.
- At least 27 amphibian species are on record.

Although present in the park, lion are seldom seen.

There are several small forest patches in sheltered gullies containing **wild olive** (*Olea europaea*), **ironwood** (*Olea capensis*), **candelabra tree** (*Euphorbia ingens*), **real yellowwood** (*Podocarpus latifolius*) and **broom cluster fig** (*Ficus sur*). There are also wetland areas, mainly annual or perennial seepage points forming waterlogged sponges, dominated by **sedges** and **mosses**. Along some streams the **water berry tree** (*Syzgium cordatum*), favoured as a 'scratching' tree by leopard, produces its abundant purple fruits in summer.

Wildlife
Mammals

In addition to the Big Five and **wild dog**, Marakele has an extremely rich mammal fauna. Most smaller species are elusive and nocturnal. The day-active **short-snouted** and the **eastern rock sengis (elephant shrews)** may be spotted with a bit of patience, the former in the lower-lying sandy areas and the latter sheltering in rock crevices, which it often shares with **spiny mice** and **Namaqua rock mice**. The **tree squirrel** is found in the bushveld areas and the **southern African ground squirrel** in more open sandy areas at lower levels. **Chacma baboons** are commonly seen at high levels, while **vervet monkeys** occur at lower altitudes. There are small numbers of **savanna elephant**, **hook-lipped** and **square-lipped rhinoceros**, **giraffe**, **savanna buffalo**, **lion** and **spotted hyaena**. No fewer than 20 species of antelope include **common eland**, **greater kudu**, **sable antelope**, **tsessebe** and **blue wildebeest**. Viewing is good for **klipspringer**, **mountain** and **common reedbuck**, but **grey rhebok** may be more elusive. Large carnivores are hard to spot because of the broken terrain and limited road network, but several common and day-active smaller species may be observed, including the troop-living **banded** and **dwarf mongooses**, as well as the **yellow mongoose**.

Birds

Records show 363 bird species, including rarities and seasonal migrants. Birds from the large breeding colony of **Cape vultures** may be observed from the end of the Lonong Loop road – access to the breeding cliffs is not permitted, but these can also be seen from the public road along the southern border of the park. A further 44 species of raptor have been recorded, including several rarities. **Verreaux's eagle** and **jackal buzzard** are quite commonly seen, as are **rock kestrel** and **tawny** and **Wahlberg's eagles**. The high-altitude road to the vulture viewing site offers species such as **short-toed rock-thrush**, **Gurney's sugarbird** and **buff-streaked chat**. Both the tented camp, on a dam, and the campground in the lower-lying bushveld area are extremely productive for birds. The park hosts an amazing eight species of owl, ranging from the diminutive **pearl-spotted owlet** to the largest of all, **Verreaux's eagle-owl**. It is useful to know their calls, as they are not easily observed. There are nine kingfisher species, six bee-eaters, 12 swallows and martins, five francolin and spurfowl species, and 13 shrike species, including the **magpie shrike**.

Unlike most woodpeckers, Bennett's commonly forages on the ground.

Reptiles and amphibians

No fewer than 62 reptiles are believed to occur in the park. The very localized **Lobatse hinged tortoise** occupies low-lying country, and **marsh terrapins** inhabit dams and other water bodies. As many as 30 snake species may be present, including **southern African python**, **black mamba**, **snouted cobra**, **Mozambique spitting cobra**, **rinkhals**, **boomslang**, and the sluggish **puff adder**. Only a few of the lizards allow easy identification. South Africa's two largest lizards, **rock** and **water monitors**, are common, and the latter is often seen at the Tlopi Tented Camp dam. In rocky areas, watch for the brightly coloured males of the **common flat lizard** and the

Bottom left: Most births of banded mongoose take place during the early summer months when food is likely to be most abundant.

Bottom right: Wild dogs range widely in the park and are only infrequently sighted.

Waterberg flat lizard; the latter is found up to 2 000 m above sea level. In the lower bush areas the large **southern tree agama** is common but well camouflaged against the tree bark, unless the male is active with his bobbing display. The tiny (70 mm) **Cape dwarf gecko** is commonly seen foraging on trees, as well as on the decks in the tented camp. The brightly marked **Waterberg dwarf gecko** lives in rock crevices in sandstone boulders. The males of the 27 amphibian species will be heard calling during the rains; the most obvious sign you are likely to see is the white froth 'brood chambers' of the **foam nest frog** hanging over water bodies.

Fish

Sharptooth catfish are abundant in the dam near Tlopi Tented Camp; unfortunately the alien **carp** is also present. More than 20 fish species are known in related river systems but probably not all enter the park.

Top: The black mamba is one of 30 snake species in Marakele.
Above: Milkweed grasshoppers feed on the poisonous milkweed plant.

- Beware of dangerous game, both in unfenced camps and when leaving your vehicle.
- Weather conditions in this region are changeable, especially at higher altitudes.

Waterberg Biosphere Reserve

The Waterberg Biosphere Reserve comprises Marakele National Park, several outlying provincial reserves and many private game farms and nature reserves, but we have chosen to feature only the national park in the book. This is mainly because land claims of uncertain outcome are being contested on many of these properties. The better-known private properties include Lapalala, offering an education and tourism centre, as well as a management area for such endangered species as hook-lipped rhinoceros; and Entambeni, near the provincial reserve at the Doorndraai Dam in the south-east. The adjoining map shows the location of the more important properties falling within the Waterberg Complex.

38 Limpopo

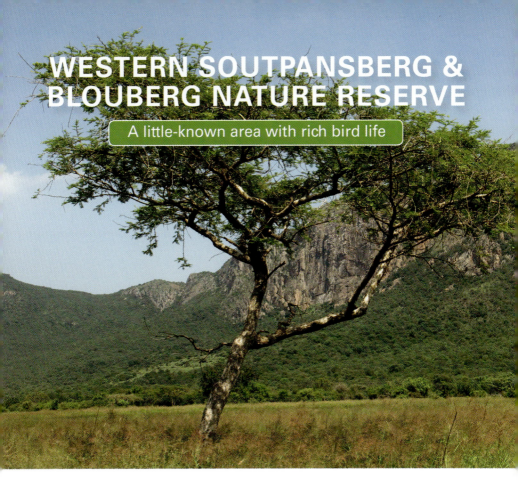

WESTERN SOUTPANSBERG & BLOUBERG NATURE RESERVE

A little-known area with rich bird life

Lie of the land

The western Soutpansberg mountain range runs east-west for about 70 km, from the town of Makhado (Louis Trichardt) to the settlement of Vivo, along the southern fringe of the Limpopo plains, and is bordered to the west by the Kalahari sands. Blouberg Nature Reserve lies to the south-west of the western tip of the Soutpansberg and encompasses the north-east sector of the Blouberg massif. The range includes one small provincial reserve, Happy Rest, and several private nature and game reserves, including Lajuma Mountain Retreat, Leshiba Wilderness and Medike Mountain Reserve.

The western Soutpansberg comprises the main east-west ridges of the range and includes its highest peak, Lajuma, at 1 747 m above sea level. The Sand River, rising in the south near Polokwane, has carved a gorge about midway along the western range. After good rains, other streams form tributaries to the Limpopo. From the highest ridges one looks north over the Limpopo valley and south over the Pietersburg plain, with the Blouberg massif rising to the south-west. Blouberg consists of rolling plains at 840 m above sea level surmounted by 2 000 ha of cliffs, steep slopes and mountains reaching 1 450 m above sea level.

LOCATION

Blouberg Nature Reserve is dominated by a dramatic backdrop of steep cliffs.

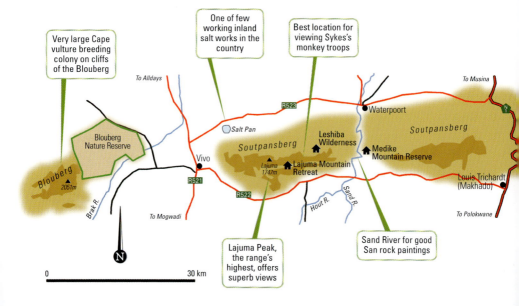

HIGHLIGHTS

- Western Soutpansberg covers just 900 km² but has rich diversity in fauna and flora; Blouberg (9 350 ha) has several endemic species and a very large Cape vulture colony.
- Dramatic scenery throughout.
- Very few people and no crowds.

The area has a rich heritage of rock art.

Brief history

Early humans and their ancestors have been influencing the western Soutpansberg and Blouberg for about a million years; sites in the area represent Earlier, Middle and Later Stone Ages as well as the three distinct Iron Age periods. Evidence takes the form of stone structures, pottery and artefacts in caverns and overhangs, as well as San and other rock paintings. The Greater Soutpansberg biosphere project has mapped 700 such locations. Before the arrival of the first white hunters and explorers in the early 19th century, the mountains were inhabited by San hunter-gatherers and peoples associated with Zimbabwean and Sotho-, Venda- and Zulu-speaking cultures.

The first Dutch-speaking settlers arrived in the late 1830s, followed by missionaries in the 1860s. White farmers were given title to mountain land from 1880. Fortunately, the upper reaches were unsuited to large-scale farming and were left relatively unscathed.

Geology and landscape

The range is composed mainly of very old basalts and sedimentary rocks laid down almost 2 billion years BP. The site of the Soutpansberg, initially a rift valley, filled with material eroded from the surrounding rock over millions of years. This flat and featureless landscape was strongly block-faulted and then uniformly tilted northwards about 150 million years BP. The sediments, hardened by pressure and time, eroded more slowly than their surroundings. In places these rocks are overlaid by younger sedimentary rocks belonging to the Karoo strata, or penetrated by dolerite intrusions. All of these rocks form part of what is known as the Soutpansberg Group.

Vegetation

The vegetation of the Soutpansberg and the Blouberg is complex and very rich, with nearly 600 tree species and more than 2 500 plants across the range, and a wealth of endemics. Three broad vegetation types can be recognized: mistbelt forest patches between 1 000 m and 1 600 m above sea level, Soutpansberg summit sourveld from 1 200 m above sea level to the very summit of Lajuma, and Soutpansberg mountain bushveld from 600 m to 1 500 m above sea level. The mistbelt forests can become very dry in winter, but in summer benefit from the rains and frequent mists. Some typical trees are the **Outeniqua yellowwood** (*Afrocarpus falcatus*), **real yellowwood** (*Podocarpus latifolius*), **lemon wood** (*Xymalos monospora*), **forest bushwillow** (*Combretum kraussii*), **silver oak** (*Brachylaena discolor*) and **red currant** (*Rhus chirindensis*). In the forest pockets, usually close to streams, are **forest waterwood** (*Syzgium gerrardii*) and **tree ferns** (*Cyathea* spp.) Here also are many species of fern, moss and liana. The mountain bushveld forms a complex mosaic with subtropical moist thickets on the southern slopes, mistbelt bush clumps in upland grassed areas, and semi-arid bushveld including **baobab** (*Adansonia digitata*) on lower north-facing slopes. The distinctive

Many flowering plants, such as Plectranthus spp. occur here.

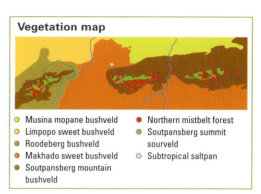

Vegetation map

- 🟡 Musina mopane bushveld
- 🟡 Limpopo sweet bushveld
- 🟠 Roodeberg bushveld
- 🟠 Makhado sweet bushveld
- 🟠 Soutpansberg mountain bushveld
- 🔴 Northern mistbelt forest
- 🟢 Soutpansberg summit sourveld
- ⚪ Subtropical saltpan

The cliffs of Blouberg are home to one of South Africa's largest Cape vulture colonies.

Western Soutpansberg & Blouberg Nature Reserve **41**

CLIMATE

The Soutpansberg lies within the summer rainfall zone. Annual rainfall, averaging 350–400 mm, is higher in the east, on the south-facing slopes and in the high mountains, where mist adds considerable precipitation. The average temperature in the mountains is 23°C in January and 14°C in July, but greater extremes occur on the plains.

The leopard population in the Soutpansberg is one of the highest in South Africa.

common tree euphorbia (*Euphorbia ingens*), seen especially on southern slopes, can grow to 10 m. The summit sourveld grassland consists of coarse tussock grasses and scattered bush clumps with a number of interesting and endemic species, including such shrubs as *Callilepis coerulea*, *Berkheya carlinopsis*, and the two species of **grass aloe** (*Aloe soutpansbergensis; A. vossii*) that are only found in the higher reaches of the southern ridges and produce their flowers January to March. Blouberg has large stands of **common cluster fig** (*Ficus sycomorus*) and **tamboti** (*Spirostachys africana*).

Wildlife
Mammals

Western Soutpansberg is home to 95 mammal species, and **savanna buffalo**, **sable antelope**, **tsessebe** and other game species have been reintroduced to Blouberg and several private game reserves. Species

FACILITIES AND ACTIVITIES

- On Lajuma there is a magnificent exclusive-use lodge overlooking a waterfall, as well as other accommodation; Leshiba and Medike also have options. Blouberg has a rustic bush camp.
- Lajuma has a network of hiking trails allowing access to all major habitats and the highest peak.
- Fuel and supplies are available only in Vivo and Makhado.
- Access roads are rough and a high-clearance or 4x4 vehicle is recommended.

Lajuma has a self-catering lodge overlooking a waterfall.

Limpopo

The southern lesser galago, or bushbaby, is nocturnal and, like this juvenile of the species, is seen mostly in trees.

WILDLIFE FACTS

- The 95 mammal species in these mountains include red duiker, Gambian giant rat, Sykes's monkey, leopard and brown hyaena.
- There are 298 bird species with a number of rarities and several at their southern range limits; 232 species are known at Blouberg, which has arguably South Africa's largest Cape vulture colony.
- There are 93 reptile species, several endemic to these ranges, and 28 amphibian species.
- The mountain streams in the area contain 17 fish species.
- In one limited area near Lajuma, more than 130 spider species have been collected, including several new to science. The area is also rich in butterflies, moths and beetles.
- More than 500 tree species have been recorded, especially in the west of the Soutpansberg range. Several of the plant species occur only in these mountains.

such as **Sykes's monkey**, **red duiker** and the **Gambian giant rat** live on this montane 'island' in complete isolation from other populations. All three species are numerous, although only Sykes's monkey is regularly seen, especially on Lajuma where there are habituated troops. Other primates include several troops of **Chacma baboon**, **vervet monkey** – more abundant on the lower slopes – and **thick-tailed** and **southern lesser galago**. The area has one of the highest **leopard** densities in South Africa and there is also a healthy **brown hyaena** population. Of the 18 species of carnivore, troops of **banded** and **dwarf mongoose** are most likely to be spotted. **Rock hyrax** outnumbers **yellow-spotted rock hyrax**, though both are common. Red duiker, **common duiker** and **bushbuck** are common in the thicket clumps amid high open grassland.

Birds

Blouberg may contain the largest **Cape vulture** colony in South Africa with perhaps 700 breeding pairs and a good view of the cliffs. There is another colony of about 100 birds at the entrance to Buffelspoort, west of the Sand River. Both **Verreaux's** and **crowned eagles** are common, with at least 22 pairs of the former west of the Sand River. **Jackal buzzard** is commonly seen but **forest buzzard** is also regularly sighted. **Martial eagle** and at least six pairs of **African hawk eagle** nest in the baobabs north of the mountain. **Bat hawks** occur in the mistbelt forest and several pairs of **peregrine falcon** nest on the steep south-facing cliffs west of the Sand River. Several species of owl occur, including **Pel's fishing owl** in the riparian forest along the Sand River. More commonly heard than seen, the **narina trogon** inhabits the forest pockets, like **Knysna turaco**, **crested guineafowl**, **chorister robin-chat**, **gorgeous** and **olive bushshrikes**, **African olive pigeon**, **Meyer's parrot**, **black-headed oriole**, **buff-streaked chat** and **starred robin**. On the dry north slopes, such arid-area species as **crimson-breasted shrike** may be seen.

Top: The leopard tortoise is one of the largest tortoise species in southern Africa.
Above: At least 28 species of amphibian can be found in these mountains.

Reptiles

A remarkable 93 reptile species occur in the western Soutpansberg region, and several additional species on the Blouberg. A number of species and subspecies are only found on these mountains. Three land tortoises, the **leopard tortoise** and **Speke's** and **Lobatse hinged tortoises**, are found on the lower mountain slopes. At least 39 species of snake occur, including **southern African python**, common and **southern brown egg-eaters**, **snouted** and **Mozambique spitting cobras**, while **black mamba** and **twig snake** are both common. These mountains are particularly rich in lizards, with 53 species occupying virtually every habitat. Among the more colourful species endemic to the mountains are the **flat lizards**. The **Soutpansberg flat lizard**, whose male has markings of dark green and yellow-green with a bright orange tail, and the **common flat lizard** with similar, but variable male coloration. The Blouberg has the only known population of the **orange-throated flat lizard**, with its bright brick-red tail and blue legs. A tally of at least 12 different geckos includes three of the **dwarf geckos** with the **black-spotted dwarf gecko** only found in the Soutpansberg and Blouberg. A race of the **spotted dwarf** is only found on rocky outcrops above 1 500 m on the Soutpansberg.

Fish

Most of the 17 fish species in the western Soutpansberg are found in the Sand River, although the **common (stargazer) mountain catfish** occurs in several of the clear, rocky-bottomed mountain streams.

Invertebrates

Work done on Lajuma (just over 40 km^2) suggests a great wealth of species in the region. Some 90 species of butterfly occur there, including a number of endemics. More than 130 spider species, including several new to science, have so far been collected on Lajuma.

The Soutpansberg has a rich butterfly fauna, including the ragged skipper.

- Weather conditions are changeable – always carry water and warm clothing. In heavy mist it is advisable to stay put, as it is very easy to fall or get lost.
- Ticks may be abundant at certain times of the year.

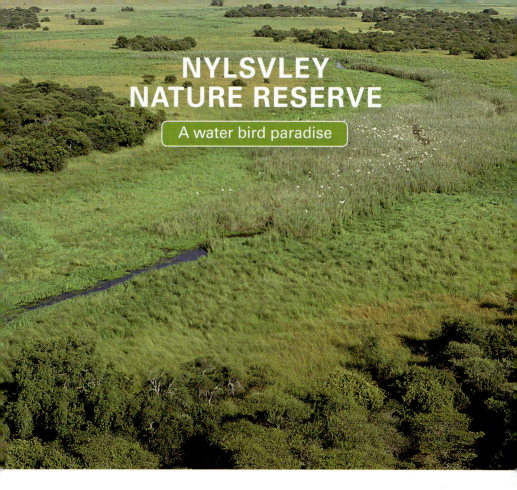

NYLSVLEY NATURE RESERVE
A water bird paradise

Lie of the land
Nylsvley lies east of the N1 highway between Modimolle (Nylstroom) in the south-west and Mokopane (Potgietersrus) in the north-west. It covers 3 100 ha of the Nyl River floodplain, centred on the part that forms the headwaters of the Mogkalakwena River, a major tributary of the Limpopo River to the north. The entire floodplain runs south-west to north-east, is 70 km long and 7 km wide at its widest point and extends over some 16 000 ha. Its waters rise in the Waterberg Plateau, visible on the western horizon.

LOCATION

Brief history
According to legend the Nyl River and Nylsvley were given their names by early settlers who mistakenly believed that they had stumbled on the source of the Nile, which – we now know – rises in Uganda and Ethiopia, emptying its waters into the Mediterranean Sea many thousands of kilometres further north. The first influx of European settlers was in the 1830s, followed by hunters and missionaries who visited the floodplain before 1850.

Nylsvley centres on an extensive floodplain and wetland, attracting many water birds.

Nylsvley Nature Reserve 45

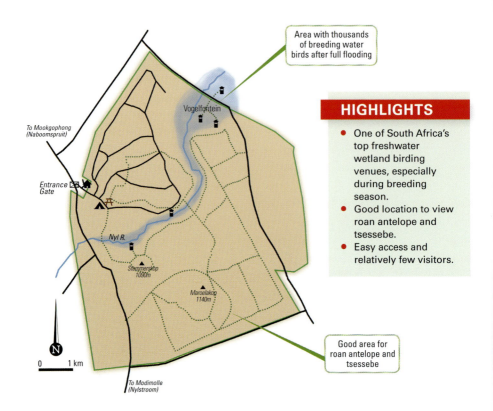

HIGHLIGHTS

- One of South Africa's top freshwater wetland birding venues, especially during breeding season.
- Good location to view roan antelope and tsessebe.
- Easy access and relatively few visitors.

Geology and landscape

Much of the area lies at about 1 100 m above sea level and the floodplain is about 20 m lower, although Maroelakop in the south-east is somewhat higher. The Nyl River and its floodplain occupy the centre of the reserve. The underlying rocks are sandstones and conglomerates belonging to the Waterberg System, with rock outcrops in the south near Maroelakop.

Vegetation

The most important plants in the reserve are associated with the floodplain, predominantly **rice grass** (*Oryza longistaminata*) and *Elytrophorus globularis*, both of which are restricted to this region in South Africa. Rice grass can remain dormant, with its rhizomes buried in the baked earth, for three to four years awaiting the return of flood waters. The floodplain is flanked by belts of thornveld that includes such species as **umbrella thorn** (*Vachellia tortilis*), **scented thorn** (*V. nilotica*) and **sickle bush** (*Dichrostachys cinerea*). Many of these thorn-tree areas are believed to be the sites of local villages abandoned more than 70 years ago. Areas in the north-west and south-east are mixed broadleaf woodland and grassland with tree

The goliath heron is Africa's largest heron.

46 Limpopo

Small numbers of plains zebra have been introduced.

Vegetation map

- Grassland
- *Combretum*-dominated broad-leafed woodland
- *Burkea*-dominated broad-leafed woodland
- Acacia thornveld
- Floodplain

and bush species such as **wild seringa** (*Burkea africana*), **sandpaper raisin** (*Grewia flavescens*), **spine-leaved monkey-orange** (*Strychnos pungens*) and **corky monkey-orange** (*S. cocculoides*). There are slight variations in species composition between the two major broad-leaved woodland areas. Grasses here include **broom love grass** (*Eragrostis pallens*) and **long-awned grass** (*Aristida stipitata*). In the Maroelakop area the tree structure and composition is somewhat different and includes **hornpod tree** (*Diplorhynchus condylocarpon*) and **velvet bush willow** (*Combretum molle*).

Wildlife
Mammals
Among the 77 mammal species, a few game animals include reintroduced populations of **roan antelope** and **tsessebe** as well as naturally occurring **impala**, **common reedbuck, common duiker, steenbok** and **greater kudu**. Also present in the reserve are small herds of **plains zebra** and **giraffe**. **Warthog** range throughout and, in the wooded areas, **vervet monkey** can be seen. There is a total of 11 species of carnivore but the only ones regularly observed are troops of the small but distinctive **banded mongoose** as well as the solitary **slender mongoose**. The large, shaggy-coated **white-tailed mongoose** is common but strictly nocturnal. **Black-backed jackal** are more frequently heard calling than seen.

Purple swamphens, with their long toes, are able to walk on floating vegetation.

CLIMATE

This is a summer rainfall area with very dry winters, and up to 98% of the annual average 630 mm falls between October and March. The floodplain depends on 12 streams, the largest being the Klein Nyl, Groot Nyl and Olifantspruit, that carry rain from the Waterberg Plateau in the west. Usually flooding takes place as late as January/February. Complete inundation occurs only in about one year out of 10, while partial flooding occurs in six years out of 10.

Mean maximum temperature in January is 35°C; mean minimum in July is -2°C but it may approach -10°C. Frost occurs on about 20 days during winter.

FACILITIES AND ACTIVITIES

- Small campground, group camp and self-catering accommodation in the reserve; several options in neighbouring towns or on nearby farms.
- Limited gravel road network.
- Several walking trails; guided walks can be arranged through Friends of Nylsvley.
- Picnic site and bird-watching hides.
- No fuel or supplies in the reserve; full services available at Modimolle and Mokopane.

The white-backed duck is one of about 17 species of duck and goose that occur at Nylsvley.

Birds

Nearly everyone comes to Nylsvley for its extremely rich bird life, especially the 102 species of water birds that have been recorded along the floodplain. At least 50 of these breed during a good flood year, which will also see up to 12 000 herons and egrets of 17 species, 19 000 ducks of 17 species and an estimated 43 000 crakes flocking here. At least 85 of the 95 water bird species known to breed in southern Africa have been recorded on the Nyl. Spring and especially late summer are the most productive for bird-watching, although not every year brings floodwaters. Species breeding here, such as **great egret**, **purple heron**, **yellow-billed egret**, **black heron**, **dwarf bittern** and **reed cormorant**, make up a significant portion of South African populations. The largest South African breeding populations of **Allen's gallinule** and **lesser moorhen** nest here during full flood years. Some species that normally migrate only as far south as the Zambian, Zimbabwean and Botswana wetlands, carry on to Nylsvley when the flooding is good. Like the avocets, black-winged stilts and flamingoes that find newly filled pans in the Kalahari and Karoo, this creates a mystery: how do they know?

The array of **crakes** recorded here is quite astounding and includes **African**, **Baillon's**, **spotted**, **striped** and the elusive **corncrake**. Apart from the wetland birds there are also many bushveld species, including **kurrichane buttonquail**, **southern pied babbler**, **barred wren-warbler** and **crimson-breasted shrike**, close to the eastern limits of its range here. Three of South Africa's 'pygmy' owls occur, **African scops**, **white-faced scops** and **pearl-spotted owlet**, all best tracked by their calls. **African grass owl** also breeds here, but it is difficult to locate.

A small population of tsessebe thrives in the reserve.

Reptiles and amphibians

There are 58 reptile species so far recorded, including 18 lizards. The largest of these are the **rock** and **water monitors**, and among the most

The frog-hunting spotted bush snake is common in the Nylsvley reserve. It is especially adapted for climbing, and spends most of its time in trees.

abundant is **Cape dwarf gecko** with a density of 195–262 animals per hectare in suitable habitat, far more than the **Cape rough-scaled sand lizard**. The large **leopard tortoise** is the most frequently seen of the three tortoise species that occur here. The most commonly seen of the 26 snake species on record are **spotted bush snake**, **herald snake**, **vine snake**, **short-snouted sand snake** and the **Cape centipede-eater**. There are perhaps three snakes per hectare in the reserve. Recorded amphibian species number 23. Many thousands converge on the floodplains when the Nyl River overflows, where they, their eggs and their tadpoles make an important contribution to the diet of many of the water bird species.

Fish

The 13 fish species in the wetland range in size from the large **sharptooth catfish** to the 15 cm **straight-fin barb**. The fish population is essential to the diet of many bird species such as kingfishers, herons and cormorants, and 600 metric tons of fish is estimated to be present on the plain during heavy flooding.

Invertebrates

An estimated 2 000 species of above-ground invertebrates, mainly insects, inhabit the reserve, with an unknown number of underground and arboreal species. There are more than 15 species of termite, 194 butterfly species and at least 55 different dragonfly species with such delightful names as **red-veined dropwing**, **jaunty dropwing**, **common tigertail**, **grizzled pintail** and **red basker**.

WILDLIFE FACTS

- The 77 mammal species include roan antelope and tsessebe.
- Records show 380 bird species, including 102 water birds, more than for iSimangaliso in KwaZulu-Natal or the Okavango Delta of Botswana.
- Home to South Africa's largest breeding populations of Allen's gallinule, lesser moorhen and no doubt several others.
- There are 58 reptile species and 23 different amphibians.
- The 13 fish species are an important attraction for the many piscivorous birds.
- Among invertebrates, there are 194 butterfly species and 55 different dragonflies.
- Approximately 600 plant species are known to grow in the reserve.

!
- Summer days can be hot and humid.
- If you plan to walk the trails, especially in summer, make sure you carry enough drinking water.

The red-veined dropwing dragonfly is one of 55 species encountered in the reserve.

Nylsvley Nature Reserve **49**

NORTH WEST

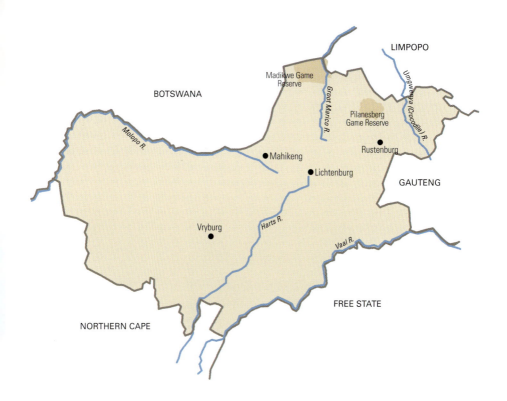

This province has two major conservation areas and 17 smaller reserves, many of the latter associated with dams and orientated towards recreation. The province is bounded by Botswana to the north-west, Limpopo to the north, Gauteng to the east, Free State to the south and Northern Cape to the west. A long-term goal of the North West parks authority is to link their two premier reserves, Madikwe Game Reserve on the Botswana border and Pilanesberg Game Reserve in the south-east, with a broad corridor of cooperative land use. This noble aim is fraught with difficulties in view of the growing human population and resource demands in the area.

The province's western region is dry, and hence sparsely populated. Towards the east of the province, however, higher rainfall, development and urbanization have resulted in higher settlement densities, which has already had major impacts on the natural environment. Pilanesberg in particular is ringed by towns and other settlements and infrastructure, with the glow of electric lights at night disturbing some, especially those visitors wanting a true African savanna experience.

Much of the south-eastern province falls within the Highveld, an area of flat, open country. Before the arrival of the first Europeans this country was covered by a vast ocean of grassland, home to great herds of antelope and zebra. Today much of this has gone under the plough, but some unspoilt patches survive.

The province also has many privately owned game farms, especially in the west, and particularly towards the Botswana border.

Summers are warm, with rainfall throughout the region. Winter days are mild to cool, with cold and usually clear nights. Despite meagre rains the west and north have extensive seasonal grasslands, and acacia woodland is widespread. In the south-west, where rainfall is lowest, elements of arid-adapted karroid scrub are common.

Giraffe are present in substantial numbers in several North West parks.

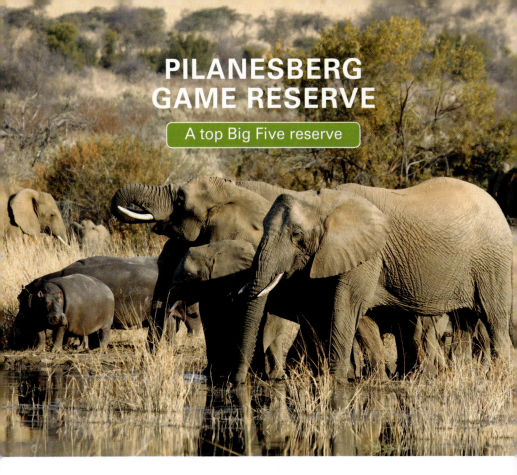

PILANESBERG GAME RESERVE

A top Big Five reserve

LOCATION

Lie of the land

Pilanesberg covers about 50 000 ha in the north of North West province, just south of the Limpopo province boundary. It is 62 km from Rustenburg, and Pretoria and Johannesburg lie to the south-east, in Gauteng. The reserve lies almost entirely within a near-circular caldera resulting from ancient volcanic activity. Much of it is hilly, eroded and broken rock country, crisscrossed by narrow valleys. The surrounding country is largely flat. Most of the reserve lies between 1 100 m and 1 500 m above sea level, the highest point being Matlhorwe, 1 687 m above sea level, in the north.

Brief history

Many thousands of years of prehistory have been documented in Pilanesberg. Visible relics include the remains of walls, widely scattered through the reserve and dating from the 17th century. These Iron Age Batswana settlements were mostly located at the foot of hills. In the 19th century the area was settled and farmed by Afrikaners at the end of their 'Great Trek'; a few scattered graveyards from this period remain.

Mankwe Dam attracts many game species, including savanna elephant.

52   North West

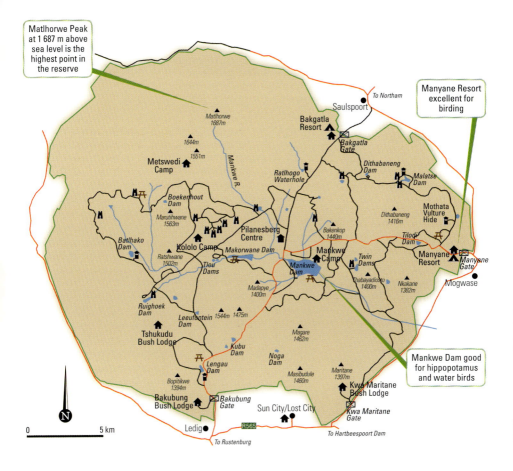

The Pilanesberg National Park was established and proclaimed in 1979 in the then 'homeland' of Bophuthatswana. It gave rise to one of the largest game-stocking programmes on record, started in the 1970s, and led to the reintroduction of much of the wildlife that was present before white settlement.

Geology and landscape

The origins of Pilanesberg, the third-largest alkaline rock ring complex in the world, lie in a massive volcanic eruption about 1 300 million years BP. The vast volcanic caldera has been heavily eroded over time, leaving a plain surrounded by three concentric rocky rings about 25 km in diameter. The landscape's volcanic history can still be seen in remnants of lava flows and angular rock fragments called breccia. The park contains geological formations and rocks of great geochemical interest; these include volcanic tuff, a fine-grained pyroclastic rock, and several colour forms of syenite, an igneous rock containing alkali feldspars and feldspathoids.

HIGHLIGHTS

- A great diversity of game species, including the Big Five, in an easy viewing environment.
- Malaria-free and readily accessible from Johannesburg and Pretoria, two of South Africa's largest cities.
- Great bird diversity with eastern bushveld and Kalahari thornveld influences.

Several species of bushwillow grow in the park.

Vegetation

The mountain bushveld of the Pilanesberg dominates the reserve, with minor challenges from Zeerust thornveld in the south and west, sandy bushveld in the extreme east and Dwaalboom thornveld patches in the north. Broad-leaved deciduous trees and bushes dominate, with a good grass layer on slopes and in some valleys. The densest bush and tree stands appear in the sheltered gullies. The succulent **common tree euphorbia** (*Euphorbia ingens*) can reach a height of 10 m, and in summer **marula** (*Sclerocarya birrea*) produces delicious greenish-yellow fruits, sought out by many mammals and birds. This tree, among others, hosts the larvae of the large and beautiful moon moth (*Argema mimosae*). Several species of bushwillow include the **red bushwillow** (*Combretum apiculatum*), the **velvet bushwillow** (*C. molle*) and the **large-fruited bushwillow** (*C. zeyheri*), all easy to place in this genus by their distinctive four-winged fruits. Several thorn tree species, such as the common **black thorn** (*Senegallia mellifera*), form an important food source for browsing mammals.

CLIMATE

This is a summer rainfall area, and most of the annual average of 650 mm falls between November and March. Almost no rain falls from May to September. In the valleys, frost is frequent. Mean monthly maximum temperature in February is around 36°C, and mean monthly minimum temperature in July is slightly above -2°C.

Wildlife
Mammals

Pilanesberg, with its broad spectrum of species, is one of the finest game-viewing reserves outside the malaria zone. There are good populations of **savanna elephant**, **hippopotamus**, **savanna buffalo**, **square-lipped rhinoceros** and **hook-lipped rhinoceros**. No fewer than 15 species of antelope range from the largest of all, the **common eland**, to the delicate **steenbok**, and include several rare species such as **sable antelope** and **tsessebe**. Among the more abundant mammals are **blue wildebeest**, **impala**, **greater kudu** and **red hartebeest**, and there is a substantial population of **plains zebra**. Alongside these, all of the large predators have also been reintroduced, including **lion**, **leopard**, **cheetah**, **wild dog**, and **spotted** and **brown hyaena**. There

Vegetation map

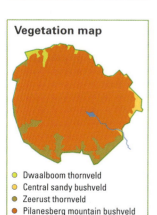

- Dwaalboom thornveld
- Central sandy bushveld
- Zeerust thornveld
- Pilanesberg mountain bushveld

Blue wildebeest are one of the many game species that have been reintroduced to Pilanesberg.

A grey heron in flight.

The endangered hook-lipped rhinoceros finds sanctuary in the park.

are also smaller predators such as **caracal**, **serval** and **African wild cat**, but the most commonly seen are the day-active mongooses: the troop-living **banded mongoose**, the diminutive **dwarf mongoose** and the solitary **slender mongoose**.

Birds

The area has 354 recorded bird species, including vagrants and rarities, and is a meeting place for species from the eastern bushveld and the Kalahari to the north. At least another six species are expected to be added to this count. We strongly recommend spending time in camps, picnic sites and at the viewing hides. Manyane Resort area is good for such species as **crimson-breasted shrike**, **southern pied babbler**, **Kalahari scrub robin** and **chestnut-vented tit-babbler**. As in many reserves where walking is restricted, it really pays to park near thicket, or other promising bird habitat, wind down the windows

The hide at Mankwe Dam offers good game- and bird-viewing.

FACILITIES AND ACTIVITIES

- Game-viewing road network of more than 100 km.
- Guided night and day game drives, and accompanied game trail walks.
- Strategically located game- and bird-viewing hides.
- Picnic sites.
- Several camps with a mix of huts and safari tents; large (100-stand) caravan/camping ground at Manyane; and large luxury hotels (Sun City and Lost City) on the southern boundary of the reserve.
- Restaurant and shop at Manyane.

Pilanesberg Game Reserve 55

WILDLIFE FACTS

- At least 87 mammal species, including Big Five and wild dog, and 15 antelope species.
- Scene of one of the world's largest game translocation exercises.
- The 354 birds are a blend of bushveld and Kalahari species.
- At least 62 reptile species, including Nile crocodile and southern African python.
- There are 18 confirmed species of amphibian, and a further five are expected to be added to this count.
- Some 132 tree species and approximately 70 different grasses.

and wait. **Black-faced** and **violet-eared waxbills** occur along with other small species. In the rugged areas, watch for **short-toed rock-thrush** and **cinnamon-breasted bunting**, as well as **flappet lark**. This is also a good raptor park with several vulture and eagle species as well as **secretarybird**, with **African fish eagle** often present at the Mankwe Dam.

Reptiles

The **Nile crocodile** was introduced to the reserve, possibly without historical justification. The **water** and **rock monitor lizards**, South Africa's largest, are frequently seen, but most other lizards are seen fleetingly if at all. On trees, even at camps and picnic sites, watch for the large (more than 30 cm) but well-camouflaged **southern tree agama** whose head-bobbing display often gives it away. **Flap-neck chameleons** are common but largely arboreal; they are sometimes spotted crossing a road or path. All of Pilanesberg's six gecko species are nocturnal, but **Moreau's tropical house gecko** emerges at night to feed on insects attracted to lights around buildings. Although the area has 35 snake species, most are secretive, nocturnal, or subterranean, hence hard to observe. The **southern African python** is the largest by far but its local population size is unknown. Dangerous species include the **black mamba**, **boomslang**, **twig snake**, **snouted cobra** and **Mozambique spitting cobra**, and the **puff adder**. The two species of land tortoise are the large **leopard tortoise** and the **Lobatse hinged tortoise**, whose very limited range covers northern South Africa and adjacent Botswana.

Above left: Although present, the snouted cobra is seldom seen. Above right: As its name implies, the water monitor prefers to remain close to water bodies.

> **!** • Beware of dangerous game; only alight from your vehicle where this is allowed.

56 North West

MADIKWE GAME RESERVE
A top reserve but not 'free-drive'

Lie of the land

The 75 000 ha Madikwe reserve borders Botswana to the north and South Africa's Limpopo province to the east. Gaborone, the capital city of Botswana, lies just a few kilometres to the north-west, and the closest South African town, Zeerust, is 85 km south of the reserve.

Madikwe offers a pleasing blend of mainly flat to undulating plains, interspersed by broken ridges, hills and isolated outcrops. The Groot Marico River lies on the eastern boundary of the reserve. A range of broken hills known as the Dwarsberg Mountains, topped by Brandwacht at 1 228 m, lies to the south. The southern plain drops at the Tweedepoort Escarpment in the north to a low flat plain interrupted by inselbergs and the Tshwene Tshwene hills, reaching 1 328 m. Hills on the western flank include Abjaterskop, 1 377 m, and Lotteringskop, 1 144 m.

LOCATION

Brief history

The prehistory of Madikwe may extend back to the Earlier Stone Age (1 million years to 250 000 years BP), as a possible site has been identified from stone artefacts on the banks of the Groot Marico River. Three Middle Stone Age sites and four Later Stone Age sites (25 000 to 500 years BP) have also been identified. Several Middle to Later Iron Age sites are found in the hill ranges and inselbergs. Most of these sites, dating from 600 to 300 years BP, are identified from potsherds,

A large termite mound surrounds the base of a stink shepherd's tree.

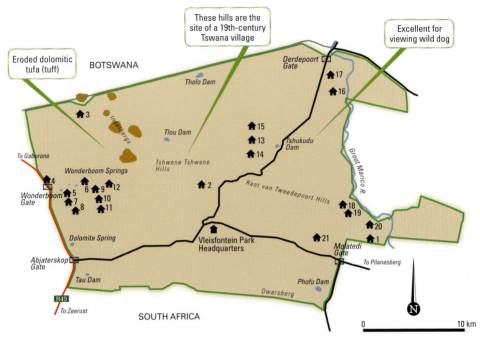

1. Thakadu River Camp	8. Rhulani	15. Etali
2. Masethla Bush Camp	9. Buffalo Ridge	16. Madikwe River Lodge
3. Tau Game Lodge	10. Tuninga	17. Makanyane Safari Lodge
4. Madikwe Bush Lodge	11. Madikwe Mooifontein	18. Jaci's Safari Lodge
5. Impodimo	12. Motswiri	19. Jaci's Tree Lodge
6. Rock Fig Lodge	13. Madikwe Hills	20. Morukuru
7. Royal Madikwe	14. Mateya	21. Jamala Royal Safari Lodge

HIGHLIGHTS

- A great diversity of game animals, including the Big Five and wild dog, in a malaria-free area.
- Lodges provide experienced ranger-guides who know the area intimately.
- Excellent guided bird-watching possibilities.

relics of copper-smelting furnaces and other remains. There is also evidence that San and Khoekhoen inhabited the area sporadically over a period of perhaps 2 000 years.

At times in the 17th and 18th centuries the area was unoccupied, apparently because of drought. During the 19th century, Sotho-Tswana peoples settled here and a large Tswana village – the reputed capital of Gaborone, chief of the BaTlokwa tribe – is located at Tshwene Tshwene. The first European missionaries arrived in the early 19th century, and David Livingstone made several visits to the Madikwe area. A number of skirmishes took place here between the renegade Zulu Mzilikazi with his impis, and the Voortrekkers with their native allies, whereafter the Dutch-speaking settlers started to farm the area. The first specimen of sable antelope known to science was collected here by William Cornwallis Harris in 1836.

The reserve was established and proclaimed in 1991, although by then little game remained. Operation Phoenix, one of the largest game translocation exercises ever undertaken, introduced 10 000 animals of 25 species, mostly within the first two years of the operation.

Geology and landscape

Madikwe's extensive plains slope gently eastwards to the bank of the perennial Groot Marico River. The quartzitic Rant van Tweedepoort hills run in an east-west line across the reserve. The northern plains are underlain by granitic, gneiss and andesite lavas; the rolling southern plains, underlain with dolerite, are bounded in the south by the Dwarsberg range, with its mix of quartzites, shales and andesite lava. Scattered across the north are several impressive inselbergs standing up to 200 m above the surrounding plains. In the hills, impressive formations of water-eroded dolomitic tufa, relics of a much wetter period, are exposed under overhangs and resemble frozen waterfalls.

Vegetation

The vegetation of Madikwe can be classified into two principal groups: broad-leaved woodland dominated by bushwillow (*Combretum* spp.), and regions dominated by acacia (*Senegalia* and *Vachellia* spp.). As a broad simplification, the north is principally acacia and the south mainly bushwillow dominated. A third type, Dwarsberg-Swartruggens mountain bushveld, is a mix of these and a number of additional flora. Among the most important bushwillow species are **red bushwillow** (*Combretum apiculatum*) and **leadwood** (*Combretum imberbe*). The greatest variety of acacia trees and bushes is found on the northern plains but a good diversity exists in the south too. Species include **blue thorn** (*Senegalia erubescens*), especially in the east, **black thorn**, (*S. mellifera*), **red thorn** (*S. gerrardii*) and **umbrella thorn** (*Vachellia tortilis*). Areas in the north-east and the hill country have fine examples of **stink shepherd's tree** (*Boscia foetida*). **Sickle bush** (*Dichrostachys cinerea*), although an indigenous species, can form dense thickets that exclude most other

CLIMATE

Most rain falls in summer between November and March, while May to August is very dry. Annual average rainfall ranges from 500 mm in the north to 600 mm in the south near the Dwarsberg. Summer days are hot with mild nights, while winter days are mild with cold nights and frequent frost.

Vegetation map

- Old lands
- *Senegalia erubescens*
- *Senegalia mellifera* and *Boscia foetida*
- Old lands with *Vachellia tortilis* and *Senegalia gerrardii*
- Mixed acacia woodland
- *Senegalia erubescens* and *Combretum* spp.
- Mixed acacia closed woodland
- *Terminalia sericea* veld
- *Combretum imberbe* woodland
- *Senegalia mellifera* on red sand
- Mixed acacia and *Ziziphus mucronata*
- Ficus on bare rock
- *Senegalia erubescens* infested with *Dichrostachys cinerea*
- *Combretum apiculatum*, *Vitex* spp. and *Tarchonanthus* spp.
- *Combretum apiculatum* broad-leaved mountain veld
- *Sclerocarya caffra* and *Senegalia erubescens* woodland
- *Vachellia tortilis* and *Senegalia gerrardii* on vleis
- Mixed acacia and *Combretum* veld

The inselbergs have unusual rock formations.

FACILITIES AND ACTIVITIES

- Must pre-book with a lodge to enter this reserve.
- There are 15 public-access lodges and 16 private, corporate-owned lodges.
- Public lodges, ranging from luxury chalets to fully equipped safari tents, are primarily upmarket, fully catered and serviced.
- Use of own vehicle permitted only to reach the lodge.
- Accompanied day, evening and night drives in open reserve vehicles.
- Guided walks can be arranged.

An accommodation unit at Madikwe Safari Lodge.

Above: Some overhangs contain volcanic tufa formations.
Right: The dwarf mongoose moves in small troops.

plants and often indicate past overgrazing. Among the inselbergs in the north-west are excellent and abundant examples of **large-leaved rock fig** (*Ficus abutilifolia*), its fruit prized by many mammals. Two other rock-splitting figs also grow here on these seemingly barren, broken slopes, the **red-leaved fig** (*Ficus ingens*) and the **Wonderboom fig** (*Ficus salicifolia*). Many of the open, grassy plains in the north are a legacy of bush-clearing in the area's agricultural past, but now offer important grazing and have been left undisturbed by conservation authorities. These plains have also acquired a strong admix of other plant species.

Wildlife

Mammals

Madikwe is a Big Five reserve where the use of mandatory guides will greatly help to improve your chances of seeing a good variety of species. The artificial repopulation of the reserve has been fraught with the difficulties of creating a delicate balance between predator and prey; an example is the unfortunate preference of the **lion** population for the rare **sable antelope**. There are healthy populations of **elephant**, **hook-lipped** and **square-lipped rhinoceros**, and **savanna buffalo**, and **hippopotamus** have been introduced to some of the larger dams. A broad variety of antelope species do well here, from those favouring grassed broad-leaf woodland to those that thrive in acacia country. Hence one can observe **tsessebe** and **impala** as well as **southern oryx** (**gemsbok**) and **springbok**. **Greater kudu** are widespread but **klipspringer** are restricted to the rugged hill country. All the large predators, introduced in the 1990s, are thriving, perhaps too well in the case of the lion. In all there are 23 carnivores, including many that were here before the reserve was proclaimed, and five species of mongoose.

Birds

As with the mammals, birds typical of the Kalahari mix with those of the eastern Bushveld. The **arrow-marked babbler**, a broad-leafed

60 North West

Many grazers, such as these blue wildebeest, feed on open, recovering farmland.

woodland species, is neighbour to the Kalahari thornveld-loving **southern pied babbler**. Three vulture species are regularly seen here, **Cape**, **white-backed** and **lappet-faced**, as well as an additional 26 raptor species. Among gamebirds there are four species of francolin, and the reserve is a courser hotspot with **double-banded**, **Temminck's**, **Burchell's** and **bronze-winged coursers**, and is also one of the best locations for seeing the elusive **yellow-throated sandgrouse**. The rugged inselbergs are home to an interesting mix including **Verreaux's eagle**, **short-toed rock-thrush**, **mocking cliff chat**, **cinnamon-breasted bunting** and **freckled nightjar**.

Reptiles and amphibians

Three species of land tortoise inhabit Madikwe: the **Lobatse hinged tortoise** of very limited range, the **Kalahari tent** or **serrated tortoise**, and the giant **leopard tortoise**. Although 25 species of snake are on record, they are seldom seen. Near the rock outcrops you have a good chance of seeing the **southern ground agama** and the common **Transvaal girdled lizard**. **Tropical house geckos** can usually be found around the lodge lights at night. A small but day-active lizard to watch for, the **Cape dwarf gecko**, is another lodge resident that hunts tiny insects, especially on verandahs. Both **rock** and **water monitor** lizards occur, the latter mainly at the Groot Marico River. The 20 amphibian species keep a low profile and are difficult to observe, even in the rainy season. The polystyrene-like nests of **Gray's foam-nest frog**, attached to branches or rocks, contain eggs that hatch and drop the tadpoles into the water below.

WILDLIFE FACTS

- There are 74 mammals listed, including the Big Five and wild dog, and 16 antelope species.
- Park is said to hold some of the largest greater kudu bulls in South Africa.
- At least 340 bird species recorded, including a number of vagrants.
- Reptiles include five species of tortoise and terrapin, 26 snake species, 22 lizard species and the Nile crocodile.
- No fewer than 20 amphibians, including African and giant bullfrogs.
- There are 50 identified butterfly species.
- At least 98 species of trees and bushes, and some 60 different grasses.

- Beware of dangerous animals. Camps are elephant-proof but not predator-proof.

Madikwe Game Reserve 61

KWAZULU-NATAL

This province covers a relatively small area but has a great diversity of habitats, ranging from subtropical forest to a great mountain chain that rises more than 3 000 m above sea level. In the south it borders the Eastern Cape, in the west its boundaries are shared with Lesotho and Free State, and to the north lie Mpumalanga, Swaziland and Mozambique. The warm waters of the Indian Ocean lap the highly popular eastern coastline. Most people know the province for two of its greatest drawcards, the Drakensberg and iSimangaliso, formerly known as the Greater St Lucia Wetland Park. Many smaller conservation areas have been incorporated into these two giants.

KwaZulu-Natal can be divided into three broad landscape features, the Drakensberg range in the west, with the thick underlying beds of sandstone overlaid by a great blanket of basaltic lava, the Midlands, and the largely flat coastal plain. Its most famous reserves, which are also South Africa's oldest, lie in the north-east, centred on the Maputaland region and its inland fringes.

The vegetation more or less follows the three landscape features. Coastal dune and swamp forest dominate the coastal plain where this has not been destroyed by urbanization and agriculture; the Midland belt, now farmland, was originally a mix of savanna woodland with scatterings of forest; and the foothills and mountains are mostly grassland.

Most rain falls in summer which can be hot and humid, sometimes uncomfortably so in parts. Winters are usually mild, although it can be cool at night, especially in the interior.

The vegetation in Hluhluwe Game Reserve is typical of most Zululand conservation areas, with a mix of wood- and grassland.

KwaZulu-Natal 63

UKHAHLAMBA-DRAKENSBERG PARK

A major scenic park

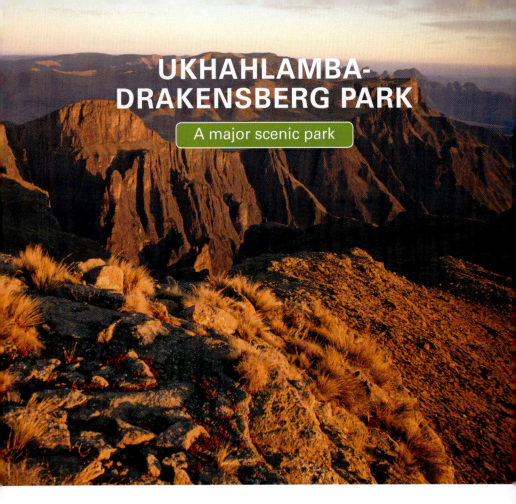

LOCATION

The view north along the crest of the Drakensberg range, the 'Barrier of Spears', is breathtaking.

Lie of the land

This World Heritage Site, covering almost 250 000 ha, follows a great eastward bulging arc, from just north of Cathedral Peak (3 004 m) where it adjoins uKhahlamba State Forest, southwards to Bushman's Nek, clinging to the Lesotho border in the west for its full length of more than 200 km. In the south it adjoins Lesotho's only national park, Sehlabathebe. A proposed transfrontier park will greatly expand the protected land in eastern Lesotho, linking in the north with Royal Natal Park, and several conservation areas in the Free State. The park is dominated by uKhahlamba, or the mighty Drakensberg, as it all falls within the foothills ('Little Berg') and escarpment ('High Berg') of this magnificent range. Several of the highest peaks in South Africa are here, including Giant's Castle (3 315 m), Mafadi (3 450 m), Champagne Castle (3 377 m) and, the tallest in southern Africa, Thabana Ntlenyana (3 482 m), just 10 km over the Lesotho border. The 'High Berg' consists of a series of near-vertical cliffs, while rugged to rolling hills make up the 'Little Berg'. Many of Natal's rivers have their sources in these mountains.

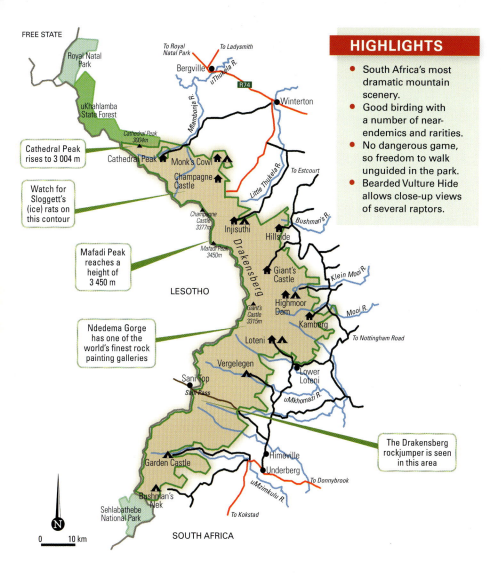

HIGHLIGHTS

- South Africa's most dramatic mountain scenery.
- Good birding with a number of near-endemics and rarities.
- No dangerous game, so freedom to walk unguided in the park.
- Bearded Vulture Hide allows close-up views of several raptors.

Brief history

There is ample evidence of early human presence in the Drakensberg region from at least the Middle Stone Age. However, it is the rock art left by the San of the Later Stone Age that is best documented. There are hundreds of locations with thousands of rock paintings from at least the past 1 500 years, although some have argued that they are mostly under 800 years old. Some of the paintings depict ox-wagons, men with rifles and cattle, and thus date from approximately the first half of the 19th century. There are about 4 000 paintings in the Ndedema Gorge alone.

The park protects some of the finest rock art sites in Africa.

uKhahlamba-Drakensberg Park **65**

Vegetation map

A naturally occurring population of eland roams widely.

- Drakensberg foothills moist grassland
- Northern Drakensberg highland grassland
- Southern Drakensberg highland grassland
- uKhahlamba basalt grassland
- Drakensberg Afroalpine heathland
- Northern Afrotemperate forest
- Afromontane heathland

The arrival of the first Nguni cattle farmers and, later, white settlers, sealed the fate of the San in uKhahlamba. As the black and white settlers decimated the wild game in the area, including eland, the San saw their neighbours' cattle as a legitimate food source. Pursued by the disgruntled cattle owners, the San hunters moved up into today's Lesotho. Many of these escape routes were dynamited and the San, now regarded as vermin like leopards, jackals and baboons, were gunned down on sight by white and black alike. Several military operations were mounted expressly to wipe them out. The British colonial authorities established a belt of black tribal reserves in the foothills to serve as a buffer against incursions by the remaining San. The last recorded San raid was in 1872. In 1873 a rebellion led by Langalibalele, a local tribal chief, against the colonial authorities was suppressed by a military detachment and the remnants of his people fled through what is now the Giant's Castle sector of uKhahlamba.

Giant's Castle was proclaimed a conservation area in 1903 in order to save the last eland, and other areas were added until the 1960s.

Endemic plants include these Christmas bells, also known as Chinese lantern lilies.

Geology and landscape

Whether one calls it uKhahlamba (Zulu for 'Barrier of Spears'), Drakensberg, Dragon Mountains, or the Dragon's Teeth, this is one of South Africa's most dramatic natural landscapes.

From the western edge of the Midlands, one sees first the foothills, then rising vertically behind them the great cliffs of basaltic lava and peaks towering more than 3 000 m above sea level. These cliffs are the last remnant of a vast basalt plain that resulted from eruptions of the so-called Drakensberg lavas some 180 million years ago. These erosional mountains are estimated to recede by 1.5 m per year. The basalts average about 1 500 m in thickness and overlie four different sedimentary formations, all of which are visible. The layer in contact with the basalt is the yellowish to pink Clarens sandstone (about 100 m thick), followed by the multicoloured mud- and sand-stones of the 200-m Elliot Formation and then the shale and sandstone layered Molteno Formation, which in its turn tops the sandstone and multicoloured mudstones of the Tarkastad Formation. The 'Little Berg' has lost its dolerite capping and is entirely composed of the above-mentioned sedimentary rocks, undergoing more rapid erosion. These sedimentary strata are rich in fossils, ranging from dinosaurs in the Elliot, to plants and insects in the Molteno.

Vegetation

The dominant plants are grasses, and you will see grassland everywhere you look. In the highest reaches, from about 1 800 m to 3 300 m, the basalt grasslands lie just below the edge of the highland plateau of Lesotho, with a strong mix of herbaceous plants. The tall **giant turpentine grass** (*Cymbopogon validus*), **Munnik fescue** (*Festuca scabra*), **Mahem's crest** (*Rendlia altera*) and **red grass** (*Themeda triandra*) are just a few examples. Highland grasses near Giant's Castle consist mainly of tussock grasses with fewer herbs, based on sedimentary rocks between 1 400 m and 2 000 m. **Red grass** is here, as are several **fescue** species (*Festuca* spp.), various 'love grasses' (*Eragrostis* spp.), **spear grass** (*Trachypogon spicatus*) and **vlei bluestem** (*Andropogon appendiculatus*). The high grasslands extending northwards from Giant's Castle are predominantly short, sour grasslands rich in non-grass plants, including scatterings of tall **common sugarbush** (*Protea caffra*) and **silver sugarbush** (*Protea roupelliae*). We again meet red grass here but there are many other species too, such as **bristle grass** (*Setaria sphacelata*), **finger grasses** (*Digitaria* spp.) and **spear grass** (*Heteropogon contortus*). Scattered in small patches in the grasslands are clusters of Afromontane heathland (fynbos) growing in deep valleys. Small-leaved, evergreen shrubs that grow up to 3 m dominate, including such species as **lip-flower sugarbush** (*Protea subvestita*) whose cream-white to pink flowers bloom in summer through autumn, **Drakensberg proteas** (*Protea dracomontana*) whose big cream to rusty-pink blooms appear from January to March, and **mountain cypress** (*Widdringtonia nodiflora*). There are also several heaths, including the tall **water tree heath** (*Erica caffra*) that produces its numerous small white flowers in spring. There are many endemic plant species. As with the heathland there are also tiny patches of Afrotemperate forest, which are mostly protected from fire in deep gorges and on steep slopes from 1 450 m to 1 950 m above sea

CLIMATE

This is a summer-rainfall area but climatic extremes and sudden weather changes are possible at any time of the year. Rainfall in the upper reaches averages 1 234 mm to 1 820 mm annually. At lower altitudes, annual falls range from 780 mm to 1 000 mm. The annual mean temperature is 12°C but may reach 30°C in summer. Frost is common in winter, with snowfalls at high altitudes. Morning mists, hot, dry winds and impressive thunderstorms are common in summer, from July to October.

Most camps, resorts and camping grounds in the Ukhahlamba-Drakensberg Park have dramatic backdrops, such as the Loteni campsite in the southern section of the park.

FACILITIES AND ACTIVITIES

- Several hotels on boundary; huts and lodges at several points including Giant's Castle, Kamberg and Loteni; several campgrounds within and outside the park.
- Many walking and hiking trails ranging from one hour to several days.
- Mountain bike trails.
- Guided walking trails to San rock art sites.
- Bearded Vulture Hide near Giant's Castle – booking essential.
- Trout fishing.
- Few sites have fuel, and supplies may be limited or nonexistent.
- Nearest towns with full services are Ladismith and Estcourt, with Underberg in the far south. Pietermaritzburg is 180 km away.
- There are at least 12 entry points to the park, including (starting from the north) Cathedral Peak, Champagne Castle, Giant's Castle, Highmoor, Kamberg, Loteni, Vergelegen, Sani Pass (through to Lesotho), Drakensberg Garden and Bushman's Nek.

Didima Resort is near Cathedral Peak.

Mountain reedbuck avoid the most rugged terrain.

level. Larger trees include real yellowwood (*Podocarpus latifolius*), **mountain hard pear** (*Olinia emarginata*), **white stinkwood** (*Celtis africana*) and **cheesewood** (*Pittosporum viridiflorum*).

Wildlife
Mammals

This is not a rich game area but several larger species, including **red hartebeest**, **black wildebeest** and **blesbok**, have been reintroduced into the Giant's Castle area. **Common eland** here are survivors from the free-ranging herds. Today they occur in good numbers throughout the park. Other naturally occurring antelope include **bushbuck** (in forest pockets), **common reedbuck**, **mountain reedbuck**, **oribi**, **grey rhebok**, **common duiker** and **klipspringer**. Although there are occasional reports of **leopard**, the main predators are **caracal**, **black-backed jackal** and **serval**. The jackal is regularly seen and heard and if you are lucky you may see a hunting serval. Other small carnivores, such as the **African striped weasel**, are generally secretive and nocturnal. **Chacma baboons** are found throughout the park; there are believed to be more than 300 troops. Some of the small mammals live at particularly high altitudes. The record is taken by **Sloggett's**, or **ice**, **rat** that lives in rock crevices on the highest crests between 2 750 m and 3 000 m in the alpine zone. It is day-active and will forage even in frost or snow, reaching densities of 100 animals to a hectare. A few other small rodents also live above 2 200 m, such as the **pygmy mouse** and **four-striped grass mouse**, while the **woodland dormouse** has been found in forest pockets at 2 700 m in the Giant's Castle sector. **Sclater's golden mole** lives more than 3 000 m above sea level but spends most of its life underground.

Birds

The Drakensberg is an excellent birding destination, and at least 340 species, including vagrants, can be seen here. This is the prime location for the **bearded vulture**, or **lammergeier**, usually above

Bearded vultures are resident in the Drakensberg.

The Drakensberg rockjumper is a local endemic.

1 500 m above sea level. About 200 breeding pairs live in the Drakensberg, but not all within the park. From May to September, the bearded vulture hide is often good for this species as well as **Cape vulture**, **lanner falcon**, **jackal buzzard** and **Cape raven**. Several of the Drakensberg specials require some stiff hiking, although a drive to the top of the Sani Pass will usually show some results. The **Drakensberg rockjumper** lives above 2 450 m in summer but descends a few hundred metres in winter. Likewise, the **Drakensberg siskin** prefers the heights at 2 600 m to 3 000 m during the warmer months but drops to about 2 000 m in winter. Four species of francolin have been recorded, including the **grey-winged francolin** that can be seen even on high-altitude grasslands. This is a good area for the **southern bald ibis**, which favours the 1 200 m to 1 800 m belt. Other open grassland birds include **southern ground hornbill**, **yellow-breasted pipit** and **mountain pipit**. At least three species of flufftail are recorded, including the **buff-spotted flufftail** from about 2 500 m above sea level, but these are elusive birds and a knowledge of their calls will help. Scan the skies for the hyrax-hunting **Verreaux's eagle** and the **forest buzzard**. Other specials include **ground woodpecker**, **Cape eagle-owl** (recorded above 3 000 m and elsewhere), **Gurney's sugarbird** and **malachite sunbird**, especially where there are proteas or aloes in flower. As always, bird-watching in the camps is worthwhile.

Reptiles and amphibians

Although many of the 54 reptile and 28 amphibian species are found at lower altitudes, a few Drakensberg endemics occur higher up. Although not endemic, the venomous **berg adder** has been observed as high as 3 000 m, and two of the three **mountain lizards** of the genus *Tropidosaura* live among the highest peaks. **Lang's** and **Drakensberg crag lizards** also occupy high-altitude areas, as does the **spiny crag lizard** which favours the 1 500 m to 2 500 m range. Another Drakensberg endemic, the **mountain flat gecko**, has been found up to 2 750 metres above sea level, and there are even two

WILDLIFE FACTS

- Some 62 species of mammal, of which the largest is the common eland.
- Oribi, mountain reedbuck and grey rhebok present.
- Some 340 bird species, including several Drakensberg endemics or near-endemics.
- At least 54 reptiles and 28 amphibian species. Several are largely restricted to uKhahlamba and its close vicinity.
- Introduced brown and rainbow trout are predators of indigenous fish.
- More than 1 000 plant species.

The Drakensberg river frog is only found in high mountainous grassland regions in KwaZulu-Natal and Lesotho.

chameleons, the **Drakensberg dwarf** and the **Emerald dwarf**, that occupy suitable habitat up to 2 500 m. The mildly venomous **cream-spotted mountain snake**, was unknown until 1980 when the first specimen was collected at Cathedral Peak. Several frogs are only found in the Drakensberg, including the **Drakensberg river frog** that lives in streams on the top of the plateau. Another high-altitude dweller is the **large-mouthed frog**, which spends virtually its entire life in water. The **Drakensberg stream frog** is another endemic as is the **long-toed tree frog**. The latter is a misnomer as it never goes near a tree and lives on the ground, 1 800 m or more above sea level. You have little chance of seeing any of these frogs, but several species of toad may be seen foraging for insects at night around the accommodation areas. They, too, prefer higher altitudes, and the widespread **Karoo toad** lives at over 3 000 m.

Fish

Unfortunately, exotic carnivorous **brown** and **rainbow trout** have nearly eliminated the indigenous fish, of which about six species survive. The endemic **Drakensberg minnow** has not been recorded here since the 1930s but survives in Lesotho's Sehlabathebe National Park at uKhahlamba's southern border.

Although fly-fishing is popular here, the trout species found in these rivers are not endemic to South Africa and have been responsible for the decline of indigenous species.

- Be prepared for changing weather conditions at all times if you are hiking.
- Be alert for unstable ground conditions, such as slippery rocks.

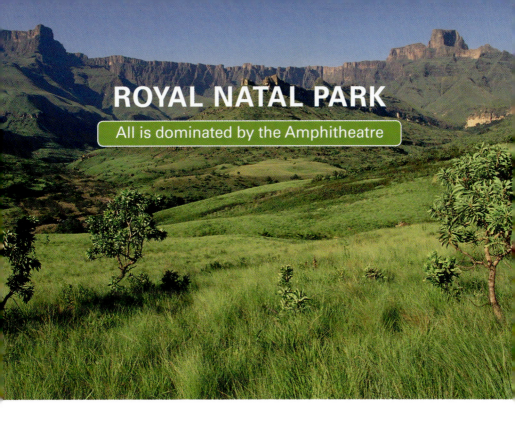

ROYAL NATAL PARK
All is dominated by the Amphitheatre

Lie of the land

Royal Natal covers just over 8 000 ha, was proclaimed in 1916, and lies 46 km west of the small town of Bergville, west of the Oliviershoek Pass. The park is focused on the great sheer crescent-shaped rock face of the Amphitheatre, averaging 2 926 m and dominating all below it. On the east of the Amphitheatre is the mighty uThukela (Tugela) waterfall that tumbles an almost sheer 850 m and the 3 282 m Mont-aux-Sources where this river rises. Flowing north-west from Mont-aux-Sources are the feeder streams forming the headwaters of the Orange (Gariep) River that cuts westwards across South Africa to the Atlantic Ocean. To the east of the Amphitheatre is the second highest peak, the Sentinel at 3 165 m, although several others to the south top 3 000 m. Below the cliffs are the foothills, or 'Little Berg'. Royal Natal is now part of uKhahlamba-Drakensberg Park and shares many similarities with other parts of the range and its foothills.

LOCATION

Brief history

The San people had probably been here for thousands of years before the first Nguni farmers and cattle herders arrived, followed much later by the first white hunters and settlers. The last San here, possibly the last in uKhahlamba, are believed to have left by 1878. Rock art testifies to their residency.

The source of the uThukela and Orange (Gariep) rivers was discovered and named Mont-aux-Sources by the missionaries Arbousset and Daumas in 1836.

The Amphitheatre in the Royal Natal Park is one of the best-known features in the Drakensberg.

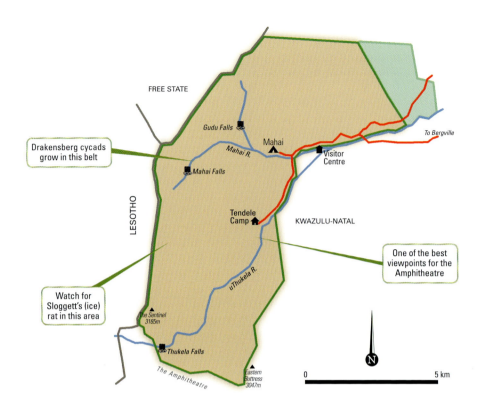

HIGHLIGHTS

- Spectacular scenery, centred on Amphitheatre rock formation.
- Focus on hiking trails (minimal roads).
- Good birding.

Sloggett's (ice) rat can be seen along the escarpment crest.

Much of the foothill country was surveyed in 1884 and a few farms were purchased. Large numbers of hardwood trees, especially yellowwoods, were felled, a practice that continued into the 1930s.

The park was proclaimed in 1916 but the final land purchases were only made in 1950. The park was named for a visit by the British royal family in 1947.

Geology and landscape

As you drive towards the park, the scene is dominated by the mighty cliffs of the Amphitheatre, with its thick dolerite capping and the lower strata of sand, silt and mudstones. These multi-coloured sedimentary strata also make up the foothills usually called the 'Little Berg'. As the great dolerite escarpment erodes it exposes the softer strata to even more rapid erosional forces.

Vegetation

The higher and western reaches of the park are dominated by grassland on basaltic soils, but on the summit you will find mainly low heath plants such as small-leaved heath (*Erica* spp.) and everlastings (*Heliochrysum* spp.), and no trees. On the moist south-facing slopes

The leaves of the Drakensberg tree fern grow up to 1 m long.

CLIMATE

The overall climate here is very similar to that of the main sector of uKhahlamba to the south, with summer rains, at higher altitudes exceeding 1 000 mm per annum (see page 67). Mists and winter snow are frequent in the higher reaches. Extremes of weather must be expected at any time of year.

and elsewhere the temperate evergreen grasslands are characterized by the **fescue** (*Festuca costata*), and abundant **red grass** (*Themeda triandra*), valuable for grazing. This grassland dominates the park but it is studded with small patches of Afromontane heathland (fynbos) and Afrotemperate forest, mainly restricted to sheltered slopes and deeper valleys where there is some protection from the fires that periodically sweep across these mountain slopes. Look out for the **Drakensberg cycad** (*Encephalartos ghellinckii*), stands of the **Drakensberg protea** (*Protea dracomontana*) that are fire-adapted by having underground stems and large rootstocks, and the **common sugarbush** (*Protea caffra*) that is more restricted to sandstone-derived soils and forms open woodland in places. In the wetter places you will see **common tree ferns** (*Cyathea dregei*), some 5 m high. The diversity of trees in the forest pockets is similar to that found throughout the uKhahlamba, with **white stinkwood** (*Celtis africana*), large **yellowwood** (*Podocarpus* spp.) and **Cape chestnut** (*Calodendrum capense*) (see page 67). In fact more than 900 species of tree and bush have been recorded in the park. The uThukela River valley, where you enter the park, is foothill moist grassland and the vegetation structure here differs somewhat from that of the higher altitude grasslands, though some species are shared. Much of the road from the entrance to the park office passes through bushland that includes **oldwood**, or **ouhout**, (*Leucosidea sericea*), also found in pockets at higher altitudes. Dominant grasses here include red grass and **hairy trident grass** (*Tristachya leucothrix*).

Wildlife
Mammals

Eland occupy high grasslands in summer but during the harsh winter months they descend to more sheltered areas to feed. **Bushbuck** and **common duiker** are seen in the forest and bush pockets, mostly in the early morning and late afternoon, and below 1 900 m. On the

Drakensberg proteas are well adapted to surviving fire.

Vegetation map

○ Northern KwaZulu-Natal moist grassland
○ Northern Drakensberg highland grassland
● Afroalpine heathland
● uKhahlamba basalt grassland
● Northern Afrotemperate forest
● Afromontane fynbos

FACILITIES AND ACTIVITIES

- Tendele Camp has 28 accommodation units (2–6 beds); Mahai campground can accommodate up to 400 people; Mont-aux-Sources Hotel is on the eastern boundary.
- Extensive network of footpaths and hiking trails (about 130 km) – permits required for the latter.
- San rock paintings in Sigubudu valley and elsewhere.
- No internal roads except to camps.
- Take own supplies.

Chacma baboons are prevalent throughout the park.

The insect-eating Cape batis is commonly seen at picnic sites.

open grassland there are small family parties of **oribi** and **mountain reedbuck**, as well **grey rhebok**, with **klipspringer** on the broken upper slopes, rarely above 2 800 m. **Chacma baboons** occur throughout, from the alpine crests to the lowest riverine bush- and grasslands, but troops in the high areas tend to be smaller than those in the more hospitable low altitudes, and they tend to migrate downward in winter. **Rock hyrax** are common wherever there are suitable rock piles and crevices, but rarely higher than 2 600 m above sea level. As elsewhere in uKhahlamba **Sloggett's**, or **ice**, **rat** is common on the highest ridges throughout the year.

Birds

The birds you are likely to see here are widespread in the mountain range and include the raptors, **bearded vulture** (watch for the 'diamond-shaped' tail), **Cape vulture**, **Verreaux's eagle** the hyrax hunter, **jackal buzzard** and the small **rock**, or **common**, **kestrel**. In suitable habitat, such as the bush along the entrance road, watch for **red-necked spurfowl**, **Drakensberg prinia**, **bush blackcap** and **swee waxbill**. Wherever there are stands of protea, or other nectar-producers, scan for **Gurney's sugarbird** and **malachite sunbird**.

Reptiles and amphibians

The herpetofauna in Royal Natal closely follows that for the rest of uKhuhlamba and needs little further explanation (see pages 69–70).

Rock hyrax frequently cross some of the access roads.

WILDLIFE FACTS

- Some 56 mammal species in the area.
- Bird life is rich, similar to the rest of the mountains to the south.
- More than 900 plant species, including some near endemics.

- When walking always be prepared for sudden changes in the weather, at any time of year.
- When above 2 500 m, be alert and prepared for the onset of altitude sickness.
- Baboon can be a nuisance in places. Do not feed them or leave food unattended.

KwaZulu-Natal

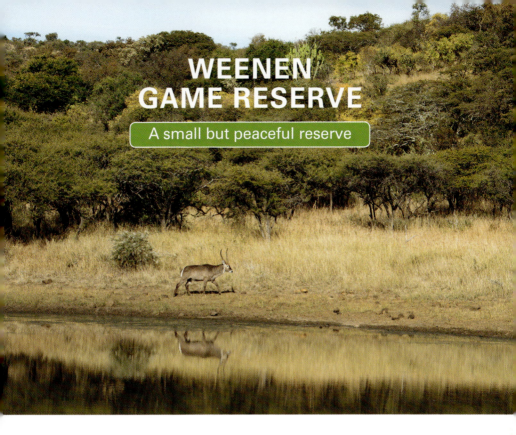

WEENEN GAME RESERVE
A small but peaceful reserve

Lie of the land
The 5 000 ha Weenen Game Reserve lies in the KwaZulu-Natal Midlands, some 25 km north-east from Estcourt, 20 km from Colenso and 8 km from the Weenen settlement. The northern boundary extends to the Colenso-Weenen road and all boundaries are fenced. The reserve is flat to undulating with rugged hills in parts, notably in the south and south-east, and surrounded by cattle-grazing farmland. Altitudes range from 1 000 m to 1 240 m above sea level. The Bushman's River flows through a steep valley in the southern part.

Brief history
There is evidence that Stone Age hunter-gatherers lived in this area for several hundred thousand years, followed by Iron Age settlers from about 1000 AD. By 1500 AD the area was quite densely populated. There are relics from the Stone Ages and Iron Age, while larger stone structures are the remains of cattle enclosures (*isiBaya*) from more recent settlement. There is a San rock painting site along the Bushman's River but its age is unknown.

The first whites to move through the area were the Voortrekkers during the 1840s. One of the farms proclaimed shortly thereafter was 'Onverwacht'. The first owner sold the property in 1862, and it was eventually bought by the government in 1948 before eventually becoming part of the Weenen reserve.

Much of Weenen Game Reserve is covered by thornveld.

Weenen Game Reserve 75

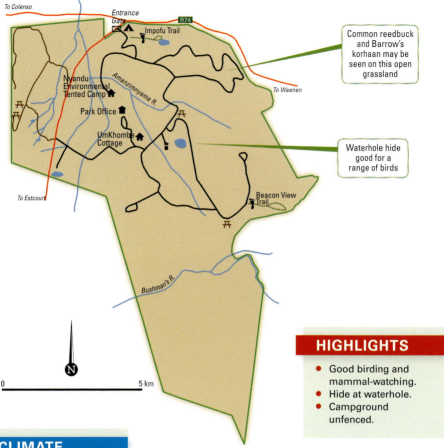

HIGHLIGHTS

- Good birding and mammal-watching.
- Hide at waterhole.
- Campground unfenced.

CLIMATE

This is a summer rainfall area, averaging 56 thunderstorms each summer. Annual rainfall averages 750 mm but it is erratic, ranging from 429 mm to more than 1 000 mm. Temperatures may reach 37°C in summer (the record is 41°C) and 1°C in winter. Mean daily temperatures in January are 17°C to 29°C; in June 2°C to 21°C. Frost may occur on higher ground for up to 10 days each winter.

From the Mtunzini picnic site, looking down into the valley, you can see an irrigation channel dug by the Voortrekkers in 1841. There are also the remains of a narrow-gauge railway between Estcourt and Weenen that was commissioned in 1907 and closed in 1983.

Geology and landscape

Flat to undulating country with steep, rocky hills in the south and south-east. Rock formations of the Karoo system and the Beaufort Series predominate, with dolerite intrusions forming plateaux in the southern hill country. The Bushman's River, a tributary of the uThukela River, is perennial but other streams only flow during the summer rains. Soils are shallow and despite reclamation work necessitated by bad farming practices in the past, evidence of soil erosion can still be seen.

Weenen consists mainly of flat to undulating country, well wooded in parts.

Vegetation
Much of the north of the reserve is known as Thukela thornveld: open grassy woodland and in places dense thicket dominated by acacia trees. Trees here include **scented thorn** (*Vachellia nilotica*), **paperbark thorn** (*Vachellia sieberiana*) with its flaking, paper-like bark, **Natal thorn** (*Vachellia natalitia*) and the **umbrella thorn** (*Vachellia tortilis*). In the north-central and south-west parts of the reserve the vegetation is classified as highland thornveld but is similar in many ways, with paperbark thorn and scented thorn, as well as **sickle bush** (*Dichrostachys cinerea*), among others. Grass species include **weeping love grass** (*Eragrostis curvula*), **common thatching grass** (*Hyparrhenia hirta*) and **red grass** (*Themeda triandra*), all important grasses for herbivores. Between the two blocks of highland thornveld and in the south are areas of Thukela valley bushveld; look for **cabbage tree** (*Cussonia spicata*), the succulent **candelabra tree** (*Euphorbia ingens*), **Natal fig** (*Ficus natalensis*), **wild olive** (*Olea europaea*) and **weeping boer-bean** (*Schotia brachypetala*). In places, such as along the Bushman's River, the valley bushveld forms dense thickets.

Wildlife
Mammals
There are 48 recorded mammal species, including 14 that have been introduced or reintroduced. Both **square-lipped** and **hook-lipped rhinoceros** are present; the latter is more difficult to find as it tends to keep to dense thickets during the day, whereas the former is a grazer,

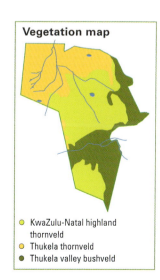

Vegetation map

○ KwaZulu-Natal highland thornveld
○ Thukela thornveld
● Thukela valley bushveld

FACILITIES AND ACTIVITIES

- UmKhombe cottage for up to five people; 12 caravan/camping sites at entrance gate.
- 8–10 km guided walking trail.
- Good 4x4 trails; network of 2x4 game-viewing roads.
- Picnic sites good for birding.
- No fuel or supplies in the reserve.
- Services in Colenso or Estcourt; minimal services in Weenen.
- Access roads are tarred; internal roads are gravel.

A single giraffe calf is normally born after 450 days of gestation, though twins do occur occasionally.

feeding in more open areas. Commonly seen game species include **plains zebra**, **giraffe**, **savanna buffalo**, **greater kudu**, **common waterbuck**, **red hartebeest**, **common duiker** and **common reedbuck**. Watch for **mountain reedbuck** in the broken hill country. The largest predator is the seldom-seen **spotted hyaena**. **Black-backed jackal** are occasionally seen but more commonly heard calling in the evening. The most visible predator is the day-active and solitary **slender mongoose**. Most of the 10 rodent species known are nocturnal and secretive. Although only two bat species have been recorded it is likely that several more are present permanently, or seasonally. One small mammal you might see in the rocky hill country along the Bushman's River valley is the **rock hyrax**.

Black-headed herons hunt at dams and in open grassland.

Square-lipped rhinoceros are grazers and favour open areas.

Birds

At least 267 species of bird have been observed, including vagrants and migrants. The **black-bellied korhaan** and the secretive **Barrow's korhaan** are found on the open grassland. No fewer than eight cuckoo species and 29 different raptors have been recorded. These include **crowned eagle**, **brown snake eagle**, **long-crested eagle**, **Wahlberg's eagle**, **African cuckoo-hawk** and **secretarybird**. Commonly seen are **Natal** and **Swainson's spurfowl**, **helmeted guineafowl**, and several of the nine recorded species of pigeons and doves. You have a good chance of hearing several of the six owls, including the **western barn owl**, **African scops owl** and **spotted eagle-owl**. If you enjoy the LBJs then you can search here for no fewer than 24 warblers and warbler-types, six different pipits and five larks. One of our favourite groups, the shrikes, has had 13 species recorded here, including **black-backed puffback**, **brubru** and **gorgeous bushshrike**. **Red-billed oxpeckers** are present, as are six sunbirds including **scarlet-chested sunbird**, and three buntings including the **golden-breasted bunting**.

Reptiles and amphibians

The two land tortoises, the **leopard tortoise** and the **Natal hinged tortoise**, are seldom seen. Although only 13 lizard species have been recorded, several more are known from neighbouring areas. Both the **rock** and **water monitor** lizards occur, and you are most likely to see **flap-neck chameleon**, the common **tree agama** and the tiny **Cape dwarf gecko**, which is day-active and inhabits the trees in the campground. The 13 amphibians are seldom seen, although during the rainy season the courtship calls of the males cannot be ignored. As with many South African reserves it is usually the toads that draw attention to themselves by hunting insects attracted to the lights at night around the accommodation sites. Watch for **guttural**, **raucous** and **red toads**.

Fish

Of the seven species of fish recorded here, three of them are exotics, namely **carp**, **grass carp** and **large-mouth bass** but it is believed that the grass carp is no longer present. The indigenous species found in the Bushman's River are **chubby-headed minnow**, **three-spot barb**, **mottled eel** and **KwaZulu-Natal yellowfish**, or **scaly yellowfish**.

> **WILDLIFE FACTS**
> - Some 48 mammals, including both rhinoceros species and roan antelope.
> - For a small reserve the bird-list of 267 species is very respectable.
> - At least 28 reptile and 13 amphibian species.
> - Only seven fish species have been recorded, of which three are exotics.

The long-crested eagle is one of 29 raptor species in the reserve.

- The campground, picnic sites and the cottage are not fenced so be alert for dangerous animals.

Southern tree agamas are superbly camouflaged.

Weenen Game Reserve

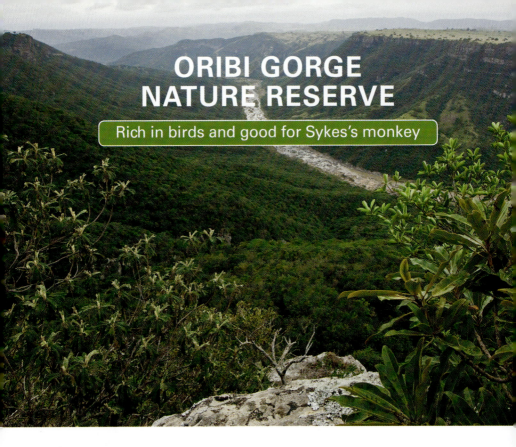

ORIBI GORGE NATURE RESERVE

Rich in birds and good for Sykes's monkey

LOCATION

Lie of the land

The 1 837 ha Oribi Gorge Nature Reserve is located just 25 km from the Indian Ocean coastline, inland from Port Shepstone, and about 150 km south of Durban. It is focused on a 24 km stretch of the Oribi Gorge, through which the uMzimkulwana River has carved its path, leaving sheer cliffs in many places. The bottom of the gorge lies at about 120 m above sea level, with the highest point at some 680 m above sea level.

Brief history

Prior to its proclamation as a nature reserve in 1950 the area fell within the uMzimkulwana State Forest, established in 1920 and 1928. Land was added up to 1970. The surrounding area is predominantly commercial farmland.

Geology and landscape

The uMzimkulwana River has cut through a 500 m-high plateau to create the Oribi Gorge. The rock formations are thick strata of sandstones belonging to the Karoo Supergroup, overlying granite, with the latter only exposed at the bottom of the gorge.

The spectacular Oribi Gorge is the dominant landform feature of this reserve.

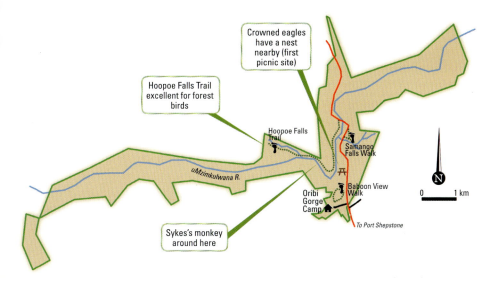

Vegetation

Four distinct vegetation types can be recognized within Oribi Gorge: scarp forest, valley bushveld, coastal sourveld and Ngongoni veld. Scarp forest is the most obvious, dominating the slopes and bottom of the gorge. Trees tend to be tall, from 15 m to 25 m, species-rich and the forest multi-layered. A few of the characteristic trees are **fluted milkwood** (*Chrysophyllum viridifolium*) with its distinctive fluted lower trunk, **red quince** (*Cryptocarya wyliei*), **forest ironplum** (*Drypetes gerrardii*), **forest elder** (*Nuxia floribunda*), **wild pepper tree** (*Loxostylis alata*) and **Cape ebony** (*Heywoodia lucens*). Valley bushveld is semi-deciduous savanna woodland that generally flanks the scarp forest and includes a scattering of thickets and several species of succulent euphorbias and aloes. Coastal sourveld, known as Pondoland-Ugu sandstone coastal sourveld, occurs in small patches on the outer edges of the reserve and is a species-rich grassland with a scattering of low shrubs and small trees; these include **silver sugarbush** (*Protea roupelliae*). Ngongoni veld is a small area of dense tall grassland in the extreme south-west of the reserve, away from the tourist area, dominated by the unpalatable **Ngongoni grass** (*Aristida junciformis*), and species diversity is low.

HIGHLIGHTS

- Dramatic and rugged scenery.
- Excellent forest birding.
- Several rare and localised mammals, including blue duiker, Sykes's monkey and tree hyrax.
- Easy access.

Vegetation map

- Ngongoni veld
- Sandstone coastal sourveld
- Eastern valley bushveld
- Scarp forest

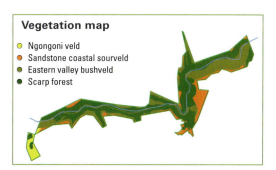

Wildlife
Mammals

Although many of the mammal species in the Oribi Gorge reserve are small, secretive and nocturnal, several interesting mammals are to

CLIMATE

A very variable summer rainfall area, annual totals range from 570 mm to as high as 1 625 mm (in 1965). Most rain falls between October and March; July is the driest month. Mean January temperatures are 16.6°C to 32.2°C; July 5.8°C to 20.5°C. The recorded extremes are 1.7°C and 41.1°C. Frost does not occur here.

Blue duiker are secretive and seldom seen.

be found here. The forests of the reserve offer one of the best chances in South Africa to observe **Sykes's monkey**, with about 600 animals. There are about 150 **vervet monkeys**. Since they avoid dense forest, suitable habitat is more limited. **Chacma baboons** number about 90 animals in several troops within the gorge. If you sleep in the reserve you are likely to hear the blood-curdling call of the nocturnal **tree hyrax**; their close cousin, the **rock hyrax**, is day-active and commonly seen. Do not confuse the harsh call of the **thick-tailed galago** with that of the tree hyrax. **Leopard** occasionally move through the gorge as evidenced by kills, and an additional 11 carnivores are believed to be present, including five species of mongoose. Despite the reserve's name no **oribi** occur in this conservation area though they are known from surrounding properties, but **bushbuck** are the most frequently sighted antelope. **Blue duiker** are also fairly abundant but secretive, hence seldom seen.

Oribi Gorge reserve is one of the best locations to observe Sykes's monkey.

The tree hyrax is one of two hyrax species in Oribi Gorge.

Birds

Oribi Gorge is an excellent and accessible forested reserve to see, and hear, many species tied to this habitat. Although there are several walking trails, some of the best bird-watching can be had by stopping at the picnic site, along the tarred access road, or at the camp. Look out for **Knysna woodpecker**, **Narina trogon**, **crowned eagle**, **trumpeter hornbill**, **brown scrub robin**, **spotted ground thrush** and **green twinspot**. Just above the first picnic site is the long-established nest of a pair of **crowned eagles**. The river is good for a number of species, including **mountain wagtail**, **African black duck**, **African finfoot** and several species of kingfisher. The open grassland beyond the picnic site, towards the camp, is good for seed-eaters such as **red-backed mannikin** and **green twinspot**, with the possibility of hearing **African broadbill** on the forest edge.

The malachite kingfisher is one of several species of kingfisher that can be seen along the river.

Reptiles and amphibians

This small reserve has at least 21 reptile and 14 amphibian species. South Africa's two longest snake species, **southern African python** and **black mamba**, are seldom seen but a further 10 snake species are known. Most lizard species are cryptic but **tree agamas** are obvious and can often be seen in the camp, like the small diurnal **Cape dwarf gecko**. Watch also for **rock agamas** along the upper edge of the gorge and in other rocky situations. As usual the amphibians you are most likely to see will be toads, three species in this case, in the camp. During the rains you will hear the males of several species calling. An interesting but diminutive frog, 30 mm to 35 mm, that occurs in the streams that pass through the forest is the **kloof frog**. Males have a very soft clicking call that is repeated at irregular intervals. The female attaches 75 to 100 eggs to vegetation or rocks overhanging water, and the tadpoles undergo partial development before dropping into the water below.

Fish

The largest species present is the **Natal**, or **scaly**, **yellowfish**, said to be common here; the river is a probable breeding location.

- Bilharzia is present and one should not enter water, even on a hot day.

FACILITIES AND ACTIVITIES

- Six 2- or 4-bed chalets and a 7-bed cottage, all self-contained; tent camping; Oribi Gorge Hotel just outside reserve.
- Picnic site offers excellent forest birding.
- Hiking and walking trails of 1–9 km.
- Closest town with range of services is Port Shepstone.
- Access road to the bottom of the gorge.
- Vulture viewing hide just outside reserve boundary; must be booked in advance.

WILDLIFE FACTS

- Some 48 mammal species; the eponymous oribi occur only on neighbouring farmland.
- At least 230 species of bird. Best place in KwaZulu-Natal to see Knysna woodpecker.
- There are 21 reptile and 19 amphibian species in the immediate area.
- Six species of fish have been recorded.
- More than 700 plant species, including many trees and bushes.

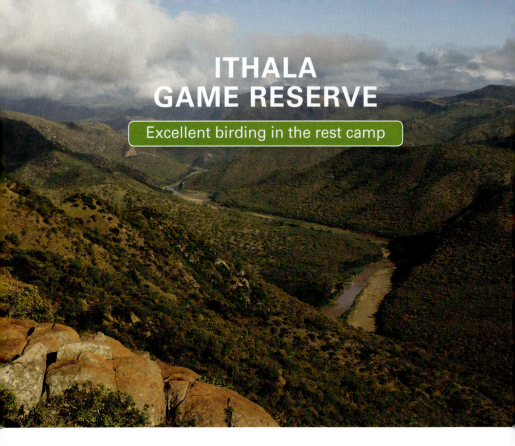

ITHALA GAME RESERVE

Excellent birding in the rest camp

LOCATION

Lie of the land

Located in northern KwaZulu-Natal, the 30 000 ha Ithala, proclaimed in 1972, is about 60 km north-east of Vryheid, with entry to the reserve through Louwsburg. The reserve is bordered to the north by the Pongola River, which flows into the Manzana River in the north-west. This is a mountainous reserve, with the high hills of Nkwambase, Nkangala and Madibe to the west, rugged ridge-lines intersected by deep stream beds throughout, and the land falling steeply to the Pongola in the north. The highest hills are about 1 400 m above sea level, dropping to some 400 m. Ngotshe Mountain rises to 1 450 m above sea level. The reserve is fenced along its southern, eastern and western boundaries but the Pongola River boundary is unfenced.

Brief history

Stone tools testify to the presence of people in the Middle Stone Age, and the San in the Later Stone Age. Surprisingly, few rock paintings have been discovered although there is some San art in an overhang near the Mhlangeni Bush Camp. There are also Iron Age sites where iron ore was excavated for smelting.

The present-day reserve formed part of a vast tract of land that the Zulu king Dinizulu granted to 800 Boers for settlement in 1884. In this 'Nieuwe Republiek'

The Pongola River gorge forms the northern border of Ithala.

84 KwaZulu-Natal

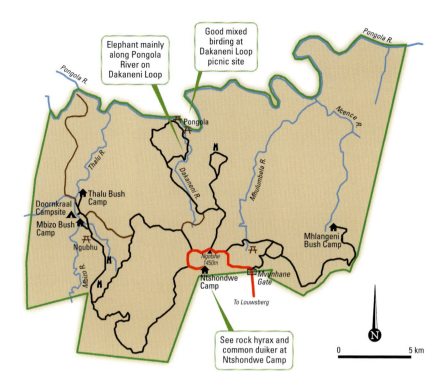

the once abundant game was over-hunted, then depleted by the rinderpest of 1896, and finally devastated by the attempt to eradicate nagana, the cattle disease carried by the tsetse fly.

The land that was set aside for conservation had been badly abused in the past and had suffered overgrazing and consequent erosion. Since its proclamation as a reserve, Ithala has shown remarkable signs of recovery. It has been restocked and some 23 species of larger mammals have been reintroduced.

Geology and landscape

Ithala has a great diversity of geological features, including rocks of the Mozaan Group of the Karoo Sequence that were originally laid down some 3 000 million years BP. Much of the reserve is covered by bands of shales and quartzites, with areas of higher ground capped or intruded by dolerite and diabase. The most recent rocks in the south of the reserve are little more than 200 million years old, and made up of sandstone and shales of the Ecca Group, as well as sandstones, shales and tillite of the Dwyka Formation. It is this rich geology and the soils derived from it that have allowed such rich plant diversity to evolve here. The landscape is dominated by the rugged hills and deeply incised plateau, and the deep valley cut by the Pongola River.

HIGHLIGHTS

- Excellent game-viewing, all of Big Five except lion.
- Diverse bird populations, including several rarities.
- Unfenced main and bush camps.

Sweet thorn in flower.

Ithala Game Reserve 85

CLIMATE

Ithala is a summer rainfall region averaging about 800 mm each year; most falls in midsummer. Rainfall may exceed 1 000 mm at higher altitudes. Mist in the hills is not unusual in spring and summer, and there are occasional frosts in winter. Mean annual temperature is about 17°C but summers can be hot and humid, especially along the Pongola River.

There is a small population of spotted hyaena in the reserve.

Familiar chats are regular visitors to the camp.

Vegetation

Large areas of the reserve are covered by Ithala quartzite sourveld, a mix of tall grassland with a mosaic of woody shrubs and small trees especially in the more rocky areas. Important grasses here include **spear grass** (*Heteropogon contortus*), **yellow thatching grass** (*Hyperthelia dissoluta*) and **Natal panicum** (*Panicum natalense*). Trees here are generally short and include the widespread **sweet thorn** (*Vachellia karroo*). Near the park entrance on the steep slopes you will see short mountain grassland. The woodlands are dominated by various Senegalia species, such as **flame thorn** (*Senegalia ataxacantha*), which stands out in late summer and autumn with its attractive red pods, **black monkey thorn** (*S. burkei*), **common hook-thorn** (*S. caffra*) and **knob thorn** (*S. nigrescens*). Other obvious trees include the tall succulent **Transvaal candelabra** (*Euphorbia cooperi*) and **common tree euphorbia** (*Euphorbia ingens*), **Zulu cabbage tree** (*Cussonia zuluensis*), **wild teak** (*Pterocarpus angolensis*) and **Lebombo cluster-leaf** (*Terminalia phanerophlebia*), to name but a few. The banks of the Pongola River host some fine trees, including the **sycamore fig** (*Ficus sycamorus*). Several species of protea grow on the slopes. There are botanically important species, including the **pepper bark tree** (*Warburgia salutaris*), that because of its supposed medicinal uses has become extinct over much of northern KwaZulu-Natal. The high cliffs of the reserve are home to the endangered **Lebombo cycad** (*Encephalartus lebomboensis*).

Vegetation map

- ○ Short mountain grassland
- ○ Undulating tall grassland
- ● Basin bushveld or thicket and mixed thornveld
- ● Wooded rocky outcrops
- ● Tall deciduous woodland
- ● Sparsely wooded hill slopes
- ● Riverine and scree forest

Wildlife
Mammals

Savanna elephant and **buffalo** keep mainly to the dense bush along the Pongola River. **Hook-lipped** and **square-lipped rhinoceros**

are here, but species most frequently seen include plains game, such as **plains zebra**, **blue wildebeest**, **red hartebeest**, **common eland**, **common waterbuck**, **tsessebe** and **impala**. The perennial Pongola provides animals with a regular water source and therefore movements and sightings tend to be more unpredictable than in the 'waterhole parks'. Good viewing areas include the Ngubhu Loop road, as well as the Dakaneni Loop, which is said to be particularly good for hook-lipped rhinoceros sightings, especially in the late afternoon and early morning hours. Elephant, or at least their signs, are also commonly sighted here. Leopard occur naturally here, as well as both **spotted** and **brown hyaenas**, and if you are lucky you may glimpse **serval** on the open grassland. **Common large-spotted genet** often enter the camps at night, and during the day, watch for **slender mongoose**. In Ntshondwe Camp there are many **rock hyrax**, some of which spend the night on the windowsills of the chalets. **Thick-tailed galagos** are also visitors, as are **common duiker**, and the **vervet monkeys** have become a nuisance. Camera traps have spotted **Meller's mongoose** and confirmed that this park has the highest **leopard** density of any conservation area of South Africa.

Birds

Some 323 bird species have been recorded in Ithala, including vagrants and seasonal migrants. Among the best birding locations are Ntshondwe Camp and the picnic site on the Dakaneni Loop, Pongola River. In the rocky terrain of the camp **familiar chat**, **buff-streaked chat** and **mocking cliff chat** are regularly seen, as are **trumpeter hornbill**, **purple-crested turaco** and **African green pigeon**. Along the Pongola River watch out for **brown-headed parrot**, **broad-

FACILITIES AND ACTIVITIES

- Ntshondwe Camp has 39 fully equipped 2-, 4- and 6-bed chalets; three 4- to 10-bed bush camps; rustic campground. Because of the steep access road, no caravans are allowed.
- Extensive game-viewing roads; 4x4 trails.
- Guided day and night drives.
- Guided walks and self-guided walking trail in the camp.
- Restaurant and coffee shop.
- Fuel is available and there are basic supplies in Louwsburg, but the nearest town with a full range of services is Vryheid.
- Road to Ntshondwe Camp is tarred.

Ntshondwe Camp is located at the base of the escarpment.

Ithala Game Reserve 87

WILDLIFE FACTS

- Some 84 mammal species; extensive reintroductions of game species, including elephant.
- About 323 bird species, including rarities.
- Almost 100 species of reptile and amphibian.
- About 20 fish species in the Pongola River.
- More than 900 plant species, including 12 species of *Senegalia* and *Vachellia* trees.

Red-pod acacia trees are common in parts of Ithala.

The red primary feathers of the purple-crested turaco are dramatically displayed when the bird is in flight.

billed roller and **bearded scrub robin**; riverine forest is also good for **crowned eagle** and the cliffs should be scanned for the hyrax-hunting **Verreaux's eagle**, with **secretarybirds** on the open grassland. Other species that you might see on the grassland are **southern bald ibis**, **Denham's bustard** and **black-winged lapwing**. Reintroduction of **red-billed oxpeckers** has seen numbers grow substantially, along with increase in big game populations.

Reptiles and amphibians

Nile crocodiles are present in the Pongola River and this is also a good area to look for the **water monitor** lizard. The **rock monitor** occurs throughout the reserve but shows a preference for broken, rocky country. Smaller lizards that may be seen, especially in the main camp, are various species of skink. No fewer than 41 species of snake occur in the area, the largest being the **southern African python**. The visitor is less likely to see the 23 known amphibians than to hear the males calling, especially during the early part of the rainy season. The **guttural**, **raucous** and **red toads** may be seen in the camp at night, foraging for insect prey.

Fish

Some 20 species of fish have been recorded in the local stretch of the Pongola River.

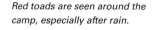

Red toads are seen around the camp, especially after rain.

- There is a low risk of contracting malaria in the park, although it is present in the wider Pongola Basin.
- Be careful of dangerous game in the unfenced camps and picnic sites.

HLUHLUWE-IMFOLOZI PARK
The reserves that saved the square-lipped rhino

Lie of the land

This 96 000 ha reserve lies about 280 km north of Durban in north-eastern Zululand. The Hluhluwe section of the park, in the north, is hilly and rugged in parts with ridges up to 540 m above sea level. On a clear day, from Hilltop Camp, one can see the high coastal dunes of iSimangaliso to the east. The Hluhluwe River flows through the northern sector of the reserve and the White and the Black Mfolozi rivers traverse the southern sector. The iMfolozi sector is a mix of rugged hills and wide valleys, the two rivers separated by a wedge-shaped area about 20 km wide in the west, narrowing to the confluence near the eastern boundary. Highest point in the southern sector is 650 m above sea level.

LOCATION

Brief history

Although the area may have been occupied during the Stone Age, the first evidence of human habitation takes the form of iron smelting and metal-working sites from about 1 500 years BP. In more recent times the area was settled by the Mthethwa clan under their leader Dingiswayo. Later still the Zulu ruler Shaka used the area, particularly between the two Mfolozi rivers, as his private hunting reserve. Zulu kings coordinated elephant hunts from the hill Nqolothi.

Despite the presence of perennial rivers in Hluhluwe-iMfolozi, many game animals drink at pools and waterholes.

HIGHLIGHTS

- Excellent game-viewing, especially in iMfolozi section.
- Big Five and a great diversity of other game.
- Good bird-watching, especially in the Mbhombe scarp forest at Hilltop Camp.

The ripening fruits of the waterberry tree are favoured by birds.

From the mid-1800s white hunters and traders also made heavy inroads into the game populations. The discovery of a remnant square-lipped rhinoceros population prompted the establishment of Hluhluwe and iMfolozi game reserves in 1895. Later there were calls for their deproclamation and the eradication of the game to control the tsetse-borne nagana that killed the neighbouring farmers' cattle. More than 100 000 head of game were killed in a 10-year period, though the square-lipped rhinos were spared.

Only in 1952 was the little surviving wildlife again protected. In 1989 the so-called Corridor between iMfolozi and Hluhluwe was incorporated into the reserve.

Geology and landscape

Hill country, mainly in the extreme north and south, is intersected by three major river courses and several minor streams that cut through lower-lying flatter areas. The park lies within the foothills of the first escarpment rising from the coastal plain. iMfolozi and especially Hluhluwe contain many of the different rock types found in KwaZulu-

Vegetation map

○ Zululand lowveld
○ Northern Zululand sourveld
● Scarp forest

Much of the park consists of Zululand lowveld with grassland and scattered thickets.

Natal, including those of volcanic, glacial and sedimentary origins, mostly belonging to the Karoo Supergroup. Erosion of these rocks has produced the many different soils that allow for a great diversity of plants, especially in Hluhluwe.

Vegetation

This reserve has three distinct vegetation types: Zululand lowveld is the most widespread, while northern Zululand sourveld occurs mainly in higher areas, and scarp forest appears in small pockets at altitude. Some of the most significant scarp forest, also known as moist semi-deciduous forest, is found in the north-west of Hluhluwe and includes **white pear** (*Apodytes dimidiata*), **Cape chestnut** (*Calodendron capense*), **forest fever-berry** (*Croton sylvaticus*) and

CLIMATE

Hluhluwe-iMfolozi is a summer rainfall region and most rain is between October and January. The rainfall increases from the west, with an annual average of 700 mm, to the Hluhluwe hills, with an annual average of almost 1 000 mm. Summers are hot, wet and often humid, with temperatures sometimes exceeding 38°C. Mean temperatures in Mpila Camp range from a maximum of 38.5°C in February to a minimum of 7.8°C in June. Winters are dry and cool but frost is very rare. Mist is common in the hills and in the valleys of northern Hluhluwe.

Savanna buffalo frequently wallow in mud.

Hluhluwe-iMfolozi Park 91

FACILITIES AND ACTIVITIES

- Approximately 90 accommodation units in Hilltop and Mpila camps; a 9-unit safari tent camp at Mpila; several bush lodges/camps. There is no campground.
- Hilltop has fuel and a shop, restaurant and bar; Mpila has fuel only.
- Guided game-viewing walks; day and night game-viewing drives.
- Self-guided walk at Hilltop Camp; overnighting trails in wilderness area of southern iMfolozi.
- Guided boat cruise – good for a number of water birds.
- Some 200 km of all-weather roads.
- Access from the north via Hluhluwe town at Memorial Gate, from the south-east via the N2, Mtubatuba and St Lucia at Nyalazi Gate, and from the south-west via Ulundi at Cengeni Gate.

Hilltop Camp.

The square-lipped rhino is the largest of the two African species.

forest bushwillow (*Combretum kraussii*). Hilltop Camp adjoins the Mbhombe scarp forest with a self-guided walking trail at its edge. These forests harbour an array of epiphytic orchids that cling to the tree branches. The Zululand sourveld is mostly wooded grassland and the dominant trees are thorny species, such as **knob thorn** (*Senegalia nigrescens*), **umbrella thorn** (*Vachellia tortilis*) and **sweet thorn** (*Vachellia karroo*). The two Mfolozi river courses show clear evidence of scouring by cyclone Domoina that destroyed much of the magnificent riverine forest in 1984, though some sheltered patches did survive.

Wildlife
Mammals

A Big Five reserve with growing populations of **elephant**, the second largest population of **square-lipped rhinoceros** after Kruger National Park, and numerous **hook-lipped rhinoceros**, although the latter are elusive as they prefer dense bush and are mainly nocturnal. Most square-lipped are in the south, while the hook-lipped are more densely concentrated in the north. Spend a few hours in one of the hides at water points if you want to see a variety of savanna game. **Chacma baboon** and vervet monkey can be seen throughout the park but to see **Sykes's monkey** or hear **thick-tailed galago** you will need to stay at Hilltop Camp, though the galago also occurs along some of the river courses with stands of woodland. The scarp forest at Hilltop is where most **red duiker** occur, as do **blue duiker**, in much lower numbers; the most commonly seen antelope here is the **bushbuck**.

Steenbok and **klipspringer** stick to their favoured habitats in the iMfolozi sector. The **common** and **mountain reedbuck** are two other antelope largely restricted to the south. The **savanna buffalo**, and most antelope, are widespread. Although **lion**, **leopard**, **cheetah**, **wild dog** and **spotted hyaena** occur they are usually not as easy to observe as in some other reserves. You may well hear them, especially at night, as they all now range widely. A smaller carnivore, the **black-backed jackal**, occurs throughout and its distinctive yipping call is commonly heard.

Birds

More than 330 species of bird are residents, migrants or regular visitors, so this is yet another top birding destination. Some of the specials include **African finfoot** (search for it particularly at the Gontshi stream crossing near Memorial Gate), and **southern bald ibis** that breed, from May to October, in small numbers on a cliff that can be viewed from Siwasamakhosikazi picnic spot just south of Hluhluwe River. Watch here also for **striped pipit** and **mocking cliff chat**. Linger close to fig trees in fruit along the river courses as a great variety of frugivorous birds are attracted, including **crowned** and **trumpeter hornbills**, **purple-crested turaco**, **African green pigeon**, **black-bellied starling** and several species of barbet. The Mbhombe self-guided trail at Hilltop Camp is ideal for seeing some of the scarp forest birds, including **Narina trogon**, **lemon dove**, **crested guineafowl**, **olive bushshrike**, **Cape batis** and **green twinspot**. A slow wander along the trail is good but even better is to sit quietly and wait, not only for the birds but for whatever mammals might show themselves. In the open game areas to the south watch

> ### WILDLIFE FACTS
> - Big Five reserve with at least 96 species of mammal.
> - More than 330 bird species are residents or regular visitors, with a further 70 or more rare vagrants.
> - Excellent birding in camps and at picnic sites, especially Hilltop.
> - Some 26 amphibians and 58 reptiles on record.
> - At least 21 fish species in the river systems.

Giraffe have a long tongue which they use to strip leaves from twigs.

The flap-neck chameleon is widespread in southern Africa.

There is a great diversity of spiders in the park.

for **white-backed** and **lappet-faced vultures**, **secretarybird** and **tawny eagle**. Bird-watching from the hides at the various waterholes is always productive, especially during the dry season. At least five owl species are present and several can usually be heard calling from the camps, with **African wood-owl** a near certainty at Hilltop.

Reptiles and amphibians

Nile crocodiles are present in the rivers, and both **water** and **rock monitors** occur. Most species are seldom seen but the observant visitor will see the large **tree agama** and the male's bobbing display as it clings to a vertical tree trunk. In the camps, picnic sites and hides watch for the small, day-active **Cape dwarf gecko** as it hunts for small insects. The **flap-neck chameleon**, difficult to spot in the trees, is obvious and vulnerable to predators when crossing the road. The only other lizard you are likely to see for long enough to identify it is the **striped skink**, which is common throughout, including on and around the camp buildings. Two land tortoises, the large **leopard tortoise** and **Bell's hinged tortoise**, may be seen crossing roads, especially after rain. Two species of terrapin bask along rivers and at waterholes. You will be lucky to see any of the 31 snake species, even though several, including the venomous **black-necked spitting cobra** and **puffadder**, frequent the camps. You are unlikely to encounter many of the frog species, except by hearing the males calling during the rainy season. The **guttural** and **red toads** are commonly seen in the camps, emerging at night to hunt insects around the buildings. The **grey tree**, or **southern foam nest, frog** lurks in the hides and occasionally in buildings, and during the rains its characteristic white foam nests, looking from a distance like rounded blocks of polystyrene, are clearly seen in branches above pools and waterholes.

Fish

There are 21 species of fish, augmenting the diet of the Nile crocodile, the Cape clawless otter and a number of bird species. Many of the species are common, including the **scaly**, or **Natal**, **yellowfish**, **three-spot barb**, **leaden labeo**, and **Mozambique tilapia**. The large **sharp-tooth catfish**, said to be extremely common in the rivers and larger pools, will readily move overland between water bodies at night, especially during rain. It will eat virtually anything, which explains its success throughout its African range.

- This is a malaria area.
- Dangerous animals include elephant, lion and buffalo, and caution should be exercised at all times.
- Summer days can be uncomfortably hot and humid.

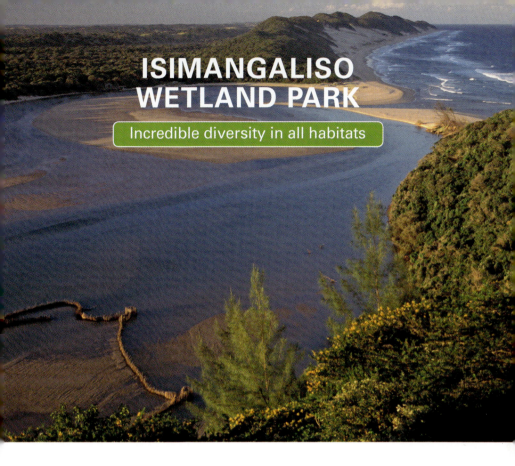

ISIMANGALISO WETLAND PARK

Incredible diversity in all habitats

Lie of the land

Covering 332 000 ha, including a marine sanctuary, and extending from the Msunduzi River in the south to the Mozambique border in the north, this is one of South Africa's largest conservation areas. (See pages 103–107 for a separate chapter on the uMkhuze section). It is a narrow strip of land, especially towards the north. A band of vegetated sand dunes, running almost the length of the park, separates the interior from the ocean. The interior is mostly flat with Lake St Lucia (actually a vast estuary for the Hluhluwe and other rivers), 80 km long and up to 23 km wide, dominating the south. Towards the north are the smaller Lake Sibaya, South Africa's largest freshwater lake, and four interlinked lakes at Kosi Bay. The Indian Ocean forms its eastern boundary and a marine protected area extends outwards from the coastline. St Lucia town is situated 26 km east of Mtubatuba in the south, and Hluhluwe town is 13 km from the False Bay Park sector.

Brief history

Much of our knowledge of the human prehistory of this area comes from excavations in Border Cave in the Lebombo Mountains, almost due west of Kosi Bay. Artefacts found here range from about 125 000 BP to 33 000 BP in the

Kosi Bay is in the north of iSimangaliso Wetland Park.

iSimangaliso Wetland Park 95

HIGHLIGHTS

- Phenomenal biodiversity on land, in freshwater and rich offshore reefs.
- Wide range of game animals, including elephant, buffalo and both rhinoceros species.
- One of best places in Africa to view common reedbuck and Sykes's monkey (Cape Vidal).
- Breeding locations of two marine turtle species.
- One of South Africa's top dive locations.

early Later Stone Age. These early humans left pierced seashells, presumably decorative, and certainly foraged near the shoreline of present-day iSimangaliso. Iron Age sites at Enkwazini, east of Lake St Lucia, date from 290 AD. The first southward-migrating Bantu peoples reached the area in about 1440 and profoundly impacted the environment through bush clearance, livestock grazing and hunting. Tribes that passed through included the amaThonga, who settled, and the Thukela-Nguni, who continued into the interior.

Trade beads found at uMkhuze suggest that Arab traders may have visited the coastline as early as 1250. Vasco da Gama and his crew were the first Europeans to set eyes on the iSimangaliso coastline in December 1497. The Portuguese were the first whites to explore and map the Maputaland coast, and the Dutch landed a party at the St Lucia estuary in 1670. The first British exploration had to wait until 1822, and the first ventures into the interior, with a ship exploring Lake St Lucia and penetrating 50 km up the uMkhuze River, took place in 1853. These explorers were soon followed by hunters seeking ivory, traders and of course the ever-present missionaries.

The initial St Lucia reserve (not today's extent) was established in April 1895, making it and Hluhluwe-iMfolozi the oldest conservation areas in Africa. The current name of the park, iSimangaliso, means 'miracle and wonder'. It was proclaimed a World Heritage Site in 1999. The inhabitants today are mainly an Nguni-Thonga mix known as the Shangana-Tsonga. Local people have fished the Kosi lakes for several centuries, and there is an intricate network of permanent fish traps in place.

Vegetation map

- ○ Subtropical seashore vegetation
- ○ Maputaland wooded grassland
- ● Maputaland coastal belt
- ○ Subtropical dune thicket
- ● Freshwater wetlands
- ● Northern coastal forest
- ○ Subtropical saltpans

Geology and landscape

The reserve consists of slightly undulating plains whose highest points are in the coastal sand dunes, 138-m St Mary's Hill near the north-eastern tip of Lake St Lucia, and 159-m Nyathikazi just north

Blue-banded snappers and flame goat fish are among the many fish species that can be seen at Sodwana Bay.

Sodwana Bay's Nine-mile Reef has many caves and overhangs.

CLIMATE

This is generally a summer rainfall area, albeit less so along the coastline; St Lucia town, for example, has year-round showers, with more than 40% falling in the winter months. Annual precipitation ranges between 964 mm and 1 200 mm. The mean annual temperature is about 22°C, with mean maximum in January around 35°C and mean minimum in June around 5.5°C. The summer months can be hot and uncomfortably humid.

of Lake Bhangazi South. Wind action during the late Pleistocene and in recent times gave rise to the extensive north-south dune topography that one sees today. At odd places along the coastline one sees outcrops of grey-white sandy limestone such as at Black Rock north of Rocktail Bay. These underlying limestone rocks are some 30 m thick along the iSimangaliso coastline. The marine sediments within the park date from the Cenozoic and recent eras and the sands forming the dunes are calcareous and from the Quaternary.

Vegetation

This subtropical vegetation area can be divided into two Maputaland types, coastal belt and wooded grassland. The coastal belt is characterized by grassland, forest and thicket patches with scatterings of stands of the **lala palm** (*Hyphaene coriacea*) and the **wild date palm** (*Phoenix reclinata*). The stand of **Kosi** (**raffia**) **palms** (*Raphia australis*) in the north of the park in swamp forest, is the only naturally occurring population of this tree in South Africa. It is a massive palm, growing to 24 m, with feather-like leaves reaching 10 m in length. The wooded grassland zone also supports a variety of grasses and is particularly rich in dwarf shrubs, low trees and herbaceous plants. The forest and woodland associated with the sand dunes may be classified into coastal forest and dune thicket. Trees include such species as the **flat-crown** (*Albizia adianthifolia*), **coastal red milkwood** (*Mimusops caffra*), **ironplum** (*Drypetes reticulata*) and **white milkwood** (*Sideroxylon inerme*). Small areas of sand forest are present in the False Bay Park sector, with dominant trees including **Zulu podberry** (*Dialium schlecteri*) and **false tamboti** (*Cleistanthus schlechteri*). Mangrove communities are present in several places on the coast, the most extensive being around Kosi Bay in the north, where five species grow. Other common, and easily identified, trees include the **wild banana** (*Strelitzia nicolai*) and the large-fruited **black monkey-orange** (*Strychnos madagascariensis*).

The Tonga-kierie occurs in sand forest and bushveld areas.

Five species of mangrove can be found around Kosi Bay in the north of the wetland park.

iSimangaliso has a large hippopotamus population.

Wildlife
Mammals
With 115 mammal species, iSimangaliso is one of the richest mammal conservation areas in South Africa. In recent years major efforts have been made to reintroduce game species that had been hunted out. To date these include **savanna elephant**, **savanna buffalo**, **hook-lipped rhinoceros**, **spotted hyaena**, **brown hyaena**, **wild dog** and **cheetah**. The **hippopotamus** population survived and today has perhaps reached its population limit (about 800 in Lake St Lucia and several hundred elsewhere). Antelope are diverse, including probably Africa's densest population of **common reedbuck** on the open grassland, **common waterbuck**, **greater kudu** and **bushbuck**. In the False Bay sand thicket there is a small population of the diminutive **suni**, with **red duiker** occurring widely but most easily seen on the western shores, such as at Charter's Creek. Both **vervet** and **Sykes's monkeys** occur, the latter most easily observed around the camp at Cape Vidal. Smaller creatures are abundant but seldom seen.

FACILITIES AND ACTIVITIES

- Plentiful accommodation, including hotels and apartments (St Lucia), luxury lodges, huts, wilderness camps and campgrounds.
- Self-guided walking trails; guided hiking and walking trails.
- Guided game-viewing, day and night.
- Game-viewing road network in the south.
- St Lucia, Mtubatuba and Hluhluwe towns have fuel and several other facilities.
- Access to Cape Vidal is through St Lucia town; other roads access Sodwana, Lake Sibaya and Kosi Bay from outside the park.
- Access to St Lucia, Cape Vidal and Sodwana is on tar roads but most internal roads are gravel or sand 4x4 tracks.

Wilderness Safari's Rocktail Beach Camp offers luxury accommodation.

Southern, or common, reedbuck are numerous in open grassland.

iSimangaliso Wetland Park 99

Although brown hyaena have been released here, it is uncertain whether the park is within their natural range.

An exception is the **banded mongoose**, whose troops make regular 'tours' around and through the camps. There are 12 bat species, and a colony of **Egyptian fruit-bats** roosts during the day in sea-caves at Mission Rocks on the Eastern Shores. There are 21 rodent species but only the **red bush squirrel** is likely to be spotted, probably at Cape Vidal or Sodwana Bay.

Birds

iSimangaliso is one of South Africa's top birding destinations with at least 482 species. Give yourself enough time to add a host of 'lifers'. Birding is good throughout the year but late summer is best if you want to see vagrant shore- and sea-birds. As always, birding is excellent in and around the campgrounds and settlements, including St Lucia itself, as well as the grounds of the Crocodile Centre. Specials include **great white** and **pink-backed pelicans**, with large numbers of the former breeding here. The sandspit at the estuary mouth is nearly always productive, with regulars including **Caspian**, **little** and **lesser crested terns**, and a range of palearctic waders in season. Cape Vidal and other forested locations are good for **purple-crested** and **Livingstone's turacos**, **brown scrub robin**, **Woodward's batis**, **blue-mantled crested flycatcher** and **square-tailed drongo**, among others. During the summer rains the flooded grasslands between St Lucia and Cape Vidal can be good for **African pygmy goose** and **white-backed duck**, though they are well camouflaged. Another special on the northern sector of the game-viewing loop, just below Lake Bhangazi South, is the **rosy-throated longclaw**. On the western shores False Bay is generally considered to be the best birding site, although species composition is similar in the other locations. **African broadbill**, **pink-throated twinspot** and

Among the approximately 482 species of bird that occur in iSimangaliso are the mangrove kingfisher (left), the green malkoha or coucal (middle) and the African cuckoo hawk (right).

The park is the only stronghold of Gaboon viper in South Africa.

bearded scrub robin are fairly certain. **Palmnut vultures** are most likely to be seen in the Kosi section of the park, where they favour the raffia palms.

Reptiles and amphibians

If iSimangaliso is a birder's and mammal twitcher's dream, for those interested in reptiles and amphibians this is paradise. Unfortunately, many species are nocturnal, cryptic, or both, and not easily encountered. Probably the largest **Nile crocodile** population in South Africa is found here and hereabouts. There may be 1 200 crocodiles in Lake St Lucia alone. A visit to the Crocodile Centre, close to St Lucia town, is well worthwhile if you want to learn something about these giant reptiles and see living animals close-up. This coastline has particularly important egg-laying sites for two marine turtles, **leatherback sea turtle**, from October to February, and **loggerhead sea turtle**, from November to January. The largest of the 51 snakes is the **southern African python**, which can exceed 5 m in length. The beautifully marked, and dangerous, **Gaboon adder** is present

WILDLIFE FACTS

- Whopping 115 terrestrial mammal species, ranging from elephant to pygmy mouse, and a probable marine mammal count of 20.
- Official bird-list including uMkhuze Game Reserve (see page 103), now managed as part of iSimangaliso, contains 526 species; authors' records of iSimangaliso alone show an exceptionally rich count of 482 species.
- No fewer than 100 reptile species, including a large population of Nile crocodiles.
- Real South African hotspot for amphibians with at least 48 species.
- More than 1 200 species of marine fish and about 90 freshwater fish species.
- Coral reefs offshore.

iSimangaliso's beaches are important breeding grounds for the loggerhead turtle.

Above left: Mudskippers dwell in the mangrove swamps.
Above right: Ghost crabs live near the water's edge, burrowing in sand above the high-water mark.

Butterfly species found in the park include the variable mimic (top) and gold-banded forester (bottom).

in a number of forest pockets in the park. You are unlikely to see many of the approximately 36 species of lizard but there may be exceptions. The only South African colony of the small day-active **Bouton's skink** occurs at Black Rock. Another common skink here is the **striped skink**; also watch for South Africa's largest lizards, the **rock monitor** and the **Nile monitor**. Look out for the **southern tree agama**, even in the camps. At night, on and around buildings, large numbers of **Moreau's tropical house gecko** gather to hunt insects. Of the two chameleon species here, you are more likely to see the large (up to 35 cm) **flap-neck chameleon**. There are 48 amphibian species but you are most likely to see those that gather in the buildings and ablution blocks – the authors have listed 10 species from these habitats, from ground-foraging **guttural** and **red toads**, to **greater leaf-folding frogs** and the **grey**, or **foam nest**, **frog**. During the spring and summer rains, you will undoubtedly hear a multi-species chorus.

Fish

There are at least 1 200 marine fish species and 90 living in the freshwater systems. Fish form the bulk of the diet of the Nile crocodile and a host of piscivorous birds. **Bull (Zambezi) sharks** are known to penetrate not only Lake St Lucia but also the major feeder rivers. In the mangrove areas at low tide watch for the fascinating **mudskipper** (or **mudhopper**), as it skips around on the exposed mudbanks among the trees.

Invertebrates

Apart from those insects that draw our attention by biting or stinging us, there are vast numbers of invertebrates that are worth watching. The authors have spent many fascinating hours observing crab species here, including the three species of beach-dwelling ghost crabs, at their best at night. In the morning you will see their walking trails and holes. Mangroves are hotspots for a number of species, such as various fiddler crabs whose males have one massive and one tiny pincer. Here also are the **red-clawed mangrove crabs**, coming out to feed on fallen mangrove leaves at low tide. There are well over 40 species of crab, lobster and prawn on these shores. The park is also rich in butterfly and moth species, beetles and spiders.

- This is a malaria area.
- Bilharzia is present in fresh waters.
- There are several dangerous animals, including crocodile, hippopotamus and elephant. Take great care along lake shores as crocodiles attack stealthily and very fast, even on land.

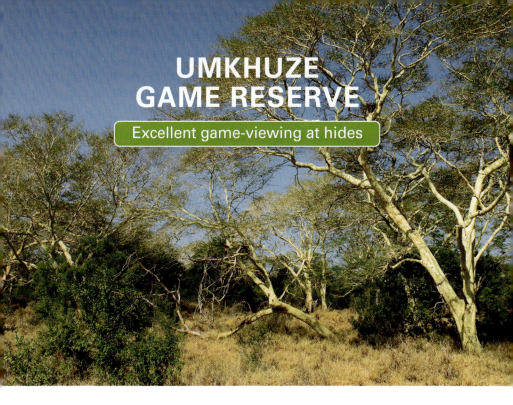

UMKHUZE GAME RESERVE
Excellent game-viewing at hides

Lie of the land

This 40 000 ha reserve, 335 km north of Durban, forms part of the iSimangaliso Wetland Park. The closest towns are Mkhuze (22 km from eMshopi Gate) and Hluhluwe. The uMkhuze River forms the northern and eastern boundaries, with the Umsinduzi River lying to the south, and the Lebombo Mountains to the west. The large Nsumo Pan in the south-east is the largest water body in the uMkhuze section. Although much of the reserve consists of plains, there is hilly country in the west and south.

LOCATION

Brief history

Stone tools and other evidence point to occupation by people from the Earlier Stone Age through the Iron Age and into modern times.

From about the late 1880s white farmers and hunters in the area began hunting buffalo, eland and greater kudu for their hides. Although malaria and the tsetse fly restricted these depredations to the colder winter months, the hunters wiped out several species. Mkuzi Game Reserve, originally proclaimed on 15 February 1912, was deproclaimed in 1939. From 1944 onwards no fewer than 38 000 head of game were slaughtered in a futile attempt to eradicate the tsetse-borne cattle disease nagana; only the hook-lipped rhinoceros were spared. Subsequently, much more successful efforts included aerial pesticide spraying and clear-cutting of dense thicket where the flies bred. The shooting was stopped in 1949. The reserve was reproclaimed in September 1954 and first opened to the public in 1958.

uMkhuze is rich in tree species, including the fever tree, easily identified by its smooth yellow-green bark.

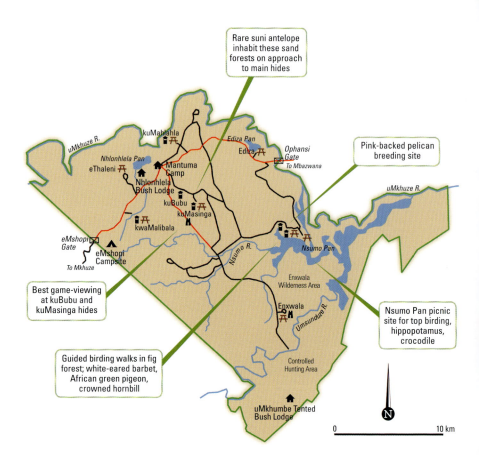

Geology and landscape

The most prominent feature is the Lebombo range to the west, rising to about 600 m above sea level, predominantly composed of resistant volcanic rhyolite lavas. To the east they disappear below the flatland, with their depth increasing closer to the coast. The reserve is mostly flat, with the Nsumo Pan and major river courses such as uMkhuze dominating the south-east. The limited sand thicket vegetation grows on orange-brown soil derived from mega-dune systems about 3 million years BP. Soils elsewhere in the reserve are sandy with variable clay content.

Vegetation

The far west of the park is largely Southern Lebombo bushveld, which is open and dominated by *Senegalia*, *Vachellia* and *Combretum* tree species, such as **knob thorn** (*Senegalia nigrescens*), **corky thorn** (*Vachellia davyi*), **red thorn** (*S. gerrardii*), **red bushwillow** (*Combretum apiculatum*) and **false black monkey-**

HIGHLIGHTS

- Excellent birding and game-viewing, especially from kuBubu and kuMasinga hides located at waterholes. Hides at Nsumo Pan offer first-class birding.
- Best location to observe nyala at close quarters, as well as the diminutive and rare suni.

orange (*Strychnos gerrardii*). Western Maputaland clay bushveld is widespread in the west, south and east of the reserve, and is a relatively low-treed (up to 10 m) mixed grass woodland. One of the most obvious trees is the **umbrella thorn** (*Vachellia tortilis*) but also look out for **knob thorn** (*Senegalia nigrescens*) and **tree wisteria** (*Bolusanthus speciosus*) with its massed blue flowers. The **sickle bush** (*Dichrostachys cinerea*) produces distinctive purple and yellow flowers through spring and summer. Interspersed with this last vegetation type is the western Maputaland sandy bushveld, running from the uMkhuze River in the north, to the west of Nsumo Pan in the south. This is woodland and open grassed bushland; a distinctive low tree is the appropriately named **silver cluster-leaf** (*Terminalia sericea*). One of the tallest trees here is the **black monkey thorn** (*Senegalia burkei*). Two iconic trees grow in the lowveld riverine forest: some of the best stands of the tall **fever tree** (*Vachellia xanthophloea*), with its yellow-green bark, grow at Nsumo Pan; and a large stand of the magnificent **common cluster fig** (*Ficus sycomorus*) occurs on the eastern side of the pan, with an accompanied trail to allow you to admire the trees and abundant bird and butterfly life. You pass through a narrow strip of sand thicket, embedded in the Maputaland sandy bushveld, on the way southwards from main camp. This has somewhat different vegetation, with species such as **red-heart tree** (*Hymenocardia ulmoides*), whose abundant and pink-winged seeds help identification in autumn. The tallest tree here is the **Lebombo wattle** (*Newtonia hildebrandtii*).

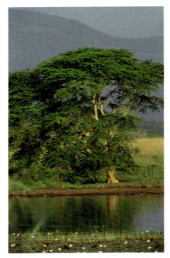

Nsumo Pan is one of South Africa's top birding locations.

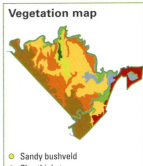

Vegetation map

- Sandy bushveld
- Clay thicket
- Clay bushveld
- Southern Lebombo bushveld
- Coastal belt
- Freshwater wetlands
- Riverine forest
- Sand forest

The sickle bush produces attractive flowers and sickle-shaped pods.

Wildlife
Mammals
Apart from big game, such as **savanna elephant**, **hook-lipped** and **square-lipped rhinoceros**, **hippopotamus**, **plains zebra**, **giraffe**, **savanna buffalo**, **blue wildebeest** and **greater kudu**, this is one of the best places to view the abundant **nyala**, especially at the kuBubu and kuMasinga waterholes. The best time for the hides is between June and October; most game arrives between 09h00 and 12h00 but there is always something moving. One of South Africa's rarest antelope, the diminutive **suni**, is only found in the area of sand thicket; with patience, you may well see it as several

CLIMATE
This is a summer-rainfall area, with 600 mm to 700 mm falling each year; in general the western sector receives less rain than the east. The mean daily maximum temperature in January is 32.5°C and mean daily minimum temperature in July is 11.7°C. The area receives no frost.

FACILITIES AND ACTIVITIES

- Eight fully equipped safari tents and 17 cottages and huts in main camp; campground with 60 sites; two bush camps with four units.
- Guided game- and bird-viewing walks.
- Guided night drives.

Guided walks to the fig forest can be arranged.

- Self-drive road network of more than 100 km.
- Fuel, basic supplies and a takeaway food outlet at Mantuma Camp.
- St Lucia, Mtubatuba and Hluhluwe towns have fuel and various other facilities.
- Access via eMshopi Gate in the north-west, or from Mbazwana and Sodwana via Ophansi Gate in the east.
- Approach and internal roads of variable condition but most vehicles will cope.

territories adjoin the road. Here and in a few other locations in the park is the largest of our elephant shrews, the **four-toed sengi**, but it is very elusive. **Chacma baboon** and **vervet monkey** are commonly seen but **Sykes's monkey** is restricted to forest patches along the rivers. Large predators include **wild dog**, **cheetah**, **lion**, **leopard** and **spotted hyaena**, with many smaller species that are mostly secretive or nocturnal, except for the troop-living **banded mongoose**.

Birds

uMkhuze is one of South Africa's top birding destinations with more than 450 species recorded. Each major habitat has its specials. The fig forest near Nsumo Pan offers **crowned** and **trumpeter hornbills**, **white-eared barbet**, **Narina trogon**, **African green pigeon** and **square-tailed drongo**. Scan the trees for **Pel's fishing owl**, among others. Nsumo Pan is excellent for both resident and migratory water birds and it is also the site of South Africa's only known breeding colony of **pink-backed pelicans**. The picnic site on the pan's northeastern extension offers good birding in peaceful surroundings, as you may see **Pel's fishing owls** roosting in the tall trees, as well as **white-throated robin-chat**. The area around kuBubu and kuMasinga hides is good for **African broadbill**, **crested guineafowl** and **helmeted guineafowl**. These waterholes are also sometimes good for **woolly-necked storks** and many other species, particularly during the dry months. **Neergaard's sunbird** nests near kuMasinga. As with many parks, the camps and campground offer excellent early morning and evening bird-watching, as does the short self-guided walk that loops from Mantuma Camp to the uMkhuze River.

Reptiles and amphibians

Nile crocodiles can often be seen basking on the edges of water including Nsumo Pan. Here you may also spot our longest lizard the **Nile**, or **water**, **monitor**, equally at home hunting on land and in water. Its close cousin the **rock monitor** occupies drier areas of the reserve.

Nyala are nearly always to be seen at the principal waterholes.

Nsumo Pan is the site of the only known breeding colony of pink-backed pelican in South Africa.

WILDLIFE FACTS

- Some 90 mammal species, including savanna elephant and cheetah.
- More than 450 species of bird with many 'specials'.
- Only breeding location of pink-backed pelican in South Africa, at Nsumo Pan.
- Over 70 species of reptile, including Nile crocodile, can be expected; 64 are definitely recorded.
- A rich amphibian fauna of 43 species.

If you are lucky you might encounter either the **leopard tortoise** or **Bell's hinged tortoise** on one of the roads but you will certainly see some of the five freshwater terrapin species. They can be spotted from the hides, sun-basking or foraging in the shallow water. With more survey work, the list of 64 reptiles could well acquire a further 21 species. Snakes are seldom seen but **black mamba**, **Mozambique spitting cobra**, **puff adder** and **spotted bush snake** have been observed. Amphibians are most obvious during the rainy season when they breed and the males call. Most of the 43 species are hard to spot. The hides harbour groups of **grey tree frogs**, and during the rains their white foam nests can be seen on tree branches. You may hear, and then see, the distinctive **red-legged kassina**, and several reed frog species appear in and near the hides and camps during the rains.

Fish

The 32 fish species that occur here support the fish-eating birds and the Nile crocodiles.

Nile crocodiles are abundant.

Leopard tortoise may be seen feeding along road verges.

- This is a malaria area and bilharzia is present.
- Beware of dangerous animals when you alight from your vehicle; camps are unfenced. Do not go to the water's edge at the Nsumo Pan picnic site as there are crocodiles.

uMkhuze Game Reserve **107**

PHINDA PRIVATE GAME RESERVE

Big Five guided viewing

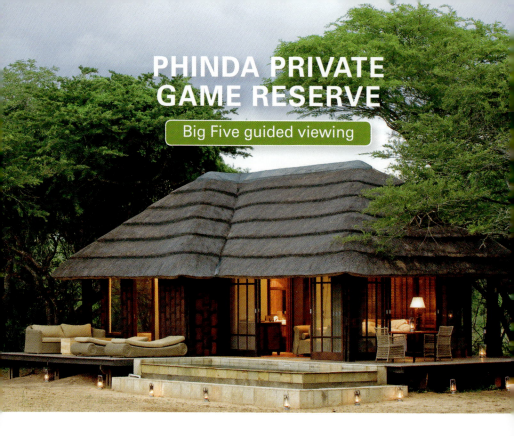

Lie of the land

Phinda, the flagship reserve of &Beyond (formerly Conservation Corporation), covers an area of about 21 400 ha, mostly flat, with some hill country. It borders the uMkhuze Game Reserve in the north, stretching eastwards from the southern Lebombo Mountains to the western Maputaland coastal plain. The Mzinene River with its associate wetlands occupies the eastern plains.

Brief history

The hunter-gatherers of the Thembe-Tonga tribe were early inhabitants. Phinda has shared much of uMkhuze's history (see page 103), including the successive depredations of the white hunters and the anti-nagana campaign.

By 1948 today's Phinda was carved into farms awarded to World War II veterans. Like other allocated areas, it suffered from bad farming practices, overgrazing and soil erosion. In 1990 Conservation Corporation was founded and Phinda was consolidated into the fine reserve it is today.

The Vlei Lodge at &Beyond's Phinda Private Game Reserve overlooks an open wetland.

Geology and landscape

The western sector of the reserve is hilly with volcanic rocks. From west to east, basaltic rocks merge into a band of rhyolite lavas; then a narrow band of siltstone-

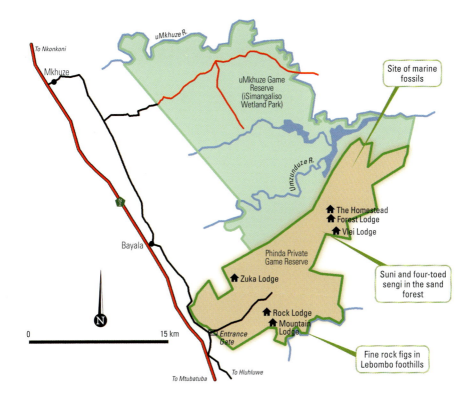

derived soils (Western Maputaland clay bushveld) gives way to the sands in the east. These sands, of various types and origins, include marine deposits rich with the fossils of extinct organisms.

Vegetation

This is similar to neighbouring uMkhuze (see pages 104–105), but Phinda has had less time to recover from land-abuse and still shows some damage. In the foothills of the Lebombo to the west, one finds a mix of interesting species, with **large-leaved rock fig** (*Ficus abutilifolia*), **red-leaved rock fig** (*Ficus ingens*), and several species of tree euphorbia growing on the steep, rocky ground. The Lebombo grassland has a scattering of woodland-forest copses and termite mounds. These rocky areas and poor soils support woodland, forest and thicket, each with its own dominant tree and bush species. The tallest trees are located in deeply incised valleys and gorges, with three species of **stinkwood** (*Celtis* spp.), **fluted milkwood** (*Chrysophyllum viridifolium*), **brown ironwood** (*Homalium dentatum*), and many more. Moving eastwards the richer soils, derived from marine sandstones and siltstones, are dominated by four types of acacia tree, each area with one dominant species,

HIGHLIGHTS

- More than 407 species of bird.
- Big Five.
- Luxury accommodation and five-star service.
- Guided walks and game- and bird-viewing drives.

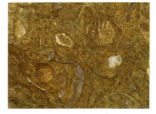

Phinda is well known for its fossil beds.

Phinda Private Game Reserve 109

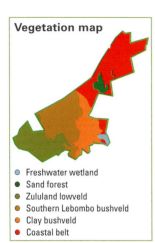

Vegetation map

- Freshwater wetland
- Sand forest
- Zululand lowveld
- Southern Lebombo bushveld
- Clay bushveld
- Coastal belt

Africa's three big cat species occur here, including leopard.

CLIMATE

Phinda's climate is very similar to that of the adjoining uMkhuze, with an average rainfall of about 578 mm each year (see page 98). Rain falls from August to March but peaks between October and February. Summers are hot and humid while winters are usually dry and mild. Temperature averages range from 25.8°C in February to 16.4°C in July.

namely **umbrella thorn** (*Vachellia tortilis*), **knob thorn** (*Senegalia nigrescens*), **horned thorn** (*Vachellia grandicornuta*) and **false umbrella thorn** (*Vachellia luederitzii*). Each area also has a strong mix of other species. Further east are nutrient-poor sandy soils and a variable water table. There are areas of seasonally flooded grasslands, dwarf shrubby grasslands, and woodland with distinctive trees such as **silver cluster-leaf** (*Terminalia sericea*), **marula** (*Sclerocarya birrea*), **large-fruit combretum** (*Combretum zeyheri*) and several species of **monkey-orange** (*Strychnos* spp.). Red sand woodland has a similar tree composition. There is also sand thicket with dense bush and short tree cover under taller trees. The sand thicket and forest is one of the rarest vegetation habitats in Maputaland, with several endemic plant species as well as two mammal, several bird, and a number of butterfly species. A few of the characteristic trees here include **torchwood** (*Balanites maughamii*), **broad-pod false-thorn** (*Albizia forbesii*), **lavender fever-berry** (*Croton gratissimus*) and the tall **Lebombo wattle** (*Newtonia hildebrandtii*).

The distinctive suni occupies the sand forest area of Phinda.

Lions doing what they do most of the time – resting.

Wildlife

Mammals

Local wildlife has recovered from its state of near-extermination before 1990. All of the large predators occur, including **lion**, **leopard** and **cheetah**. There are healthy populations of **savanna elephant**, **savanna buffalo**, **giraffe**, **hippopotamus** and both **rhinoceros** species, as well as a great diversity of antelope, including a substantial **nyala** population. The diminutive **suni**, very rare in South Africa, is reliant on the limited areas of sand forest. Here too the day-active **four-toed sengi** (**elephant shrew**) may be seen, with patience. The very localized **red bush squirrel** is also found in Phinda.

Birds

The 407 bird species are similar to uMkhuze's (see page 106) but in Phinda you have the benefit of knowledgeable guides. Among the specials ('star birds', as they are known at Phinda) are **Rudd's apalis**, **Neergaard's sunbird**, **African broadbill**, **lemon-breasted canary**, **pink-throated twinspot**, **rosy-throated longclaw**, **white-backed night heron**, **Narina trogon**, **southern banded snake eagle** and **African finfoot**.

Reptiles

The same species occur as in uMkhuze (see pages 106–107). The largest reptile present is the **Nile crocodile**.

FACILITIES AND ACTIVITIES

- Six luxury lodges with all facilities, including restaurants, bar and swimming pool.
- Guided day and night game-viewing drives.
- Airstrip allows airborne transfers.
- Not a 'free visit' area and no private driving is allowed; booking is essential.

Zuka Lodge.

The rosy-throated longclaw is one of Phinda's birding specials.

Narina trogon are more commonly heard than seen.

WILDLIFE FACTS

- Big Five have been reintroduced.
- Cheetah and many other game species are present.
- Guides help you seek out the secretive suni in the sand forest.
- No fewer than 407 bird species, several at the southernmost edge of their range.
- Diversity of reptiles and amphibians, similar to uMkhuze (see pages 106–107).

- Phinda is within the malaria belt.
- Summer days can be hot and humid.
- Always inform a guard when moving between the communal living area and your lodge at night.

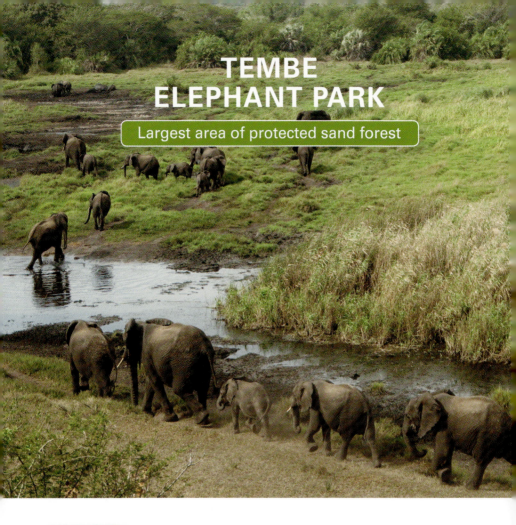

TEMBE ELEPHANT PARK
Largest area of protected sand forest

LOCATION

Lie of the land
The 29 000 ha Tembe borders Mozambique to the north, the Ndumo Game Reserve across the Mbangweni Corridor to the west, and the Kosi section of iSimangaliso in the east. Near the eastern boundary is a section of the Muze Swamp consisting mainly of seasonal pans, running from the park's Mozambique border southwards into Maputaland. The area is mostly flat.

Brief history
Tembe's prehistory was probably similar to that of the rest of the area. The park was proclaimed in 1983 to protect South Africa's last truly free-ranging elephant, unconfined by fences. The park is now fenced on three sides; although the elephant can still move freely across the border, poaching in Mozambique has driven them to seek sanctuary in the dense sand forest of the park. Part of this sand forest and thicket country is locally known as the Sihangwane.

Tembe was established to protect KwaZulu-Natal's last truly free-ranging elephants.

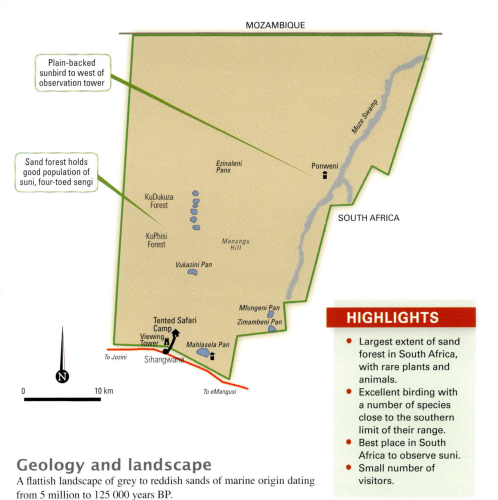

HIGHLIGHTS

- Largest extent of sand forest in South Africa, with rare plants and animals.
- Excellent birding with a number of species close to the southern limit of their range.
- Best place in South Africa to observe suni.
- Small number of visitors.

Geology and landscape

A flattish landscape of grey to reddish sands of marine origin dating from 5 million to 125 000 years BP.

Vegetation

Apart from wetland vegetation in the east, most of the park is dominated by Tembe sandy bushveld – a mix of grassland with open and closed woodland up to 10 m in height. 'Islands' of sand forest vary from 6 m thickets to tall forest reaching 15 m. Dominant trees in these forests include **Lebombo wattle** (*Newtonia hildebrandtii*), **Zulu podberry** (*Dialium schlechteri*) and **false tamboti** (*Cleistanthus*

Tembe is home to about 200 elephant.

Tembe Elephant Park 113

Although plains zebra have been introduced to Tembe Elephant Park, it is not clear whether they occurred here in the past.

CLIMATE

This is mainly a summer-rainfall regime. Rainfall averages about 650 mm, mostly brought in by clouds from the Indian Ocean. Temperatures are very similar to Ndumo to the west (see page 119).

Vegetation map

- Maputaland coastal belt
- Subtropical freshwater wetland
- Sand forest
- Sandy bushveld

schlechteri). One of the most obvious trees in the sandy bushveld is the **silver cluster-leaf** (*Terminalia sericea*). Also characteristic is the diverse shrub and grassy layer. Among the tallest trees here are the **black monkey thorn** (*Senegalia burkei*) and **marula** (*Sclerocarya birrea*). There are also areas of palm veld including the **lala palm** (*Hyphaene coriacea*) and the **wild date palm** (*Phoenix reclinata*).

Wildlife
Mammals

There are about 200 **savanna elephant** and many reintroductions have been made, including **blue wildebeest**, **eland**, **giraffe**, **greater kudu**, both **rhinoceros** species, **plains zebra** and **common waterbuck**. There are also healthy populations of **nyala**, **common reedbuck** and the tiny **suni**. Park staff should be able to point out the highly territorial suni. The still more elusive **four-toed sengi**, South Africa's largest elephant shrew, is in its ideal habitat here. **Hippopotamus** are present in the Muze Swamp area. Predators include **lion**, **leopard**, **wild dog** and several day-active smaller species such as the solitary **slender mongoose** and the troop-living **banded mongoose**. On night drives there is a chance of seeing **African civet**, **common large-spotted genet** and the **white-tailed mongoose**.

Birds

Composition of the bird-list for Tembe is very similar to that of its western neighbour Ndumo (see page 120). Some records list only 340 species but 400 seems a more accurate total. Park specials include **pink-throated twinspot, Woodward's batis, Neergaard's**

sunbird, **plain-backed sunbird** and **African broadbill** (always easier to find during breeding season because of the male's distinctive call and display).

Reptiles

The lists are probably very similar to those for Ndumo (see pages 120–121). **Nile crocodile** are present in the swamp, and both **water** and **rock monitor** lizards occur. Fairly obvious lizards are the **tree agama** and the largest of our chameleons, the **flap-neck**.

Fish

The fish species at Tembe are similar to Ndumo's but diversity is less (see page 121).

The red-faced mousebird is one of the many bird species recorded in the park.

FACILITIES AND ACTIVITIES

- Small tented safari camp and lodge.
- Viewing hides.
- Guided walks, as well as day and night drives (self-drive not permitted).
- Fuel and basic supplies are usually available at Sihangwane but it is safest to fuel up beforehand.
- Approach road from N2 via Jozini is tarred and internal roads are sand.

The displaying behaviour of Nyala rams is a means of avoiding direct fighting.

!
- This is a malaria zone.
- Dangerous animals are present, including elephant, lion and Nile crocodile.
- Summer can be hot and humid.

WILDLIFE FACTS

- At least 80 species of mammal.
- South Africa's most important location for both suni and four-toed sengi populations.
- Reserve originally proclaimed to protect the small transfrontier elephant population.
- More than 400 bird species likely, with a number of rarities.
- Reptile and amphibian diversity, composition similar to Ndumo (see pages 120–121).

Tembe Elephant Park

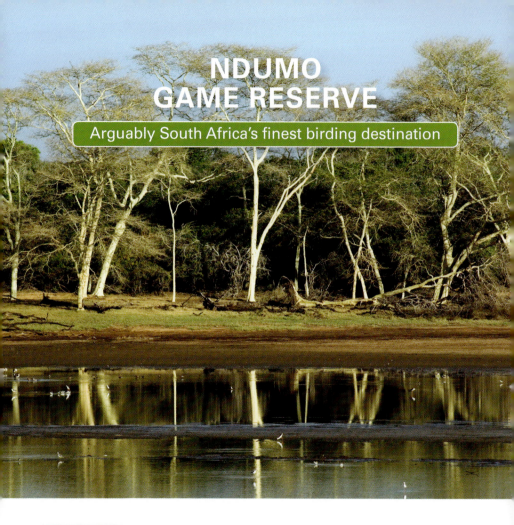

NDUMO GAME RESERVE

Arguably South Africa's finest birding destination

LOCATION

Lie of the land

Ndumo is in the far north of KwaZulu-Natal, in Maputaland. The 10 117 ha reserve is bounded to the north by the Usuthu River and Mozambique; the other boundaries are fenced. The reserve is predominantly flat except for Ndumo Hill to the south. The Pongola River runs inside the eastern boundary just before it joins the Usuthu, and the Lebombo range can be seen in the west.

Brief history

Early humans have occupied the Ndumo area since at least 500 000 years BP, throughout the Earlier, Middle and Later Stone Ages and the Iron Age from about 300 AD. An iron-smelting furnace in the reserve dates from about 630 AD.

The modern inhabitants are a mix of Nguni and Thonga people belonging to the Shangana-Tsonga group. One of the largest Thonga clans in the Ndumo area is the Tembe. These amaThonga peoples migrated down the low-lying coastal

Fever trees grow in abundance around the pans, such as at Nyamithi in the east of Ndumo.

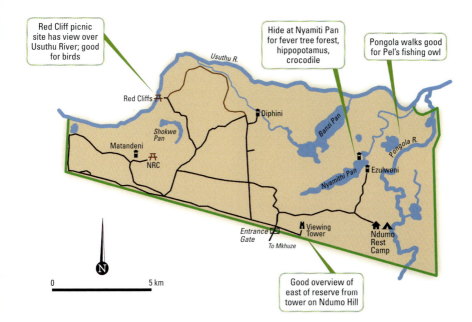

plain from eastern Africa and settled in Mozambique. Earlier another migrating Bantu people, the Thukela-Nguni settled between the Lebombo range and the ocean but then dispersed southwards. From the beginning of the 19th century they were dominated by the Zulus but retained their culture and traditions.

The first European elephant hunters entered this game-rich area in the 1840s, although the Portuguese probably made much earlier forays along the Usuthu and Pongola rivers. Among many others the legendary F.C. Selous came specifically to hunt the nyala that still abound in the area. Others slaughtered elephant and other game on a near-industrial scale. By the start of the 20th century game in the area was very scarce.

The politician Deneys Reitz, who had hunted along the Pongola River, brought about the proclamation of the Ndumou Game Reserve in 1924, declaring, 'I have now done my duty to God and the hippo.' Nevertheless, by 1954, almost 1 500 people and an ever-increasing number of cattle were living inside the reserve. The last residents left only in 1966.

HIGHLIGHTS

- Some of the best bird-watching in South Africa with great diversity and several species at the southern limit of their range.
- Excellent Nile crocodile viewing.
- Some of the best stands of fever trees and sycamore figs in the region.
- A true tropical African feel and atmosphere, unchanged by time.
- Low visitor numbers.

Geology and landscape

On the western horizon lies the Lebombo mountain range, rising to 600 m above sea level and composed of resistant volcanic rhyolite lavas. These hard rocks fractured while the East African Rift valleys were forming. In the same period the Lebombo lavas were steeply tilted in a series of blocks underlying Ndumo and extending eastwards towards the coast. They are not visible on the surface as

Ndumo Game Reserve 117

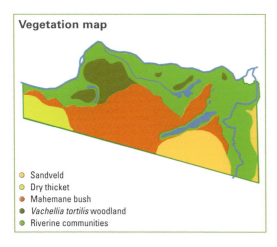

Vegetation map

- Sandveld
- Dry thicket
- Mahemane bush
- *Vachellia tortilis* woodland
- Riverine communities

they are covered by younger sedimentary rocks. Most of the reserve is covered by sands of the Berea and other formations, laid down by ancient ocean and the river systems. Sandy and clay alluvia characterize the fertile floodplain of the Pongola River.

Most of the reserve is flat and lies from 25 m to 50 m above sea level, with Ndumo Hill rising to 160 m on the southern boundary. The hide on the hill offers excellent views of the low-lying floodplains and pans. The floodplains of the Pongola and Usuthu rivers cover about one third of the park and incorporate several permanent and seasonal pans. The largest pans are Nyamithi and Banzi in the east.

Apart from yielding large sausage-like fruits, the sausage tree has impressive flowers.

Vegetation

More than 900 plant species have been recorded in Ndumo. Vegetation types include a large area of Mahemane bush in the south and central areas, patches of umbrella thorn-dominated country in the north, riverine forest and floodplain communities, dry thicket in the south-west and sandveld woodland in the south and east. Ndumo protects important vegetation types that have largely disappeared elsewhere.

Mahemane bush is often dense thicket, and trees such as thorns (*Vachellia* and *Senegalia* spp.) and false-thorns (*Albizia* spp.) dominate. The dry thicket in the south-west takes on a more savanna-like appearance in parts, with wooded grassland and the **knob thorn** (*Senegalia nigrescens*) the most obvious tree. In the south and east, sandveld woodland thrives on the orange sandy soils, with **monkey-orange** (*Strychnos* spp.), **silver cluster-leaf** (*Terminalia sericea*),

The Usuthu River, viewed here from the Red Cliffs picnic site, forms Ndumo's northern boundary.

Ndumo's hutted rest camp is unfenced.

CLIMATE

This is a summer-rainfall area with very dry winters. The annual average rainfall is around 650 to 700 mm but there have been occasional cyclonic deluges – in 1976, 700 mm fell in just three days. February averages 26°C though some days may exceed 39°C, while July averages 18°C but may drop to 3°C. October to March is generally hot and humid.

marula (*Sclerocarya birrea*), **black monkey thorn** (*Senegalia burkei*) and **large-leaved false-thorn** (*Albizia versicolor*) the dominant trees, and often good grass cover. The distinctive **umbrella thorn** (*Vachellia tortilis*) grows mainly in the north. Some of the tallest trees are to be found near the rivers and floodplains and include **sycamore figs** (*Ficus sycomorus*), which may reach more than 30 m, **water pear** (*Syzgium guineense*), **fever tree** (*Vachellia xanthophloea*), **ana tree** (*Faidherbia albida*) and the aptly named **sausage tree** (*Kigelia africana*). Riverine forest only covers about 250 ha. In the pans and floodplains there are extensive **reed beds** (*Phragmites*), other aquatic plants and large areas of short grassland sometimes called 'hippo lawns', heavily grazed by a number of herbivores but especially hippopotamus.

Wildlife
Mammals

The 75 mammal species include 11 reintroduced after having been hunted to extinction. The first game animals to be released were **impala**, **hook-lipped rhinoceros**, **square-lipped rhinoceros** and **warthog**. Later releases included **cheetah**, **blue wildebeest** and **giraffe**, although the last is controversial as it is probably exotic. Since proclamation, game animals have multiplied, especially **hippopotamus** and **nyala**. **Red duiker** were once considered to be so common that rangers were allowed to shoot them for rations. There are no large game herds but hippo viewing is good, and secretive antelope such as red duiker and **suni** may be seen, especially in the dry sand thicket country. Most commonly seen hoofed mammals are impala, nyala, giraffe (often near the dense thicket) and warthog. Elephant have not been reintroduced but a growing population is located in the neighbouring Tembe Elephant Park (see page 114). Square-lipped rhino are more frequently sighted than their hook-lipped cousins but both are scarce and **savanna buffalo** are seldom seen.

FACILITIES AND ACTIVITIES

- Small hutted camp with 7 self-contained units; campground with 14 sites.
- Bird-viewing hides.
- Guided game- and bird-watching walks can be arranged.
- Limited game- and bird-viewing gravel road network; guided or self-drive.
- No fuel or supplies in Ndumo; there is a store 2 km from the entrance gate.
- Approach road is often in poor condition.

Ndumo Game Reserve 119

WILDLIFE FACTS

- There are 75 species of mammal, including suni and red duiker.
- An amazing 444 bird species, including several species close to the southern limit of their range.
- At least 75 reptile species, including a large and healthy Nile crocodile population.
- Some 43 species of frog and toad; during the first rains, one of the best frog choruses in South Africa.
- Recorded 36 species of freshwater fish in wetlands; occasional visits by marine species such as bull shark.
- Outstanding 421 species of spider (14 new to science); further collecting is expected to yield many more.
- More than 900 species of plant, including magnificent stands of sycamore fig and fever trees.

The many pans attract a great diversity of bird life, such as this African spoonbill.

There are more than 300 hippopotamus, with some movement along the Usuthu River. Of the 18 carnivore species, only the pack-living **banded mongoose** is frequently sighted. Rare species such as **four-toed sengi** (dry thicket and riparian country), **ground pangolin** and the nocturnal **Selous' mongoose** are seldom seen.

Birds

Ndumo is one of South Africa's premier bird-watching destinations. In and around the reserve 444 species, including rare vagrants as well as seasonal migrants, have been recorded, some close to the southern limit of their range. Many palearctic and intra-African migrants are present in summer but the largest concentrations of waterfowl can be seen in the winter. With patience, as many as 100 bird species can be seen in the small tourist camp, and the Red Hills picnic site overlooking the Usuthu River is equally productive. There are many specials to be found here. Watch for **broad-billed roller**, **Neergaard's sunbird**, **pink-throated twinspot**, **African broadbill**, **white-eared barbet**, **green malkoha**, **black-throated wattle-eye** and **southern brown-throated weaver**. Naturally the water bird contingent is substantial and diverse.

Reptiles and amphibians

Nile crocodile are abundant and frequently seen in the pans and principal rivers. A research and rearing facility in the reserve was moved to St Lucia in 1974. There are at least 75 other reptile species in Ndumo including the **leopard tortoise**, **Bell's hinged tortoise**, **marsh terrapin**, **serrated hinged terrapin**, **yellow-bellied hinged terrapin**, **rock monitor**, **Nile monitor** and **southern African python**. Of the approximately 40 snake species, few are seen as they include many nocturnal and burrowing species. Many of South Africa's most venomous species are found here, such as **black mamba**, **eastern**

White-eared barbets are a local special.

A highly gregarious species, banded mongoose live in troops. They are commonly seen in Ndumo.

Park authorities ensure that all species are protected here.

green mamba, **snouted cobra**, **forest cobra**, **Mozambique spitting cobra**, **puff adder**, **boomslang** and the **twig snake**. **Moreau's house gecko** is frequently seen on the walls of buildings in the rest camp. The larger **Wahlberg's velvet gecko** is sometimes also seen here. The tiny and diurnal **Cape dwarf gecko** is common and, although cryptically coloured, is easily seen. The large **southern tree agama** is mainly arboreal and the bobbing display of the blue-headed male draws attention.

At least 43 species of frog and toad occur in Ndumo. During the rains and the breeding season vast numbers of frogs call, especially around the pans and pools of the floodplain. Toads foraging around the rest camp at night include **guttural**, **flat-backed** and **red toads**. **Grey tree frogs** hang their white foam nests just above water in bush or tree during the rains, and in the dry season they often shelter in the observation hides and the ablution block.

Dung beetles play an important role in the scheme of things.

Fish

The 36 freshwater fish species play a critical part in the diet of Nile crocodiles and piscivorous birds such as kingfishers and cormorants. Another three large marine species, **smalltooth sawfish**, **oxeye tarpon** and **bull (Zambezi) shark**, are known to penetrate the reserve along the Usuthu and Pongola rivers.

Toads forage under the camp lights at night.

!
- This is a high-risk malaria zone and precautions must be taken.
- Dangerous game is present – take extra care in unfenced camp and picnic sites and especially when entering hides.
- Never enter water as Nile crocodiles abound and bilharzia is present.

FREE STATE

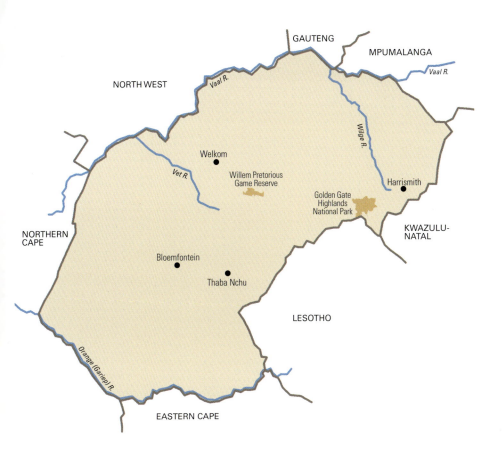

Once covered by vast tracts of natural grassland sustaining great herds of game, extensive areas of this province have been transformed for the production of maize, wheat, soya and sunflowers. Much of the province consists of Highveld plains, although the south-eastern sector bordering on Lesotho and the KwaZulu-Natal Drakensberg is mountainous and broken country. The eastern half of the province is defined as moist grassland, with the drier west strongly influenced by semi-arid Karoo scrub. This scrub dominates near the borders but blends into the grassland as it extends northwards. Monitoring has shown that there is a slow but steady spread of this semi-arid scrubland eastwards – a combined result of poor and changing land management, as well as the impacts of climate change.

The red sandstones along the southern rim, which extend into the Golden Gate Highlands National Park, are an important geological feature. The south-eastern Free State is well known for its multi-hued sandstone formations. These relatively soft sedimentary rocks erode rapidly if exposed but the basaltic layers act as a brake to this natural erosion. The southern skyline is dominated by the Maluti Mountains in Lesotho and behind them the mighty Drakensberg. Most of the province's rain falls in summer during thunderstorms.

The great game herds are gone forever, and the greatly diminished remnants are restricted to a few conservation areas and a plethora of private game reserves and farms. Most of the provincial reserves incorporate dams, and have been established principally for recreation.

The spectacular sandstone formations of Golden Gate Highlands National Park are one of the Free State's major attractions.

GOLDEN GATE HIGHLANDS NATIONAL PARK

Magnificent sandstone formations

LOCATION

Much of Golden Gate Highlands consists of sheer cliffs and steep to rolling slopes with extensive grass cover.

Lie of the land

The 32 608 ha Golden Gate Highlands park, proclaimed in 1962 and best known for its dramatic scenery, lies in the foothills of the Maluti Mountains and extends to the border of Lesotho. It is located just east of Clarens, south-west of Harrismith and south-east of Bethlehem. Throughout the park you will see exposed red and yellow cliffs and outcrops, the result of water erosion. Altitude here ranges from 1 840 m to 2 837 m above sea level on Ribbokkop. The upper parts of the park form the watershed of two separate river systems: the Little Caledon is a tributary of the westward-flowing Caledon River that eventually feeds into the Orange (Gariep) River, and the Perskeboomspruit and Klerkspruit are tributaries of the Vaal River system. The nearby 18 000 ha Sterkfontein Dam Nature Reserve will probably be amalgamated with Golden Gate Highlands as part of a greater Maluti/Drakensberg transfrontier park.

Brief history

White farmers arrived in this area in the early 19th century, long after the first humans established a presence here. Evidence shows that humans were present

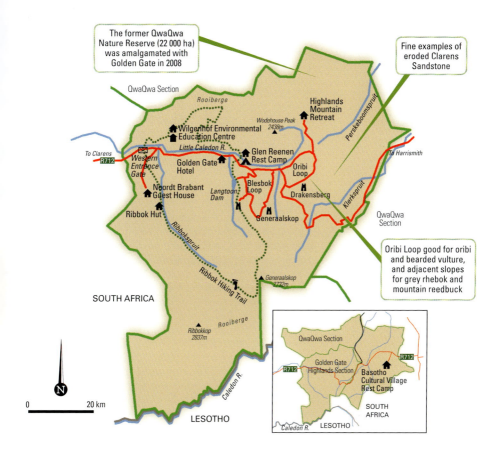

since at least 100 000 BP. The San may have been here around 2 000 BP, but the only remaining evidence lies in numerous rock paintings in the park and surrounds. Though several are worth visiting, they are generally not as well preserved as elsewhere in the Free State or in uKhuhlamba-Drakensberg in KwaZulu-Natal.

Geology and landscape

The park features colourful cliff formations and steep stream valleys such as that of the Little Caledon River. The name Golden Gate originates from the two facing cliffs on either side of the entrance road. Five main rock strata dominate the park: the top layer, or capping, consists of very hard Drakensberg basalt about 183 million years old, the cooled lava from ancient volcanic eruptions. The molten lava was also forced along rock cracks to form the dykes and sills visible throughout the park; there is an excellent example at Rooidraai just north of Glen Reenen Rest Camp. The next, rather thin layer, originally sandstone, was metamorphosed by the hot lava

HIGHLIGHTS

- Breathtaking scenery and access to high-altitude biota on fairly good roads.
- Number of Maluti/Drakensberg bird specials, including bearded vulture and southern bald ibis.

CLIMATE

Most of the 800 mm annual average rainfall occurs in summer thunderstorms from November to April. Higher areas are somewhat wetter. January mean temperatures range from 26°C down to 13°C; in July, from 15°C to a decidedly chilly -3°C. Frost is common in winter, and snowfalls fairly frequent; snow may lie for several days at high altitudes.

to form hard quartzite. The thickest and most colourful strata are Clarens Sandstone, ancient sands laid down over a dry period some 190 to 196 million years ago. This soft rock erodes easily where it is not protected by the basalt and quartzite capping. In many places, a narrow, harder, calcified stratum has formed within the Clarens layer, the result of waterborne calcium carbonate combining with the sandstone. The lowest stratum is the Elliot Mudstone, laid down as thick layers of silt and mud around 200 million years BP when the area was a wetland, then dried and compressed to rock by pressure from above. Black vertical stripes on the sandstone are manganese dioxide, leached from the basalt by water seepage.

Vegetation

Grasses are pervasive hereabouts. Three types of grassland are recognized: Lesotho highland basalt, Northern Drakensberg highland and Eastern Free State sandy gravel. Among the most important grasses to the grazing animals are **common thatch grass** (*Hyparrhenia hirta*), **curly leaf** (*Eragrostis chloromelas*) and **red grass** (*Themeda triandra*). In the low-lying areas and especially QwaQwa, short grasslands dominate, with such species as **curly leaf** and **hairy trident grass** (*Tristachya leucothrix*). There are also small areas of Afromontane heathland (fynbos) and shrubland and pockets of copse forest in sheltered gorges, especially in sandstone areas. These are dominated by **oldwood** (*Leucosidea sericea*), **wild peach** (*Kiggelaria africana*) and **sagewood** (*Buddleja salviifolia*). On some slopes below the sandstone cliffs you will see such proteas as **common sugarbush** (*Protea caffra*), **silver sugarbush** (*Protea roupelliae*) and **lip-flower sugarbush** (*Protea subvestita*), but these rarely form dense stands.

Vegetation map

- Eastern Free State sandy grassland
- Northern Drakensberg highland grassland
- Basotho montane shrubland
- Lesotho highland basalt grassland
- Afromontane fynbos

This park is one of a few places where the oribi thrives.

The hutted camp at Glen Reenen looks over majestic landforms.

Wildlife
Mammals
There are good populations of **plains zebra**, **common eland**, **black wildebeest**, **red hartebeest**, **blesbok**, **springbok** and **mountain reedbuck**. Smaller species to watch for on open grassland are **grey rhebok**, **steenbok** and **oribi** (elusive, but somewhat easier to see on the Oribi Loop). The best strategy is to scan the grassland from a high point along a game-viewing road, then drive as close as possible. Of the 14 carnivore species, you are most likely to see the **black-backed jackal** and the strictly diurnal **small grey mongoose** and the **yellow mongoose**. Very few smaller species will show themselves but the mounds of the **common mole-rat** are apparent on the lawns at the

FACILITIES AND ACTIVITIES

- Glen Reenen Rest Camp has 32 fully equipped units and a campground with 60 stands; Highlands Mountain Retreat has eight fully equipped family cottages set deep in the park; Golden Gate Hotel has various rooms and chalets; QwaQwa has 24 chalets in a camp that resembles a Basotho village.
- Hiking and walking trails. Ribbok is a 2-day hiking trail, with a communal hut.
- Mountain bike and horse trails.
- Restaurant, pub, basic supplies and fuel at Golden Gate Hotel.
- Full range of services at Clarens, Harrismith and Bethlehem.
- Tarred access roads.

The park is dominated by grassland.

Steenbok share their habitat with the oribi, which is similar in appearance but larger.

One of the birding specials in the area is the bearded vulture.

hotel and elsewhere. **Chacma baboons** are ubiquitous and often feed on the open grasslands. The park is home to 18 rodent species; the distinctive **four-striped grass mouse** may be seen by day around the camps, and on the high ridges you may glimpse the day-active **Sloggett's**, or **ice**, **rat**.

Birds

The 180 bird species and several Drakensberg endemics make this a top Free State bird destination, especially if you also have time to explore the QwaQwa section and the nearby Sterkfontein Dam reserve. The **bearded vulture** perhaps no longer breeds in the park, but is regularly seen at high altitudes. Here also are **Verreaux's eagle**, **Cape vulture** and the ever-present **jackal buzzard**. **Secretarybird** is often seen on the grasslands. There is a vulture restaurant in the park but carcasses are only placed there very infrequently. This is a good location for **southern bald ibis** and **Barrow's korhaan**, especially in areas of recent burns and short growth. Three sunbird species and **Gurney's sugarbird** frequent flowering proteas, but the **malachite sunbird** is only present in the summer months. At high altitudes, watch for **Drakensberg rockjumper**, **Drakensberg siskin** and (in summer) **mountain pipit**. As usual it is worth spending time around the camps, as many species there are accustomed to people and are more approachable. The hotel grounds are usually good for **ground woodpecker**, **mountain wheatear** and **Cape bunting**.

Reptiles and amphibians

Despite the high altitude, a surprising 28 reptile species have been recorded, although most are elusive. Several of these species are only found in the Drakensberg-Maluti area, including **mountain flat gecko**,

WILDLIFE FACTS

- At least 60 mammal species.
- Records show 180 bird species, including a variety of high-altitude specials.
- The 28 known reptile species include some Drakensberg endemics; there are 15 species of amphibian in the area, with eight so far recorded in the park.
- Only four recorded fish species, two of them indigenous.

Blesbok are herd antelope and are commonly seen in the park.

Drakensberg crag lizard, **Drakensberg dwarf chameleon** and the **spiny crag lizard**. At least one **mountain lizard** (*Tropidosaura* spp.) occurs in the higher reaches. Like the 12 snake species, the eight amphibian species are seldom seen, though **Ranger's** and **Karoo toads** are sometimes seen foraging for insects at night in the camps.

Fish

Only four fish species have been recorded. Of these, two are exotics, namely the **carp**, restricted to the Golden Gate dam, and the predatory **rainbow trout** in the river below the dam and in the Ribbokspruit. The small **chubby-head barb** is widely distributed and abundant, but the **small-mouth yellowfish**, a sometime seasonal visitor to the Little Caledon River, has not been recorded for some years.

Invertebrates

Golden Gate and surrounding areas are the only known home for several butterfly species, including the **browns** (Golden Gate widow and Golden Gate brown).

Verreaux's eagle is a cliff nester that hunts rock hyrax, found in abundance in the park.

- Weather changes are common at any time of year.
- Beware of severe cold and snowfalls in winter, and avoid high ground during summer thunderstorms as fatal lightning strikes have occurred.

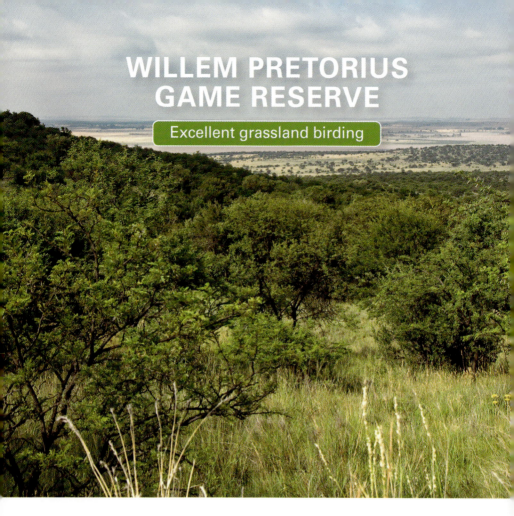

WILLEM PRETORIUS GAME RESERVE

Excellent grassland birding

There are extensive areas of shrub and bush thickets amid the grassland that dominates the Willem Pretorius Game Reserve.

Lie of the land

Willem Pretorius is north-east of Bloemfontein in the central Free State, 8 km east of the N1, 30 km north of Winburg and 19 km south of Ventersburg. The reserve is focused on the Allemanskraal Dam, its surrounding plain, and the broken hill country of the Doringberg range in the north and east. It covers 12 005 ha, of which 2 771 ha is occupied by the dam when it is full. The Sand River flows east to west through the park, feeding the dam.

Brief history

The central Free State has a number of important archaeological sites covering the Earlier, Middle and Later Stone Age eras, but these are not always immediately obvious to the visitor. Numerous small stone corbelled structures and walls are scattered through the hills, dating back to the Iron Age. These surprisingly small stone huts, mostly on rocky ridges overlooking rivers, have entrances just 45 cm

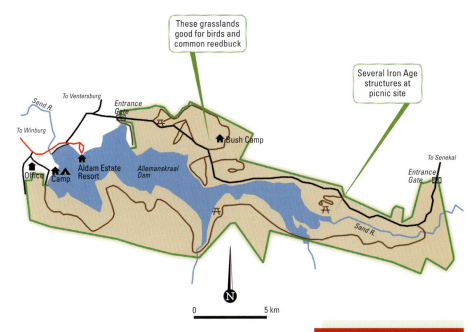

high and 40 cm wide. The first such sites were established by the Leghoja people in the 17th century or possibly earlier. A restored settlement at a picnic site in the east of the reserve has been neglected and is now reverting to the bush.

Geology and landscape

The flat area around the dam and to the south is composed of mudstones, sandstones, and the soils derived from these, with components of the Karoo Super Group. Dolerite sills form broken ridges and rugged outcrops along much of the northern boundary and in the east.

Vegetation

Much of the reserve's vegetation can be classified into two groups, the Winburg grassy shrubland of the hilly northern areas and the flat central Free State grassland that covers much of the rest. Much of the grassland consists of short species such as the important **red grass** (*Themeda triandra*), **weeping love grass** (*Eragrostis curvula*), **narrow curly leaf** (*Eragrostis chloromelas*) and **couch grass** (*Cynodon dactylon*). The **sweet thorn** (*Vachellia karroo*), with its long white thorns, dominates the flats around the dam, sometimes forming dense stands. In the hills and broken country there are grassy expanses, scattered bushes and small thickets. Here one finds **wild**

HIGHLIGHTS

- Watch the courting flight of the male long-tailed widowbird.
- While not a Big Five reserve, many large species are present.
- Easy access from the N1 between Bloemfontein and Johannesburg.

Common reedbuck favour areas of medium to long grasses.

Willem Pretorius Game Reserve   131

Vegetation map

- Eastern Free State clay grassland
- Central Free State grassland
- Winburg grassy shrubland

CLIMATE

Much of the annual average 560 mm rainfall happens in December and January thunderstorms. There is almost no rain from June to August. The area has more than 40 days of frost each winter. The mean annual temperature is around 15°C, but in summer temperatures often rise above 30°C.

olive (*Olea europaea*), **blue guarri** (*Euclea crispa*), **blue bush** (*Diospyros lycioides*) and several species of karree (*Rhus* spp.).

Wildlife
Mammals

Several large game species have been reintroduced here, including **square-lipped rhinoceros, plains zebra, giraffe, savanna buffalo, common eland, greater kudu** and **black wildebeest**. Several of the grazers, such as the **wildebeest, blesbok** and **springbok**, are concentrated in the grasslands south of the dam. **Common reedbuck** can usually be seen on the open grasslands in the east and **mountain reedbuck** also occupy this sector, preferring the rocky areas. The three most commonly seen carnivores are the solitary **small grey mongoose, yellow mongoose** and the troop-living **suricate**. The other nine carnivore species are seldom seen, though **black-backed jackal** are sometimes heard calling at night. **Chacma baboon** roam the hill country but also penetrate the grasslands and the flats around the dam.

Birds

With the dam as the centrepiece of the reserve one can of course expect a great diversity of water birds. No fewer than 14 species of duck and goose have been recorded, including sometimes abundant **Egyptian** and **spur-winged geese**. Of the nine heron species, the most numerous is the **western cattle egret**, visible in the early morning and early evening as flocks move between roost and feeding

Iron Age dwellings are found at several sites but most are collapsed and overgrown.

During late spring and into summer, male long-tailed widowbirds can be seen displaying in the longer grasslands.

FACILITIES AND ACTIVITIES

- Aldam Estate Resort on the western boundary offers fully equipped lodges, large campground, restaurant, shop, game-viewing drives and boat tours.
- Fully equipped chalets as well as a basic bush camp.
- Fishing in dam.
- Extensive network of gravel game-viewing roads.
- Western access road is tarred. No fuel or supplies available in the reserve.
- Closest towns are Bloemfontein, Winburg, Ventersburg and Senekal.

grounds. Although 18 raptor species are on record, several such as the **lesser kestrel** and **Amur falcon** are seasonal visitors. Look out for the **Orange River francolin**. Also watch for the **blue korhaan** in the grasslands. This is an excellent location for watching the breeding display flights of the male **long-tailed widowbird**. This is also a top **lark** reserve, with no fewer than 10 species, and there are seven cisticola species to seek out. The dam is a major attraction for large numbers of piscivorous birds, such as various cormorants, kingfishers, herons and the **African fish eagle**. The fish-eating **western osprey** is a rare visitor.

Reptiles and amphibians

Most of the 18 reptile species are rarely seen. With luck you may see **marsh terrapins** basking on the edge of the dam, especially in the more sheltered bays. The **southern rock agama**, especially the male, draws attention to itself by sitting on top of rocks. The 12 frog species are hard to spot, and you are more likely to hear the males calling during the rains. **Karoo toad** and **Ranger's toad** may be seen foraging at night around resort buildings and in the campground.

Fish

Eight fish species are present in the dam, and several of these attract large numbers of anglers.

WILDLIFE FACTS

- At least 47 mammal species, ranging in size from pygmy mouse to square-lipped rhinoceros.
- More than 240 bird species recorded, excluding 14 rare vagrants. Excellent for viewing grassland species.
- Of a total of 18 reptile species recorded here, nine are snakes.
- Some of the eight different fish species draw large numbers of anglers.

> **!** • Aldam Estate Resort can be very full during school holidays and summer weekends.

Willem Pretorius Game Reserve **133**

EASTERN CAPE

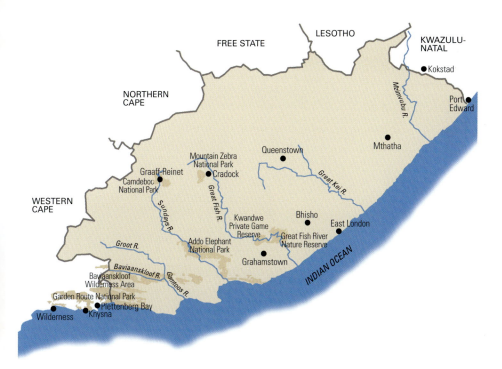

The Eastern Cape borders on Western Cape to the west, Northern Cape and Free State provinces and Lesotho to the north, and KwaZulu-Natal in the north-east. Its entire southern border is formed by the Indian Ocean. The principal mountain ranges include the southern Drakensberg range, Stormberg and Bamboesberg in the north-east, the Sneeuberg and Bankberg in the north-west, Zuurberg in Addo Elephant National Park, and the Tsitsikamma, Grootrivier, Witteberge and Baviaanskloofberge in the south-west. Many rivers rise in these ranges and pour their waters into the Indian Ocean, such as the Mzimvubu, Mthatha, Mbashe, Great Kei, Buffalo, Great Fish, Kowie, Bushmans, Sundays and the Gamtoos.

This province experiences considerable climatic variations. The northern coast has hot, humid conditions with high rainfall, but inland around Graaff-Reinet in the Karoo it is much drier and winters are cool, with snow on neighbouring mountains. Even further inland towards the Free State border, winters are cold with frequent frosts. This diversity of climate has created an equal diversity of vegetation. In the south-west, particularly near the Baviaanskloof and Kouga mountains, one finds the eastern outlier of the fynbos (Cape heathland); at places such as Alexandria, Pirie and the Amatolas rich forest. North of East London the influences are subtropical, while inland near the eastern mountains, Afromontane grasslands and forests are found. Much of the interior falls within the Karoo biome and low rainfall encourages the development of low, sparse scrub and many succulent plants. The well-known Addo bush and valley bushveld form dense, spiny thickets with a strong complement of tall succulent species including aloes and tree euphorbias. The province has great wildlife diversity and is malaria-free.

The 'flagship' park is Addo Elephant National Park, but the other parks and reserves also show outstanding diversity.

The great dolerite columns overlooking the Valley of Desolation in Camdeboo National Park are a major attraction.

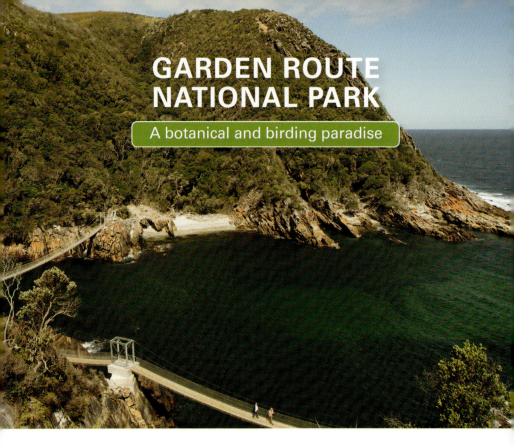

GARDEN ROUTE NATIONAL PARK
A botanical and birding paradise

LOCATION

The suspension bridge at the mouth of the Storms River affords excellent views upstream.

Lie of the land

Garden Route National Park, covering 157 000 ha, includes the former Tsitsikamma and Wilderness national parks, Knysna National Lake Area and most indigenous forests and mountain water catchment areas between Wilderness in the west and the N2/R62 road junction in the east, and the area south of the N9 and R62 to the north. It is flanked to the south by the Indian Ocean and encompasses much of the Tsitsikamma, Langkloof and the eastern Outeniqua mountain ranges. The coastal plain is very narrow and disappears in the east where the mountains descend to the sea. Numerous small streams rise in these mountains and in the east several, such as the Storms River, have cut deep gorges through the rock. Apart from proclaimed areas of national park, some areas such as the 45 000 ha Formosa Nature Reserve are managed by SANParks on behalf of other landowners. The area is a popular holiday destination and is served by towns such as George in the west, and Wilderness, Sedgefield, Knysna, Plettenberg Bay and Humansdorp to the east. The park straddles the Eastern Cape–Western Cape boundary.

Brief history

Human remains dating from about 125 000 BP have been collected from such important sites as Nelson Bay, Matjies River, Kangkara, and Storms River.

The Klasies River site consists of a number of sea caves and many interesting finds have been made here, including human skeletal remains and stone tools from about 120 000 to 60 000 BP. Evidence indicates that groups occupied the caves only for short periods, as they probably moved between the mountains and the coast to harvest seasonal foods. Because of the significant presence of marine remains, which includes shells, seal and penguin bones, it has been called the earliest known 'seafood restaurant'. This and other sites were intermittently occupied until a few hundred years BP. During the Later Stone Age, San hunter-gatherers were in the area from possibly 20 000 BP, and about 1 500 to 2 000 BP Khoekhoen herders with their livestock entered the scene.

By the 17th century and the arrival of Europeans, the main Khoekhoen group hereabouts was the Hessequa, flanked to the east by the Gouriqua and to the west by the Chainouqua. By the middle of the 18th century the San and to a greater extent, the Khoekhoen had seen their culture and economic order destroyed, and their populations shattered by smallpox. The first Europeans came mainly to hunt the abundant ivory, but by the turn of the 19th century the first settlers had arrived, planning to exploit the abundant hardwood trees. Knysna's most famous settler was George Rex, reputed illegitimate son of George III and his mistress Hannah Lightfoot, who settled here in 1804 and founded the town of Knysna. In February 1869 a fire devastated thousands of acres of forest covering the entire area of the present-day Garden Route National Park.

The Tsitsikamma National Park was proclaimed in 1964, Wilderness National Park and Knysna National Lake Area were established in 1985, and SANParks took over the management of all indigenous forests and mountain catchment areas in 2005. Several provincial nature reserves, including Rondevlei, are also now part of the new Garden Route National Park, proclaimed in 2009.

Much of the coastline in this park is wild and rugged.

CLIMATE

The park receives rain throughout the year. Diepwalle and Storms River receive an annual average of approximately 1 200 mm, decreasing to about 800 mm in the western mountain fynbos areas. North-facing slopes receive only 500 mm. Midsummer temperatures in the forests north of Knysna peak at about 25°C, but the dry north-facing slopes may be hotter. Coastal temperatures are mild throughout the year; snow occasionally falls on the higher peaks of the inland Outeniqua and Langkloof ranges, but rarely on the coastal Tsitsikamma range.

Several estuaries, including that of the Knysna River, support abundant animal and plant life.

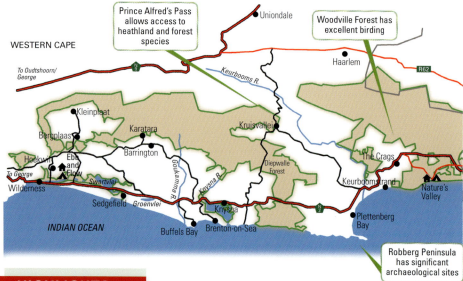

HIGHLIGHTS

- Spectacular coastal and mountain scenery.
- Great diversity of habitats, including South Africa's largest near-continuous extent of indigenous forest.
- Rich bird diversity, including range limits of some species.

Geology and landscape

The landscape contains mountain ranges, foothills, a narrow coastal plain and the rugged Indian Ocean coastline. Short streams rise in the mountains and cut precipitously to the sea. Some, like the Storms River, have formed deep gorges, while others cascade over sea cliffs. The mountains offer sheer cliffs and rolling, fynbos-covered slopes and ridges. Southern faces are generally lush and green while northern slopes are drier as they fall within the rain shadow. All the main mountain ranges and foothills here belong to the Cape Fold Belt of hard quartzites from the Table Mountain Group. This folded mountain chain with its curled and fractured strata originated in collisions of the Earth's crustal plates during the formation of Gondwanaland. Driving eastward along the estuary towards Knysna, you see roadside cliffs made up of rounded river-worn rocks belonging to the Enon conglomerates. Another feature of this coastline is the high barrier sand dunes, including notably that to the south of the Groenvlei. From the Keurbooms River, whose east bank exhibits a cut into Bokkeveld Shales, you climb 200 m to 300 m from today's coastal plain to one formed by an ancient, higher sea level. Continuing on this plain brings you to the park's eastern exit.

Vegetation

Fynbos and forest dominate the landscape here. You will encounter plantations of exotic timber trees, such as various conifers and Australian eucalyptus. The indigenous forest, scattered throughout the mountains and along the coast, is classified as southern Afrotemperate. The largest forest sector lies in an almost continuous arc that swings inland from Wilderness to just west of Plettenberg

The bush-tick berry grows in the sands of the coastal plain.

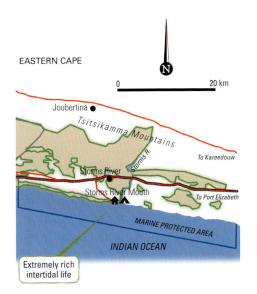

The Garden Route National Park protects the largest extent of indigenous forest in South Africa. It once covered a much greater area but a combination of fire and logging in the past reduced its extent.

Bay. The park holds the largest extent of indigenous forest in South Africa, some 43 500 ha, generally tall and multi-layered. The trees for which these forests are famous include the **Outeniqua yellowwood** (*Afrocarpus falcatus*), South Africa's tallest tree, reaching to 60 m. The **real yellowwood** (*Podocarpus latifolius*) is another giant. These and the **stinkwood** (*Ocotea bullata*) were once in great demand and over-exploited for their fine timber. Decades of protection have now restored the balance. The forest contains many other trees, including the magnificent flowering **Cape chestnut** (*Colodendrum capense*) that grows mainly in drier coastal forest patches on escarpments and slopes of river gorges, producing its profusion of large, pink flowers in spring and summer. The **keurboom**, or **blossom tree**, (*Virgilia oroboides*) rarely reaches 15 m, and is relatively short-lived. It grows near the forest edges and along the N2 to the east of Plettenberg Bay, and produces plentiful pink flowers in spring and summer. In the wetter areas, watch for the **forest** and **common tree ferns** (*Alsophila* spp.) and the **Cape wild banana**, or **white strelitzia**, (*Strelitzia alba*) can be seen at several locations. The stand at Nature's Valley is particularly impressive. In many of the forests there is a dense understorey of low bushes, shrubs and many different ferns.

The fynbos component, covering some 80 000 ha, is diverse and impressive. One can recognize five major divisions, based on their location, the type of soil and the rainfall. South Outeniqua sandstone fynbos occupies the southern slopes west of the Keurbooms River, while the north side of these mountains has a drier form. East of the Keurbooms River is Tsitsikamma sandstone fynbos that receives higher rainfall; it is found on the mountain slopes and in the east, right up to the coast. On the lower slopes, especially to the west is Garden Route shale fynbos, and from its fringes to the coast is the

The keurboom is found on forest edges.

The walkway along the water's edge in the Wilderness area is excellent for bird-watching.

The vegetated barrier dune at Groenvlei is said to be the tallest in South Africa.

Knysna sand fynbos. Many of the plant species are shared but many others are found only in one specific fynbos type. The **yellow-bushes**, or **cone-bushes**, (*Leucadendron* spp.) are conspicuous proteas, occurring in sometimes dense patches on the mountain slopes such as those seen from the Robinson and Outeniqua passes. Typical proteas on the slopes include **long-bud sugarbush** (*Protea aurea*) with its yellowish or reddish flower heads that can be present in any month. The tall **blue sugarbush** (*Protea neriifolia*), sometimes called bearded protea, with its large showy flower heads is mainly confined to south-facing mountain slopes. Altogether more than 30 protea species grow within the park. Many species of heath, or erica, (*Ericaceae*) occur across the region with several growing along roadsides, one of the most obvious being the 2 m tall *Erica canaliculata* with its small pink bell flowers. Another tall (up to 2.5 m) species is the *Erica chloroloma* which grows on the coastal sands and produces its orange tubular flowers from May to October. Masses of **blue lily** (*Agapanthus praecox*) flower impressively from December to April

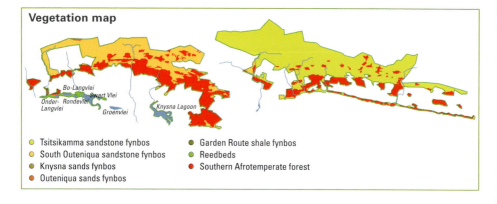

140   Eastern Cape

Cape clawless otters occupy coastal and fresh waters in the park but are rarely seen.

in the south of the park, especially near the coast. The bush known as **bush-tick berry**, or **bietou**, (*Chrysanthemoides monilifera*) grows abundantly in the sands of the coastal plain, producing many canary-yellow flowers from May to October. Near lakes and rivers, such as Rondevlei, Groenvlei, and the Serpentine at Ebb and Flow, there are extensive, dense stands of **common reed** (*Phragmites australis*), which may reach heights of 4 m and have large, showy, plume-like flower- and seed-heads. During spring and summer they are green, but they turn brown after seeding in autumn. These reedbeds are of critical importance for maintaining water quality and as habitat for a host of birds and other creatures. On mudbanks in the estuaries, such as Swartvlei, at low tide during autumn and winter you will see swathes of pinks and red; these are the succulent, jointed stems of an estuarine plant, the **glasswort samphire** (*Sarcocornia perennis*).

Wildlife
Mammals
Some 85 species of mammal occur in the area. The animal that draws most attention is the **savanna elephant**. These are some of the last free-ranging animals in the south of the country.

In the 1880s it was estimated that 400 to 600 elephant ranged the area from George to Tsitsikamma in the east; by 1970 it was believed that no more than 10 survived, and in 1992 only one. However, some experts believe as many as five survive. Current DNA work on their dung may resolve this controversy. These forests are not rich in nutrition so the elephant may also forage in the adjacent fynbos at night, but sightings are extremely rare. **Common eland** are present on the slopes in the east, with **bushbuck** wherever there is forest, even in small pockets, and in dense coastal thicket. The diminutive **blue duiker** is sparsely spread in forest pockets throughout the park; the best chance of a sighting is in the Tsitsikamma section.

FACILITIES AND ACTIVITIES

- Premier tourist destination with vast array of hotels, guest houses, campgrounds, restaurants and shops. Storms River Mouth (Tsitsikamma) has 38 cabins and huts, a campground, shop and restaurant; Nature's Valley has a small hutted camp and campground. Wilderness has a range of cottages and cabins at Ebb and Flow Rest Camp, as well as a caravan/camping site.
- Many walking and hiking trails in the parks, forest and Cape heathland (fynbos) areas. They range from just 1 km to the 5-day Otter Trail from Storms River Mouth to Nature's Valley
- There are several mountain bike trails, canoeing trails and a host of other outdoor activities.
- Shops, fuel stations and restaurants are found in all towns in the region.
- Extensive road network gives access to coast, mountains and forests.

WILDLIFE FACTS

- Some 85 species of mammal.
- At least 371 resident, migrant or vagrant bird species, with several at their eastern or western range limits.
- About 55 reptile species and 24 different amphibians.
- Some 26 freshwater and estuarine fish, and 300+ marine species.

Common duiker avoid the forests, preferring areas of thickets with clearings, such as are found along the coast. **Klipspringer** are found in the higher rocky areas, while **Cape grysbok** are largely restricted to heathland and the fringes of forest. **Chacma baboons** are found throughout, and **vervet monkeys** are widespread but avoid heathland and dense forest. One of the most commonly seen mammals, especially in places such as Storms River Mouth Camp, is the tailless **rock hyrax**, or **dassie**. Of the 24 known species of rodent, few are ever seen, except the **four-striped grass-mouse** which is day-active and commonly forages around campgrounds and picnic sites. You almost certainly will not see the **Cape dune mole-rat** but the presence of this large subterranean rodent is evident from the large, often clustered mounds of sand along most roadsides on the coastal plain. Two other species of mole-rat occur here but their mounds are smaller and are rarely so tightly clustered. You are not likely to encounter any of the five shrew species but the **long-tailed forest shrew** is largely restricted to forest pockets, with some isolated populations westwards. One of the 12 recorded bat species, the **Egyptian fruit-bat**, is a large cave-rooster; one colony shelters in a cave just above the mouth of the Storms River. They favour the fruit of the abundant Cape ash tree. Fifteen carnivore species, ranging in size from the **African striped weasel** to the **leopard**, have been recorded but only the **small grey mongoose** is regularly seen in camp areas, crossing roads, or along trails. Sometimes at night one of the two genet species may be spotted scavenging in and around the camps, and a very lucky visitor might glimpse the **Cape clawless otter** that hunts crabs, fish and octopus along the coastline, and gives its name to the Otter Trail. No fewer than 15 species of whale and dolphin have been recorded but not all are regular visitors. One of the best locations for observing **humpback dolphins** is in Plettenberg Bay, and along the entire coastline **Indian Ocean bottlenosed dolphin** and **long-beaked common dolphin** are

The long-beaked common dolphin is a regular sight along this coastline which is rich in mammal diversity.

Eastern Cape

quite commonly seen, sometimes close inshore. The largest seasonal visitor (May to December) is the **southern right whale**. It spends most time in sheltered basins such as Plettenberg Bay, where cows give birth and mating takes place, before returning to the Antarctic feeding grounds.

Birds

There are 371 species of bird recorded in the area, including 286 in the Tsitsikamma section. Of these some 45 are vagrants and seldom seen. The 24 largely oceanic species may be found anywhere along the coastline, seasonally, irregularly or as storm-driven vagrants.

Several bird species reach their eastern or western range limits here, and there is a good collection of specials. Because of the landscape, there are numerous aquatic and wading species. There are 15 species of duck and goose, including the common **Egyptian goose**, **yellow-billed duck** and **Cape shoveler**, and **African black duck** may be found in the mountain streams. With patience it is also a good park to look for **African finfoot**. The upstream Keurbooms River, the Goukamma River and the Kaaimans River near the bridge are all likely locations for this unusual bird. There are 16 Palearctic waders, usually best seen on estuaries, open lake banks and beaches. A rare resident is the **African (black) oystercatcher** that during winter may form flocks of up to 35 birds. There are three known species of flufftail, the **buff-spotted**, **red-chested** and **striped flufftail**, although all are very secretive and knowledge of their calls is of great help. Local birders say that Langvlei and Rondevlei are the best lakes for birding in the Wilderness sector of the park, and each has an observation hide on its north bank. There are 22 raptors; look out for **African cuckoo-hawk**, **crowned eagle**, and western **osprey** from September to May. This is an excellent area for the forest buzzard, easily confused with the summer-visiting **steppe buzzard**. Many visitors come in search of the forest and forest-fringe birds such as **red-necked spurfowl**,

The male African paradise-flycatcher is a dramatic presence in the park's forests.

Rock hyrax (dassies) can be seen at the Storms River Mouth camp.

Knysna turaco are endemic here.

tambourine dove, black-bellied starling, white-starred robin and forest canary. Two of the most sought-after species are the relatively common **Knysna turaco** and the **Narina trogon**; both are heard more often than seen. The best way to see forest birds is to walk the many trails; it is always good to know their calls, as many species are elusive. The heathland of both coast and mountain slopes has several species of sunbird, such as the **orange-breasted sunbird**, and the **Cape sugarbird**; in heathland and higher rocky reaches one may see the range-restricted Cape rockjumper. In the fynbos you will also see the protea seedeater and the Cape siskin.

Reptiles and amphibians

There is a substantial diversity of reptiles in the park but this is lowest in the forests. The 25 snake species on record include **Cape cobra**, **rinkhals**, **herald snake** and **brown house snake**, but few are seen. One of the most abundant is the **puff adder**, a large venomous snake that thrives in dense grass patches and coastal thicket where rodent densities are high, such as at Goukamma. There are three species of land tortoise that plod across this area, particularly on the coastal plains, and the **angulate tortoise** and **parrot-beaked padloper** are quite common. The large **leopard tortoise** is occasionally seen but this is not their usual habitat and these individuals may well have escaped or been released from captivity. The coastline is coursed by three species of sea turtle: **green**, **loggerhead** and **leatherback**. They rarely beach but youngsters sometimes get washed up. Only a few of the 21 lizard species are regularly seen, such as the trusting **Cape skink**, the rock-dwelling **Cape crag lizard**, and two species of girdled lizard. The **southern rock agama**, especially the male, is often seen sitting on rocks and boulders. At least four species of dwarf chameleons are known, although they are difficult to find in their forest or heathland homes, and additional species may yet be found. The **beardless dwarf** occurs in heathland on the dry northern slopes of the Tsitsikamma range and as yet has no specific scientific name. The **Knysna dwarf** occurs in forests on the wet south-facing slopes of the Outeniqua and Tsitsikamma mountains, often high in the canopy. The **Little Karoo dwarf** occurs in the heathland on the north-facing slopes of the Outeniqua, whereas the **Elandsberg dwarf** has a limited range on the wet heathland of the south-facing slope of the Tsitsikamma Mountains.

Most of the 24 species of frog and toad will only become known to the visitor by the courtship calls of the males. Large choruses of male **Ranger's** (or **raucous**) **toads**, sounding much like the quacking of ducks, can be heard day and night from around September. Much of the distribution of the **southern ghost frog** is in streams running through dense forest here. The **Knysna spiny reed frog**, first described near that town, is one of three species of reed frog, the others being **Horstock's**, or **arum lily**, and the **painted**, or **marbled**, **reed frogs**.

Painted reed frogs are usually found among sedges and reeds along the water's edge.

Strawberry rain frogs occur in the mountain ranges of the southwestern Cape but are also encountered at sea level near coastal mountains.

Fish

At least 26 species of estuarine and freshwater fish, including several exotics, thrive here. The **Knysna seahorse** inhabits the Knysna Estuary and a few other estuaries in the southern Cape. Another interesting freshwater species is the **Cape galaxias**, whose nearest relatives are in South America, Australia and New Zealand. More than 300 species of marine fish are found in these coastal waters, with 202 species, representing 84 families, occurring in the marine reserve (approximately 75 km long and 800 m to 5 500 m wide) that is part of the Tsitsikamma section. It is an important refuge for 17 important commercial and angling fish species. The principal oceanic influence on this coast is the north-south Agulhas Current. Among others there are 23 species of shark and shark-like species, including the **great white**, **spotted ragged-tooth**, **smooth hammerhead** and, rarely and largest of all, the **whale shark**. Other important fish here include the **black mussel-cracker**, **white mussel-cracker**, **white steenbras** and **galjoen**, with at least 10 'flat-fish', the soles and flounders. With more research, the list of species is very likely to expand.

Commonly washed ashore, 'bluebottles', or Portuguese-man-o-war, have tentacles that carry venomous stinging cells.

Invertebrates

Marine invertebrates, especially molluscs, have been well inventoried and diversity is high. One can just study the rock pools, or snorkel the underwater trail at the Storms River Mouth in the Tsitsikamma sector. Not much research has been done on the terrestrial invertebrates here but diversity, particularly of the insects, is high. A number of insects are restricted to this area, including the **Knysna forest ground katydid** which has a body length of about 25 mm with very long legs and antennae, and is covered with wavy cream and black longitudinal stripes. A number of forest-dwelling butterflies have their westward range limits in the park. The very large (wingspan 120 mm) and spectacular **silver-spotted ghost moth**, or **keurboom moth**, is found only in these southern forests. Its larvae bore into the wood of the keurboom about 1 m above the ground, and the adults emerge in February to March.

The rare Knysna seahorse only occurs in a few estuaries along the southern Cape coastline.

- Beware of sudden weather changes, especially in the higher mountain reaches.
- Strong currents and high seas are common.
- At the time of writing several walking trails, particularly in the Wilderness sector, were closed because of lack of maintenance and mugging incidents. It is always safest to walk in groups.

ADDO ELEPHANT NATIONAL PARK

Most diverse park outside 'malaria zone'

Lie of the land

Addo stretches over 200 km from Kenton-on-Sea in the east, to the banks of the Darlington Dam and to Waterford in the Karoo in the north-west. The park centres on the Zuurberg Mountains (part of the Winterhoek mountain range) that separate the dry, flat plains of the Karoo in the north from the southward-sloping land and hill country that runs to the Indian Ocean seaboard. Altitudes range from sea level to almost 1 000 m, including several Zuurberg peaks above 800 m. From Darlington Dam in the north-west, the Sundays River runs inside the south-western border of the park, emptying its waters into Algoa Bay at the western edge of the largest coastal dune system in the southern hemisphere. Addo covers approximately 170 000 ha but will ultimately encompass 686 000 ha, including a 120 000 ha marine reserve.

Savanna elephants frequently wallow in mud and water, especially on hot summer days.

Brief history

Several sites in the Addo area carry evidence of humankind from at least the Middle Stone Age. Some of the most significant artefacts lie within the Alexander dune field and show three distinct periods of usage. It is believed that the earliest

146 Eastern Cape

group, about 5 000 BP, came to the coast to forage only at certain times of the year. From about 4 000 BP people were living here permanently, as evidenced by the type of stones from which they made their tools. The bones of domestic livestock in the 'kitchen' middens indicate that Khoekhoen peoples had settled in the dunes by 2 000 BP. From around 1 500 BP there were at least three Khoekhoen clans in the area, the Iqua, Gonaqua and Damasqua, but they were largely wiped out by smallpox in the early 1700s.

Nomadic Xhosa tribes were also pushing into the area by this time, including the Gqunukhwebe who settled around the mouth of the Sundays River, and the Dange who established themselves along the Wit River. The Khoekhoen survivors, the Hoengeiqua, rallied under their leader Ruiter and successfully campaigned against the migrating Xhosa.

The first Boers penetrated this area in the 1740s in search of ivory and trade, but within a decade they had begun to settle and farm. Initially the Boers' chief conflicts were with the San hunter-gatherers, but by 1780 at least five Xhosa clans had settled in the area and there were more battles, chiefly with the Gqunukhwebe. These conflicts peaked in 1789 and the tribesmen retreated into the Zuurberg. Guerilla warfare ensued as about 700 Khoe and mixed-breeds allied with the Xhosa warriors to harass the Boers. In 1811 a colonial force of about 1 000 regular soldiers and settler militias drove the 'enemy' beyond the Great Fish River. In this so-called 'cleansing of the Suurveld', some 20 000 Xhosa and Khoekhoen were displaced. During the 2nd Anglo-Boer War, several skirmishes took place between Boer commandos and British troops near the present-day Darlington Dam in the north of the park.

By the early 1900s only small, isolated populations of elephant remained in the Eastern Cape. In 1919 Major P.J. Pretorius, appointed to exterminate the Addo elephant because of conflicts with agriculture, shot 114 animals in just over 12 months. When the park

CLIMATE

The area is classified as a tension zone where summer, winter and all-year rainfall regimes meet. The main game area, and the area near the park headquarters, receives year-round rain averaging 450 mm, with most in February/March and October/November. Summer and all-year rainfall regimes meet at the coast, where the Sundays River mouth area averages just 390 mm, while the Alexandria Forest on the eastern edge of the dune field gets 900 mm. The dune fields themselves lie in a 'rain shadow' and receive lower rainfall than their surroundings. Up to 720 mm per year falls in the Zuurberg, but as little as 250 mm falls in the summer-rainfall Karoo area around Darlington Dam. At the park headquarters temperature ranges are 15°C to 45°C in January and 5°C to 18°C in July. Temperatures vary greatly; the Darlington Dam area may reach 48°C in summer and freezing temperatures in winter.

Cape fur seals breed on islands in Algoa Bay that fall within the Marine Protected Area adjacent to the national park.

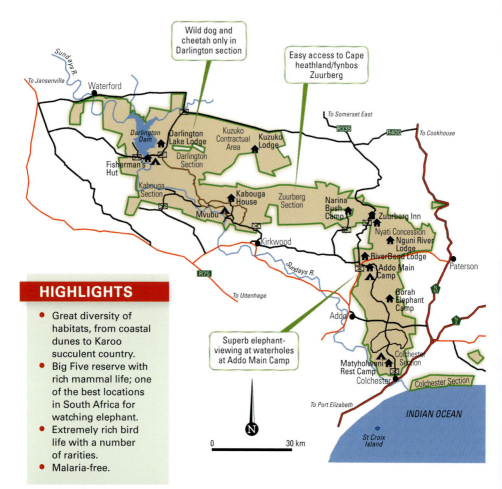

HIGHLIGHTS

- Great diversity of habitats, from coastal dunes to Karoo succulent country.
- Big Five reserve with rich mammal life; one of the best locations in South Africa for watching elephant.
- Extremely rich bird life with a number of rarities.
- Malaria-free.

The Karoo boer-bean flowers in spring, from August to October.

was proclaimed in 1931, only 11 elephant remained, and animals continued to be lost because of inadequate enclosure. In 1954, with just 22 elephant, the park manager Graham Armstrong developed an effective elephant-proof fence that stands to this day. Only one elephant ever breached the fence, the famed bull Hapoor whose mounted head can now be seen in the information centre. Today there are around 600 elephant and the population continues to grow.

Geology and landscape

The Zuurberg range can be seen from all over the park. It is an eastern outlier of the Cape Folded Belt, consisting of quartzite and sandstone sediments of the Witteberg Group, laid down about 400 million years BP. However, the islands in Algoa Bay are built of the oldest exposed rock in the park, a quartzitic sandstone formed some 500 million years BP. At the southern base of the Zuurberg range is a mix of

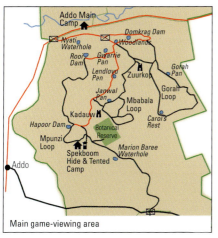
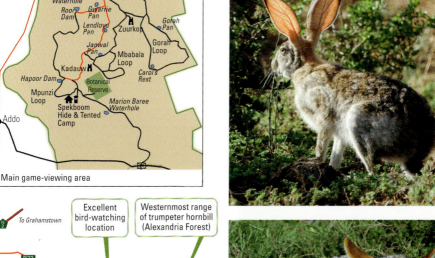

conglomerates, glacial tillites, mudstones and sandstones. Further south lies a series of ancient, undulating wave-cut platforms between 30 m and 100 m above sea level. At the northern edge of the range are rocks of the Dwyka Group, derived from glacial deposits and extending to the southern shores of Darlington Dam. In the Karoo section most of the rocks are mudstones and sandstones belonging to the Beaufort and Ecca groups, and date from 250 to 300 million years BP. The Sundays River Formation of reddish and greyish mudstones underlies much of the area south of the mountains. South-eastwards towards the coast there are extensive areas of whitish limestone of the Alexandria Formation, laid down when oceans covered the area. This white rock is quite obvious on the upper reaches of some hills within the main game area. The Alexandria coastal dune field, at 15 800 ha the largest in the southern hemisphere, dates from 6.5 million years BP and is annually augmented by about 350 000 m^3 of seaborne sand.

There are two species of hare in the park, with the scrub hare being most widespread and favouring a mix of open and bushed country (top). Black-backed jackal occur throughout the park and are commonly seen and heard (above).

Addo Elephant National Park   **149**

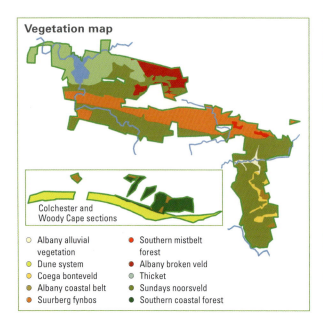

Vegetation map

Colchester and Woody Cape sections

- Albany alluvial vegetation
- Dune system
- Coega bonteveld
- Albany coastal belt
- Suurberg fynbos
- Southern mistbelt forest
- Albany broken veld
- Thicket
- Sundays noorsveld
- Southern coastal forest

The Karoo shepherd's tree flowers from August to November.

Vegetation

Of South Africa's seven biomes, five can be found in the park, more than in any other African conservation area. These are Nama-Karoo, Cape heathland (fynbos), grassland, forest, and subtropical thicket; the latter covers large areas of the park, including the main game area. Within this complex of biomes botanists have identified no fewer than 43 vegetation units, each with its own unique mix of species. The subtropical thicket includes such abundant species as **porkbush**, or **spekboom**, (*Portulacaria afra*), a favourite food of many browsing animals such as greater kudu and elephant, **white milkwood** (*Sideroxylon inerme*), the **blue-flowered plumbago** (*Plumbago*

The Alexandria coastal dunefield is the most extensive of its type in the southern hemisphere.

150 Eastern Cape

FACILITIES AND ACTIVITIES

- Main and Matyholweni camps have a variety of accommodation, comprising cottages, rondavels and safari tents. Camping sites at Main and Matyholweni camps.
- Bush camp (Narina) in the Zuurberg section and tented camp near Spekboom bird hide. Three concession lodges in the other sections, most of which are in refurbished farmhouses.
- Basic huts and campground in Darlington section.
- Two fully equipped huts in the Alexandria Forest. Excellent bird-watching location.
- Restaurant, shop and fuel at Addo Main Camp; Port Elizabeth lies 72 km south.
- A 45-km 4x4 trail.
- Hiking trail in Woody Cape section with overnight huts, and in Zuurberg section.
- Accompanied horse-riding trails at Woody Cape, main Addo game-viewing area and eastern Zuurberg.
- Sunset cruises on Darlington Dam.
- Accompanied game drives in open vehicles.
- 80 km of game-viewing roads from Addo Main Camp, including Colchester section. More routes being developed.

Addo Main Camp offers a variety of accommodation units.

auriculata), **common gwarrie** (*Euclea undulata*), **Karoo boer-bean** (*Schotia afra*) and a local agave, **Bushman's hemp** or **mother-in-law's tongue** (*Sansevieria thyrsiflora*). This thicket is very dense, rarely more than 4 m tall but with the occasional aloe or euphorbia sticking above the 'crowd', and able to withstand temperature extremes and erratic rainfall. The exotic **prickly pear cactus** (*Opuntia ficus-indica*), a noxious weed in areas with no elephants, is absent from the main game area. This is because elephant favour this plant and eat both the cladodes ('leaves') and the fruit – natural pest control at work. Large swathes of grassland clothe the south-facing slopes of the Zuurberg; the most important grazing grasses are **red grass** (*Themeda triandra*) and **guinea grass** (*Panicum maximum*). Standing above the grass are the **Zuurberg cycad** (*Encephalartos longifolius*) about 3 m tall with palm-like leaves, and the gnarled, large-leaved **Zuurberg cushion bush** (*Oldenburgia grandis*). The cushion bush grows on outcrops and produces purplish-cream flower heads up to 13 cm across, throughout the year. The richest biome is the Cape heathland, or fynbos, on the Zuurberg. It can be classified into two types: mountain fynbos exhibits the greater species diversity and is found on the wet southern slopes and here and there at lower levels, while grassland fynbos covers a much greater area, and is found along the ridges and gentle slopes in the high-lying regions. Mountain fynbos includes the rush-like members of the Restionaceae, with scattered stands of **real sugarbush** (*Protea repens*) and **giant protea** (*Protea cynaroides*) with flower heads as much as 30 cm across. The slopes harbour three species of cycad, while other species occur elsewhere in the park. Pockets of Afromontane forest are found on south-facing slopes and consist of evergreen trees with a canopy height of between 10 m and 14 m. The Alexandria coastal forest has low-growing trees with a fairly dense, dark canopy and a lower population of undergrowth plants. Interesting trees among the rich diversity include **white stinkwood** (*Celtis africana*), **white milkwood** (*Sideroxylon inerme*), **coastal red milkwood** (*Mimusops caffra*), **common wild elder** (*Nuxia congesta*) and **Cape teak**

WILDLIFE FACTS

- 95 mammal species, including savanna elephant, savanna buffalo, lion, hook-lipped rhinoceros, hippopotamus and spotted hyaena, and marine species.
- Some 417 bird species including a number of rare vagrants; many oceanic and coastal species.
- Some five tortoise, 26 snake (including five different adders) and 23 lizard species.
- About 20 species of frog and toad.
- Approximately 26 species of freshwater and estuarine fish in the Sundays River system. More than 300 marine species recorded in Algoa Bay.
- One of the last strongholds of the large flightless dung beetle.

Watch for yellow mongoose in open areas.

It is not only big game animals that are protected here but also flightless dung beetles.

(*Strychnos decussata*). The remaining major biome is the Nama-Karoo, a dry area to the north-west of the Zuurberg, and this also has some characteristic plants. These include two subspecies of the succulent **noors** (*Euphorbia coerulescens*), whose rows of thorns are not enough to put off browsers such as greater kudu and hook-lipped rhinoceros. Another prominent succulent is the **coral aloe** (*Aloe striata*), which produces its large, showy flower heads from July to October. Easily identified trees are the **sweet thorn** (*Vachellia karroo*) with its distinctive long white thorns, and the pale-barked and small-leaved **shepherd's tree** (*Boscia albitrunca*).

Wildlife
Mammals

Addo will be forever associated with its **elephants**, and many can be seen in the main game area. However, since the removal of the fence dividing the Colchester section from the main Addo area, large numbers can now move freely from the main camp in the north to Matyholweni in the south. The Addo elephant descend from the herds that once ranged freely across the eastern and southern Cape. In 2003 adult bulls were translocated from Kruger to introduce new genetic material. There are more than 40 **hook-lipped rhinoceros**, both in the main game area and in the thickets around Darlington Dam. It is believed that the park can carry as many as 300 of these animals. A small number of **hippopotamus** live in the Sundays River in the north-western Kabouga section. **Savanna buffalo** also survived early hunting and a herd of about 30 that remained in the dense bush found sanctuary. Today there are several hundred disease-free animals, particularly valuable for translocation to other conservation areas. Within the main game area **plains zebra** have been introduced, and **Cape mountain zebra** are found in the Zuurberg and the Darlington section. Antelope are well represented with 13 species, including **southern oryx (gemsbok)**, **common eland**, **red hartebeest**, **bushbuck**, **common duiker**, **steenbok** and **Cape grysbok**. **Oribi** have been reintroduced to the Langevlakte contractual area of the park. The most commonly seen ungulate, particularly in the main game area, is the **common warthog**. The 22 terrestrial carnivores include limited numbers of **lion** and **spotted hyaena** in the main game area, **cheetah** and **wild dog** in the Darlington section and **brown hyaena** in the coastal dunes and possibly elsewhere. Many carnivores are rarely seen but troops of **suricate** often forage in open areas, as does the **yellow mongoose,** which is active in the day. **Black-backed jackal** are common, and frequently heard calling in the early evening and morning. Mammal species restricted to the Alexandria Forest are the dainty 4 kg **blue duiker** and the **tree hyrax**; this is the latter's western distribution limit. You are unlikely to see this night-active creature but its blood-curdling call is a give-away.

There are very few African conservation areas that can claim to host both elephant and those marine giants, the whales. No fewer than nine species of whale and dolphin have been observed in the inshore waters, including **Bryde's**, **humpback** and **southern right whales**. Most frequently seen are the **Indian Ocean bottlenosed** and **long-beaked common dolphins**. Algoa Bay is of particular importance for the **humpback dolphin**, harbouring perhaps as much as 10% of South Africa's population.

A newborn red hartebeest is still unsteady on its legs. The red hartebeest is one of 13 antelope species occurring in Addo.

Birds

No fewer than 417 bird species profit from Addo's rich diversity of habitats. Even without the vagrants and sporadic oceanic species, birds are well represented. Large breeding populations of **African penguin** and **Cape gannet** occur on islands in Algoa Bay, and approximately 68 000 pairs of gannet breed on Bird Island. The beaches are the most easterly breeding location for the **African (black) oystercatcher**. Winter months tend to be more productive for spotting oceanic species such as the albatrosses, petrels and shearwaters. No fewer than 12 species of tern have been recorded on the coastline here and the rare **Damara tern** breeds in the dune system. The trail through the Alexandria Forest area is well worthwhile with a good chance of hearing and sighting **Knysna turaco**, **brown scrub robin**, **dark-backed weaver**, **black-bellied starling**, **white-starred robin** and **trumpeter** and **crowned hornbills**, among others. In the thicket country birding is also excellent but can be rather frustrating given the dense nature of the bush. It is often worthwhile to pull the vehicle off the road, wind down the windows and just spend a peaceful hour or so, letting the birds show themselves. Especially along roadsides around thickets watch for **red-**

The bird hide is located at a waterhole within the main camp.

The plumage of the Cape Batis is rich in colour.

Addo Elephant National Park **153**

necked spurfowl. As usual you will find some of the most productive birding in the camp, but there is also a bird hide at a pool and a short walking trail that can be very rewarding. In the Zuurberg area, among the mountain fynbos, watch for **Cape sugarbird**, **southern** and **greater double-collared sunbirds** and **malachite sunbird**. The Darlington section has resident **African fish eagle** around the dam and Sundays River, whilst **Verreaux's eagle** is seen over the rocky hills that teem with its main prey, the rock hyrax or dassie. The manmade lake, originally called Lake Menz, offers great opportunities for observing waterfowl, herons as well as kingfishers.

Reptiles and amphibians

The park's diverse habitats host a wide range of reptile and amphibian species. There are four species of land tortoise, of which the most commonly seen is the large **leopard tortoise**. The **marsh terrapin** also occurs here. There are no fewer than 26 different snakes, among them five species of adder including the very localized **Albany adder**, which is seriously endangered outside the park. Of the 23 lizard species, you are most likely to see South Africa's largest, the **rock** and **water monitor lizards**. There are at least two dwarf chameleon species, the **Eastern Cape** and **Elandsberg dwarf chameleons**. The casual visitor will probably see none of the 20 frog and toad species, but during the rains calling males will certainly be heard.

Top: South Africa's largest land chelonian, the leopard or mountain tortoise, is easy to spot in the park.
Above: The giant stick insect is one of many invertebrates in Addo. Even so, surprisingly little is known of the park's insects.

Fish

Some 26 fish species are known to occur in the Sundays River, its tributaries and the estuary but only the **Eastern Cape redfin** is at risk because of its limited range. Algoa Bay and the marine sanctuary have at least 300 species of fish, including residents, migrants and occasional visitors. The bay is an important sanctuary for the globally threatened **great white shark**.

Invertebrates

The area is rich in invertebrate species, including two rarities, the **Woody Cape dune grasshopper**, which is endemic to this dune-system, and the **flightless dung beetle**. Addo is the last major stronghold of this dung beetle, which harvests mainly elephant, rhino and buffalo dung both for food and as brood balls for its larvae. Do not drive over dung on the road as these beetles are often casualties.

Buffalo droppings are eagerly sought out by flightless dung beetles.

- Behave sensibly when encountering dangerous big game animals, especially elephants.

154 Eastern Cape

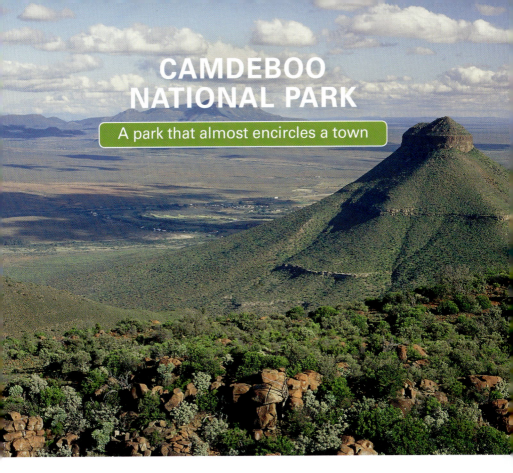

CAMDEBOO NATIONAL PARK
A park that almost encircles a town

Lie of the land
Camdeboo lies in the north-west of the Eastern Cape province, south of the Sneeuberg range. The 20 000 ha Camdeboo National Park has the town of Graaff-Reinet at its heart. It is focused in the north-west on the Nqweba Dam, the Sneeuberg range to the east and along the east-west Camdeboo Escarpment, merging into the Coetzeeberge range eastwards. Plans are afoot to create a mega-reserve, covering 520 000 ha, by linking the Camdeboo National Park and the Mountain Zebra National Park near Cradock (see page 161).

Much of Camdeboo is mountainous and rugged, except around the dam. Altitudes range from 740 m to 1 565 m above sea level with several buttes rising above 1 300 m, including the 1 316 m Spandaukop in the south-west.

Spandaukop is a prominent landmark in the south-west of the Camdeboo National Park.

Brief history
A range of stone tools at several sites, including hand axes, scrapers, blades and grinding stones, shows that humans were in the area throughout the Stone Ages. The San people of the Later Stone Age were certainly here as there are a number of rock painting locations in the mountains both within and outside the park.

Camdeboo National Park 155

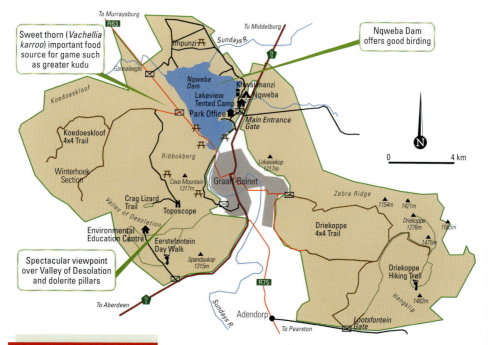

HIGHLIGHTS

- Spectacular scenery.
- Good diversity of game animals, including Cape mountain zebra, savanna buffalo and greater kudu.
- Freedom to walk unaccompanied.

Sweet thorn in full bloom.

Khoekhoen peoples arrived later with their livestock and by the mid-17th century the powerful Inqua tribe had established itself in a large area from near Aberdeen in the west to Somerset East to the east. By 1770 the first white farmers had settled in the area and in 1786 the first magistrate was appointed in Graaff-Reinet. In 1795 local farmers and other disgruntled citizens staged the first true white rebellion against the Dutch East India Company in far-away Cape Town. By 1796 the British had displaced the Dutch in the Cape and although Graaff-Reinet initially tried to resist the colonial authority, they capitulated and all but one of the rebels were pardoned. San continued to steal the settlers' livestock into the early 19th century.

Early explorer-naturalists reported vast herds of game in the area around the turn of the 19th century. Francois le Vaillant, John Barrow and Henry Lichtenstein saw tens of thousands of springbok, black wildebeest, red hartebeest and eland, along with their predators the lion, leopard and wild dog. Large numbers of springbok were still in the area in the late 19th century. During the guerilla phase of the 2nd Anglo-Boer War, several skirmishes took place in the vicinity of the Sneeuberg range, north of Graaff-Reinet. A Boer commando leader named Gideon Scheepers was caught in those mountains and executed by firing squad.

The park was first established as the Karoo Nature Reserve in 1976 and transferred to SANParks in October 2005, when it was renamed Camdeboo National Park.

Geology and landscape

Most of the park lies within the southern foothills of the Sneeuberg range and consists of broken ridges and isolated outcrops. The Nqweba Dam, fed by the Sundays River and other feeders, lies in a flat plain to the north ringed by hills, and southwards are the extensive plains of the Camdeboo Karoo. Much of the park lies between 740 m and 1 480 m above sea level. Most of the rock formations here are sandstones, siltstone and mudstone belonging to the Beaufort Group of the Karoo system, with post-Karoo dolerite intrusions in some areas. In areas such as the Valley of Desolation, this hard rock has formed jointed pillars sometimes rising 90 m to 120 m above the surrounding ground.

Vegetation

Large areas of the park are covered by Camdeboo escarpment thicket, growing mainly between 700 m and 1 200 m above sea level. It is largely restricted to the south-facing rugged slopes of the escarpment and mountains and plants rarely exceed 3 m in height. Many of the plants are succulents; the **porkbush**, or **spekboom**, (*Portulacaria afra*) is usually the dominant species, producing numerous spikes of tiny pinkish-purple flowers in summer. The tall **bitter aloe** (*Aloe ferox*) produces its spectacular orange-red flower spikes through the winter. Apart from the succulents there are also several low tree species, such as **jacket plum** (*Pappea capensis*) which is heavily browsed by game, **Karoo shepherd's tree** (*Boscia oleoides*), the aptly named **highveld cabbage tree** (*Cussonia paniculata*) and **common guarri** (*Euclea undulata*). **Sweet thorn** (*Vachellia karroo*) is most prominent near the dam, especially along the Murraysburg route. It is easy to identify by its long white thorns and in the warmer months, by its mass of small, round, yellow flower heads. Mainly above 1 300 m above sea level in the east one finds areas of Karoo escarpment grassland, with wiry grasses that grow in tussocks,

Vegetation map

○ Degraded grassland
○ Grassy open shrubland
○ Mixed shrubland
● Succulent dwarf shrubland
● Riparian thicket
● Succulent thicket

CLIMATE

This is a dry area, averaging 336 mm of rain annually. Most rain falls in summer, peaking in February/March, accompanied by thunderstorms and high temperatures. There is a little rain in autumn. Snowfalls may occur on high-lying ground in winter, and frost is quite common. Mean monthly maximum temperature in Graaff-Reinet in January is 38.6°C and minimum in July is -0.3°C.

The scenery of Camdeboo is a mix of flat plains and dominant hill ranges.

FACILITIES AND ACTIVITIES

- Campsite and tented camp. Many accommodation options in Graaff-Reinet and on surrounding farms and game ranches.
- Range of water sports and angling permitted (with licence) on Nqweba Dam.
- Several picnic sites allow good birding.
- Several walking trails of 1.5, 5, 11 and 14 km; overnight hiking trail with hut in eastern sector.
- Some 24 km of gravel game-viewing roads; the road network is set to be expanded.
- 4x4 trails in the eastern sector.
- Tarred roads enter Graaff-Reinet from Murraysburg, Middelburg, Aberdeen and Jansenville.

Suricates use their tails for balance when standing on their hindlegs.

such as **mountain wire grass** (*Merxmuellera disticha*). There is a scattering of low shrubs and bushes throughout. In the low-lying areas there is a mix of dwarf karoo shrubs and grass but many are still recovering from many years of overgrazing and erosion.

Wildlife
Mammals

Apart from such game species as **greater kudu** and **mountain reedbuck** most other species had been hunted out, or massively reduced, by the early years of the 20th century. Reintroduction programmes since the proclamation of the conservation area have seen the return of such species as **Cape mountain zebra**, **savanna buffalo**, **common eland**, **black wildebeest**, **southern oryx** (**gemsbok**) and **red hartebeest**. Populations of **klipspringer** live in the high rugged areas, whereas **mountain reedbuck** favour steep but less broken grassy slopes. The small, dainty, largely solitary **steenbok** lives on the open flats, while **common duiker**, primarily browsers, favour thickets both for cover and food. Of the 13 carnivores that are known to occur in the park you are most likely to see the day-active and pack-living **suricate**, an interesting mongoose species that has an intricate social structure and forages in groups. Like the suricate, the day-active **yellow mongoose** is found mainly in the plains, but it hunts alone although several animals usually share a burrow-system. Unlike these two, the strictly solitary and diurnal **small grey mongoose** prefers areas with some scrub cover and rarely ventures into the open country. On cool and overcast days you may spot foraging family parties of **bat-eared fox** in open areas. **Vervet monkeys** are common and they concentrate in the low-lying areas where there are stands of trees, especially sweet thorns, such as along the stretch of road entering the park from Murraysburg. **Chacma baboons** favour high ground but during cold weather they frequently descend to lower levels. Although the rodents are well represented, most are nocturnal and secretive but watch for the **four-striped grass-mouse** around the picnic sites. The burrows of the colonially living **southern African ground squirrels** can be found in open areas.

Birds

Camdeboo has a list of 225 species but about 50 of these are associated with the dam and may be absent during periods of drought. It is a meeting place of species that inhabit the arid Karoo and the thicket of the Eastern Cape. **Common ostrich** are often seen on the flats, which are also good for sightings of **Karoo korhaan**, **northern black korhaan** and **Ludwig's bustard**, though these last tend to be somewhat nomadic. **Denham's** and **kori bustards** have been recorded in the park, although these species seem to prefer the Camdeboo Karoo flats to the south. There is also a good mix of raptors, including **secretarybird**, **martial** and **booted eagles**, while **Verreaux's eagle** is most likely to be spotted on higher ground, including the Valley of Desolation viewpoint, although this eagle has

been seen hunting rock hyrax in the scree between the Murraysburg road and the dam. **African fish eagle** are resident when the dam holds water. All three of South Africa's grebe species have been recorded, as well as six species of heron, although one of these, the **goliath heron**, is a vagrant. There are 11 duck and goose species, with **red-knobbed coot** sometimes common, especially when water levels are low. The viewpoint from the Valley of Desolation is usually good for a number of rock- and thicket-loving species, such as **rock kestrel**, **pale-winged starling**, **Layard's tit-babbler**, **Cape rock-thrush** and **rock bunting**. Always well worthwhile are the picnic sites on the edge of the dam among the sweet thorn thickets.

Reptiles and amphibians

This park has four land-dwelling tortoise species besides the aquatic **marsh terrapin**. By far the largest is the **leopard tortoise**, which averages 15 kg to 20 kg, though specimens twice this size are known. At the other end of the scale is the **Karoo padloper**, which rarely weighs more than 300 g; its carapace is uniform olive- or reddish-brown in colour and it lives on high plateau grasslands where it hibernates during the winter snows. Very similar in size but with distinctive raised scales, or scutes, striped with yellow and black is the **Karoo tent tortoise**, which strongly prefers flat areas with low plants such as grass and short Karoo shrubs. Surprisingly, only six species of snake, including the **puff adder** and **Cape cobra**, have been recorded in the park, but several more will probably be found. By far the largest lizard here is the **rock monitor** and it is quite commonly seen, unfortunately sometimes as a road casualty. Of the smaller lizards most will be moving too quickly for a clear identification, but at least four are more obliging. The rocks around the viewpoint of the Valley of Desolation are good for seeing the **southern rock agama**, **Cape crag lizard** and **western rock skink**, as especially the males of these species often sit on top of rocks or at the mouths of crevices. Males of the rock agama have a distinctive blue head during

Top left: Since the proclamation of the park, a number of game species, such as the Cape mountain zebra, have been reintroduced.
Top right: Four-striped grass mice are common around picnic sites.
Above: Only six snake species, including the puff adder, have been recorded.

Camdeboo National Park **159**

WILDLIFE FACTS

- At least 43 species of mammal occur (authors' records for park and its eastern extension at 57 species) and include savanna buffalo, greater kudu and black wildebeest.
- Bird list at 225 species; more than 50 are attracted by the dam, which does not always have water.
- Of the 34 reptile species, five are tortoises; also eight amphibian species.
- About 10 species of fish are present in the dam and river, including six exotic to the system.
- Some 336 plant species have been identified, with 36 different grasses and 16 succulent crassulas.

Crowned plover can be seen around Nqweba Dam.

the breeding season, while the crag lizard has yellow and dark bands on its back. The **Karoo girdled lizard** usually lives in rock clusters on the slopes. This species is more uniformly hued and lacks the bright coloration of the crag lizard. Of the eight amphibians few are ever seen, although with the onset of rain several species will be heard calling from the dam edges and roadside pools. The most abundant when the dam holds water is the **common platanna**. This species is fully aquatic and is rarely seen, though if you watch the water surface you will see numerous bubbles and ripples made by these frogs and their tadpoles. They sometimes emerge at night during rain to move between water bodies.

Fish

Only 10 species of fish have been recorded, of which three appear to be restricted to the river, five to the dam, and two occur in both locations. There are five abundant exotics (and one rare exotic), namely the **carp**, **sharptooth catfish**, **banded tilapia**, **mosquito fish** and the **largemouth bass**. The **river goby**, which reaches a length of 12 cm, was recorded in the dam for the first time in 2008.

Nqweba Dam is mainly fed by the Sundays River and is an important bird habitat.

- Winters can be very cold and summers hot with thunderstorms, so walkers and hikers should be prepared.
- The presence of potentially dangerous animals, such as savanna buffalo, should be accounted for when walking or hiking.

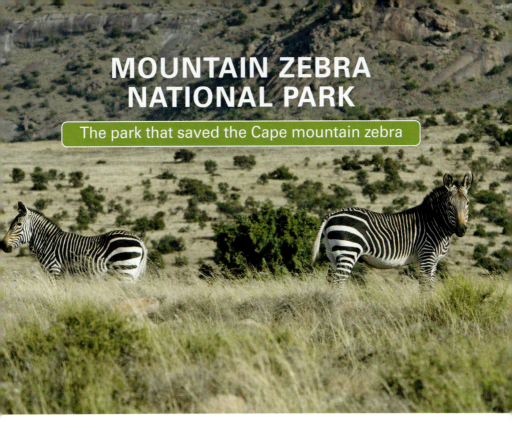

MOUNTAIN ZEBRA NATIONAL PARK

The park that saved the Cape mountain zebra

Lie of the land

Mountain Zebra National Park is backed in the south by the 1 957 m Bankberg, dropping below 1 200 m above sea level in the surrounding valleys and Karoo plain. Exposed peaks are rounded but with some deep gullies and saddles. The main stream is the Wilgerboom ('willow tree') that flows out of the park to the northeast, with several smaller annual streams feeding into it within the park. There are also several natural springs scattered through the area. The large Rooiplaat Plateau lies to the north-west. The park continues to expand, primarily westwards, and now covers about 39 776 ha. An initiative to link the Mountain Zebra and Camdeboo national parks, known as the Mountain Zebra–Camdeboo Protected Environment (MZCPE), will eventually conserve a wilderness expanse of some 520 000 ha.

LOCATION

Brief history

A number of sites of archaeological interest are in the park but they may not be visited. Most of these sites, including several on the Rooiplaat Plateau, are located along the riverbeds, and have been identified by the presence of stone tools, such as scrapers and blades. The remains are dated at 38 000 to 10 000 BP, and some of the sites are up to 100 m^2 in extent, indicating many years of usage. A few San rock paintings testify to their presence, certainly for several thousand years and up to the arrival of the first white settlers in the mid-18th century.

Founder stock of Cape mountain zebra placed in other wildlife sanctuaries came mainly from this Karoo park.

HIGHLIGHTS

- Spectacular and diverse scenery.
- Wide range of game species, including hook-lipped rhinoceros and savanna buffalo.
- One of the best locations in South Africa to see mountain reedbuck, especially on higher reaches of the Wilgerboom River circuit.
- Camp excellent for watching rock hyrax, and, if you are alert, also elusive Smith's red rock rabbit.
- Guided walks in the company of a ranger.

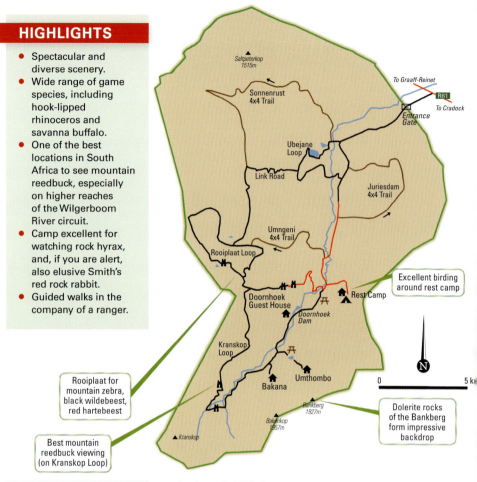

The leaves of the shepherd's tree are favoured by browsers.

By the early 1930s it was realized that numbers of Cape mountain zebra were declining to critically low levels because of hunting pressure, and efforts were made to purchase a farm to conserve the remainder. After some vicissitudes the farm Babylonstoren was purchased and in 1937 the Mountain Zebra National Park was proclaimed. By 1946 only two stallions remained; these were shot and replaced by 11 animals driven into the park in 1950 from a neighbouring farm, Waterval. By 1964, with the acquisition of additional farms and their stocks, there were 55 zebra; by 1978 this number had risen to 200. The first translocation, of 23 zebra, took place in 1979 to the newly established Karoo National Park near Beaufort West.

Geology and landscape

The most prominent feature within the park is the backdrop of the great rounded dome-hills and outcroppings of dolerite. This volcanic lava intruded into the fissures and strata of the sedimentary rocks.

The red-brown to grey-brown markings on the dolerite result from the oxidation of iron through weathering. Elsewhere in the park there are extensive areas of sandstone, mudstone and siltstone that belong to the Beaufort Series of the Karoo Supergroup. Much of the sandstone is brown, grey or yellow-brown. The finer-grained sandstone is known as siltstone, and in several places limestone is also visible. Mudstone strata are interspersed between those of the sandstone and are usually fawn-green or grey in colour; these dominate the sandstones higher than 1 400 m above sea level as can be clearly seen, for example, in the Kranskop sector in the south-west of the park. A good overview of the principal geological features can be obtained when traversing the Kranskop-Wilgerboom River route. The 1 515 m Salpeterkop lies at the northernmost point of the park and can be seen from the northern point of the Rooiplaat Loop road.

CLIMATE

The mean annual rainfall of the area is 398 mm. This is primarily a summer-rainfall area with about 70% falling from October to March; hail sometimes falls with summer thunderstorms. During the winter months snowfalls on the upper peaks and frost are quite common. In mid-winter, nighttime temperatures may drop as low as -10°C and in summer daytime levels may soar to 42°C.

Vegetation

The vegetation can be divided into three main categories, escarpment grassland, eastern upper Karoo mixed grass and shrubland, with escarpment thicket that includes areas with dwarf shrubs and open woodland. Of course many small plant communities lie within these larger areas. The escarpment grassland favours the higher ground with rather coarse, wiry, unpalatable grasses including **mountain wire grass** (*Merxmuellera disticha*), which dominates mainly above 1 400 m on south-facing slopes. There is a strong mix of shrubs and Karoo bushes here and it is known as sourveld. There is a small area of outlier Cape heathland (fynbos) on the plateau of the Bankberg. On the low slopes above the Wilgerboom River, the grass is very palatable but at higher altitudes the low bushes tend to crowd out the grass. The lower slopes in the vicinity of Saltpeterkop near the entrance to the park have very different plant structures with richer soils and many palatable species, such as

Vegetation map

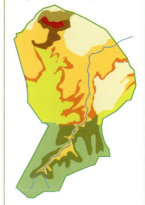

○ Degraded shrubland
○ Grassland
● Riverine sweet thorn
● Midslope shrubland
● Mixed low shrubland
● Mixed grass shrubland
● Red grass and shrubland
● *Merxmuellera* grass and shrubland
● Low karree shrubland

There is a striking view of the Karoo hills from Rooiplaat.

Mountain Zebra National Park 163

FACILITIES AND ACTIVITIES

- Some 25 fully equipped cottages and campground suitable for caravans and tents in fenced main camp; 'stand-alone' Doornhoek guest house with three bedrooms; two mountain cottages, accessible only with 4x4 or 2x4 vehicles.
- Well-located picnic sites are good for bird-watching.
- Two short self-walk trails in the camp.
- Accompanied walk to view San rock art.
- Guided trails and guided game drives, including cheetah tracking.
- 60+ km network of game-viewing roads, with new ones to be opened in the future.
- Several 4x4 trails.
- Restaurant, shop and fuel at the camp.
- Park is 24 km from Cradock, which has a full range of services.

The rest camp is particularly well located.

daggabossie (*Nenax microphylla*), **Karoo aster** (*Felicia muricata*) and **koggelmandervoet** (*Limeum aethiopicum*). Rooiplaat is one of the main areas in the park where game, such as black wildebeest, red hartebeest, springbok and mountain zebra, tend to congregate because this is so-called sweetveld with many palatable plants. Here, as in other parts of the park, one finds the much sought-after **red grass** (*Themeda triandra*). Along the valleys, many of which were cultivated in the past, you will see substantial stands of **sweet thorn** trees (*Vachellia karroo*), especially along the lower Wilgerboom. These trees, with their distinctive long white thorns, produce copious yellow pom-pom flowers in spring and summer. Greater kudu favour these linear thickets and the flanking areas in the valleys offer good grazing and browsing for many species. Upper river valley areas, such as that of the Wilgerboom, are dominated by the low thicket-producing **oldwood** (*Leucosidea sericea*) but there are also forest elements here such as **Cape beech** (*Rapanea melanophloeos*), **wild olive** (*Olea europaea*) and **sagewood** (*Buddleia salvifolia*). Lower down you will see some fine examples of the **karree tree** (*Rhus lancea*).

Black wildebeest congregate on Rooiplaat plateau.

Wildlife
Mammals

The Mountain Zebra park was founded to protect the seriously endangered **Cape mountain zebra**, but with the success of this mission and the expansion of the park in recent years, conservation is now more focused on biodiversity protection. The zebra live in family herds of one stallion and up to three mares and their young, with unattached stallions forming bachelor groups. The herds are not tied to a territory but circulate in search of the best grazing, on the plateaux in summer and the hill slopes during winter. **Plains zebra** can be distinguished from the mountain zebra by their brown shadow-stripes on the white, while they lack the throat dewlap, have no gridiron pattern on the rump, and the black ring-stripes do not extend to the hoofs. Populations of **hook-lipped rhinoceros** and **savanna buffalo** have been established but these tend to keep largely to the dense riverine thickets, generally moving out to feed at night. Especially on the Rooiplaat Plateau, one has a very good chance of seeing grassland-loving species such as **black wildebeest, red hartebeest, blesbok** and **springbok**. **Greater kudu** are most commonly seen on the mixed grass-bush slopes and in the riverbeds, especially where there are stands of sweet thorn. Two of the smaller antelope, the **mountain reedbuck** and the **grey rhebok**, are best spotted on the slopes, especially on the descent to the Wilgerboom River on the Kranskop Loop. Both live in small family groups, with one adult ram, up to three ewes and accompanying young. **Lion** have recently been reintroduced to the park. **Cheetah**, released in the park in 2007, have settled well and are breeding. The other three cat species here, **caracal, small spotted cat** and **African wild cat**, are rarely seen. The most commonly seen carnivores are **black-backed jackal, bat-eared fox, small grey mongoose, yellow mongoose** and **suricate**. **Brown hyaenas** are occasionally spotted. **Rock hyrax** occur throughout the rocky areas and are quite common in and around the main camp. **Southern African ground squirrels** are common, especially along the valley from the entrance gate. Conspicuous animals seen around the camp are the **vervet monkey**, which lives along the treed valleys, and its larger relative the dark-coloured **Chacma baboon**, which mainly favours higher ground.

WILDLIFE FACTS

- At least 68 mammal species, including cheetah, hook-lipped rhinoceros and savanna buffalo.
- Initially established to protect the endangered Cape mountain zebra, which now number about 700, though many more have been relocated over the years.
- Some 275 bird species including 112 residents.
- About 45 reptile species including 21 snakes and 10 amphibians. It is likely that more will be added over time as the park expands.
- More than 700 plant species.
- Giant earthworms (up to 4 m long) inhabit the park.

Birds

With 275 bird species there is plenty to keep the avid birder happy. As so often, the best starting point is the camp, where one can tot up a very respectable number of species. **Cape eagle-owl** are often

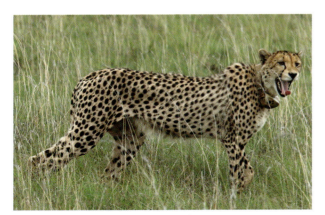

Several cheetah have been reintroduced.

Red hartebeest.

heard calling from the rock outcrops above the camp, which also attract other species including **ground woodpecker, sentinel rock-thrush, African rock pipit, mountain wheatear, Cape bunting** and **pale-winged starling**. The **white-browed sparrow-weaver** is very commonly seen in camp, where its untidy grass nests 'decorate' numerous trees. Along the river courses watch for **southern boubou, southern tchagra, acacia pied barbet** and **red-fronted tinkerbird**, though these species have also been seen within the confines of the camp. **Common ostrich** tend to favour the low-lying areas and the grassed plateaux. Of the 18 species of raptor you are most likely to see **Verreaux's eagle, rock kestrel** and **jackal buzzard**, and in summer there are periodic influxes of migrant **lesser kestrel**. Both the **blue** and **karoo korhaan** are resident but other bustards and korhaan are vagrants or occasional visitors. The two picnic sites east of the Wilgerboom River are excellent birding venues.

Reptiles and amphibians

Only a few of the 45 reptile species are likely to be seen by the visitor to the park, including the **leopard tortoise, rock monitor** and **Bibron's thick-toed gecko**, quite common around the buildings in the camp, where it hunts insects attracted to the lights at night. On the rock outcrops around the camp and near the swimming pool you may glimpse the **western rock skink** and the **southern rock agama**. Although there is a good diversity of snake species most are secretive and nocturnal. The **plain mountain adder**, one of South Africa's rarest snakes, is known to occur in the park, living above 1 600 m in a zone of severe winter frosts and snow. **Marsh terrapins** bask in the sun on the banks of the Doornhoek Dam and most other waters in the park. Partly because of the cold winters and dryness of the area, there are only 10 amphibian species. **Karoo toads** may be encountered seeking out insects at night in the camp.

Top: The approach road to the national park and the Rooiplaat plateau are good places to see the Cape longclaw.
Above: The Karoo toad is well adapted to the cold and dry conditions that characterise the habitat from which it takes its common name.

Invertebrates

Giant earthworms (*Microchaetus* sp.) may reach a length of 4 m. They are seldom seen on the surface, except after good rains. They may also emerge at night or at first light, but many are eaten by predators. Their casts evidence their visits to the surface.

- If you are walking or hiking be prepared for heat and thunderstorms in summer, and extreme cold in winter.
- Unaccompanied hiking outside the camp is no longer allowed because of the presence of lion, savanna buffalo and hook-lipped rhinoceros.

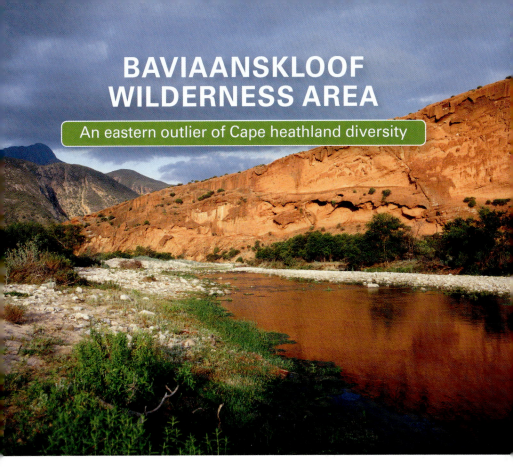

BAVIAANSKLOOF WILDERNESS AREA
An eastern outlier of Cape heathland diversity

Lie of the land

Baviaanskloof Wilderness Area, a true mega-reserve, covers 288 087 ha and comprises Baviaanskloof, Groendal and Formosa Nature Reserves. It lies mostly in the south-west of the Eastern Cape with some spill-over into the south-east of Western Cape province. Baviaanskloof Nature Reserve covers 210 000 ha and includes the Western, Cockscomb and Kouga sections as well as the discontiguous Welbedacht in the west. Groendal Nature Reserve, covering 43 428 ha, contains Kwa-Zunga in the Groot Winterhoek range, the Stinkhoutberg just north of the town of Patensie, and a small separate area known as Mierhoopplaat. A further 45 173 ha is conserved in Formosa Nature Reserve to the south-west, including the small separate Niekerksberg section 14 km to the west. The Formosa section, currently managed by the Eastern Cape authority, may devolve to SANParks in the foreseeable future.

This is a rugged, mountainous country, with streams and numerous deep gorges, often difficult to access. There are open plateaux and valleys scattered throughout the area. The long, rounded mountain ranges form the eastern extension of the Cape Folded Belt and the highest point is the Cockscomb in the Groot Winterhoek range, rising to 1 758 m above sea level. Also within the wilderness are the

LOCATION

Although a number of game species have been reintroduced here, Baviaanskloof is best known for its spectacular scenery and plant diversity.

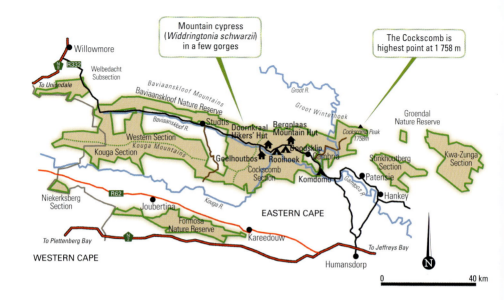

HIGHLIGHTS

- Spectacular mountain scenery.
- High plant, bird and reptile diversity.
- Proximity to the Garden Route National Park.
- Freedom to walk despite the presence of potentially dangerous game.

1 626 m Scholtzberg, and other, apparently unnamed peaks, rising to 1 562 m above the Ys River and to 1 450 m above Diepnekkloof. The Groot River rises in the Little Swartberg to the north, cuts south through the northern tip of the Groot Winterhoek range and then passes between the Baviaanskloof and Elandsberg ranges. The Kouga rises in the mountains of the same name and snakes its way east, north and then south-east to reach confluence with the Groot.

Brief history

Human habitation from all three Stone Ages is represented in the area and most of these peoples would have moved between mountains and coast in their quest for food. The presence of the San is evidenced

The Baviaanskloof area consists largely of rugged mountain terrain and deeply cut ravines.

168　Eastern Cape

Several species of aloe grow in the Baviaanskloof.

by rock art and the first livestock keepers, the Khoekhoen, arrived between 2 000 and 1 500 BP.

The first whites arrived in the mid to late 1700s, probably first as hunters and traders but later to establish farms and homesteads. Records indicate that Cape mountain zebra lived throughout these mountain ranges and their easternmost range extended to the Zuurberg, now part of the Addo Elephant National Park. Greater kudu, common eland, red hartebeest and savanna buffalo were also recorded and all have been reintroduced. Most settlement was along the valleys, and the upper mountains were largely left untouched, except for the exploitation of timber trees such as yellowwood and stinkwood in the extensive forests of the time.

Baviaanskloof was managed by the Department of Forestry from the early 1920s and the first forester was stationed at Studtis in 1930. In 1987 management was transferred from the Department of Environmental Affairs to Cape Nature Conservation, and then in 1994 to the Eastern Cape Department of Economic Affairs, Environment and Tourism. Since 2004 it has been managed by the Eastern Cape Parks Board.

CLIMATE

The region receives its rain throughout the year, although slight peaks occur in March and October/November, and summer falls increase towards the east. There are frequent thunderstorms. Snow may fall in winter on the higher peaks. Annual average rainfalls are lowest (about 365 mm) north of the Baviaanskloof and Groot Winterhoek ranges, as well as much of the thicket country in the east, although this increases as one nears the coast. Rainfall is also significantly lower on the rain-shadowed north-facing slopes of the Tsitsikamma and Groot Winterhoek ranges than on their southern aspects. The high heathland/fynbos country receives much more rain than the lowlands. Temperatures also vary according to altitude and distance from the coast. Inland and low-lying areas are generally hotter in summer, about 30° to 40°C, and colder in winter, when several frost days can occur. In the high fynbos areas, the average daily extremes range from 27°C in February to 2.5°C in July. The prevailing winds blow south to south-east in the summer and north-west in winter. The unusually dry and hot berg wind may blow in autumn and winter.

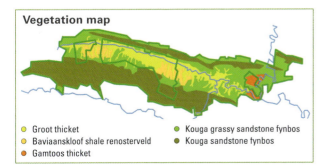

Vegetation map

- Groot thicket
- Baviaanskloof shale renosterveld
- Gamtoos thicket
- Kouga grassy sandstone fynbos
- Kouga sandstone fynbos

FACILITIES AND ACTIVITIES

- Geelhoutbos has five equipped 6-bed bungalows; overnight hikers' hut at Doornkraal; campsite with facilities at Komdomo; basic campsites at several locations. Hikers with permits can camp where they choose. Several private accommodation options on farms.
- Marked and unmarked hiking trails.
- Mountain bike trails.
- 4x4 trail but otherwise driving only permitted on public roads. Road traversing the Baviaanskloof is poorly maintained.
- No fuel or supplies in conservation area.
- Nearest town to the west is Willowmore; to the east is Patensie.

Geology and landscape

All of these mountain ranges are the eastern outliers of the great Cape Folded Belt. The sandstones and quartzites mainly belong to the Table Mountain Group but there are also quartzitic sandstones of the Witteberg Group. These rock types dominate in the east but there are also rocks and soils belonging to the Dwyka and Ecca rock series, as well as Bokkeveld influences in the far east. To the north of the Baviaanskloof there are areas of clay and loamy soils derived from shales of the Table Mountain Group.

Vegetation

This cluster of reserves lies between the arid Steytlerville Karoo to the north and the mesic southern Cape coast. Much of the complex lies within the eastern sector of the Cape Floristic Kingdom, the species-rich Cape heathland, or fynbos, biome. Some northern, and especially eastern, areas fall within subtropical thicket country, with small indigenous forest pockets located in narrow river valleys and gorges. Grassland and fynbos mix is found on the plateaux in the Kouga and Baviaanskloof ranges. Most of the Formosa sector to the south is Tsitsikamma sandstone fynbos. Botanically this reserve complex is very rich; 1 214 plant species have been identified and botanists expect to add several hundred species to the inventory over time. This richness can be judged by the fact that no fewer than 52 species of heath (*Ericaceae*), 33 species of protea (*Proteaceae*), 52 species of the succulent crassulas (*Crassulaceae*) and 11 aloes (*Asphodelaceae*) have been recorded. There are 37 species and subspecies of plant endemic, or near endemic, to the complex, including eight collected on the cliffs of the Kouga range in recent years. These include the '**painted leaf**' **aloe** (*Aloe pictifolia*) that

Grey rhebok live in small family groups and are active by day.

Baviaanskloof is an important leopard refuge.

grows on steep cliffs and flowers from July to September, *Haworthia pungensis* and the **cabbage tree** (*Cussonia gamtooensis*). Of the two **mountain cypress** known to occur here, one (*Widdringtonia schwarzii*) is restricted to the complex.

Wildlife

Mammals

There are 48 mammal species recorded, but several more species of shrew, small rodents and bats are likely to be added from further survey work in the more isolated areas. Several former residents have been reintroduced, including **hook-lipped rhinoceros**, **savanna buffalo**, **common eland**, **red hartebeest** and **Cape mountain zebra**. Populations of **greater kudu**, **bushbuck**, **mountain reedbuck**, **grey rhebok**, **Cape grysbok** and **common duiker** occur naturally. There are unconfirmed reports of **blue duiker** in some of the forest pockets but this is deemed unlikely. The most commonly seen species include **Chacma baboon**, **vervet monkey**, **rock hyrax** (**dassie**) and the **small grey mongoose**.

Although seldom seen, caracal are fairly widespread.

Birds

Approximately 300 species of bird are on record here. No fewer than 26 species of raptor are known, including populations of **Verreaux's eagle**, **crowned eagle** and **forest buzzard**. It is also a good area for spotting the bird-hunting **peregrine falcon**. **Black storks** nest here, as does the **African black duck**. There are nine species of pigeon and dove, including **African olive pigeon**, **lemon dove** and **tambourine dove**. The most westerly records for **spotted ground thrush** were made here in the forest pockets, and other species in this habitat include **starred robin**, **narina trogon** and **Knysna turaco**. The **Cape rockjumper** is close to its eastern range limit here, as are **Cape bulbul**, **Victorin's warbler**, **orange-breasted sunbird** and the **protea seedeater**. At least 20 species are at or near their western range limits.

Reptiles and amphibians

Records exist of 58 reptile species, including four species of tortoise, 24 snakes and 29 lizards. Five of the so-called **house snakes** (*Lamprophis* spp.) occur, while the principal venomous species are the **puff adder**, **berg adder** and **Cape cobra**. Among the more obvious lizards are three species of **girdled lizards** (*Cordylus* spp.), the four species of **crag lizard** (*Pseudocordylus* spp.) and the **southern rock agama**. The **rock monitor** and **water** (**Nile**) **monitor** are present but separated by their different habitat needs. There are

> **WILDLIFE FACTS**
>
> - Several of the 48 mammal species have been reintroduced, such as hook-lipped rhinoceros, savanna buffalo and common eland.
> - About 300 bird species, including several at the limits of their range.
> - Some 58 reptiles and 18 species of amphibians.
> - At least 21 fish species, including six exotic to the area.
> - No less than 66 species of butterfly have been identified, as well as nine cicadas, 27 fruit chafer beetles and 23 molluscs, including one endemic to the wilderness.
> - Whopping 1 214 species of plant from 138 families; at least another 600 are thought to lie undiscovered because of difficult terrain.

Baviaanskloof Wilderness Area 171

Many troops of Chacma baboon range across the wilderness area.

Small numbers of black stork occur in the area.

15 species of amphibian, including possibly two species of **ghost frog** (*Heleophryne* spp.), the **sand toad** at the easternmost point of its range, and the **marbled reed frog** and the **yellow-striped reed frog** at the westernmost points of their distributions.

Fish

There are 13 species of fish that are indigenous to the river systems, including the localized **Eastern Cape redfin** and an apparently isolated population of the **goldie barb**. The **Cape kurper** is close to the limit of its eastern range, as is the **small-scale redfin**. Unfortunately, there are two species introduced from other South African river systems, the **banded tilapia** and the voracious **sharptooth catfish**. Even more troubling is the presence of four exotics, including the predatory **large-mouth bass**.

Invertebrates

There are 66 species of butterfly on record of which one, the **Baviaanskloof blue**, only occurs here. A subspecies of the **giant copper** (*A. p. liversidgei*) and an as yet undescribed subspecies of **Dickson's sylph** are restricted to this area. Of the 27, mostly brightly coloured, fruit chafer beetle species, one (*Ichnestoma cuspidata*) is considered to be extremely rare. Among the terrestrial molluscs the tiny leaf-litter dwelling snail *Chondrocyclus convexiusculus* has been estimated to occur at densities of between 10 000 and 100 000 individuals per m^2. This is one of 23 snails, freshwater limpets and slugs collected within the Baviaanskloof complex.

The leopard tortoise has a pronounced domed carapace.

> **!**
> - Be prepared for weather extremes at any time of the year.
> - Road conditions can deteriorate rapidly after heavy rain. Be prepared for poor road conditions.
> - Dangerous animals should always be borne in mind.

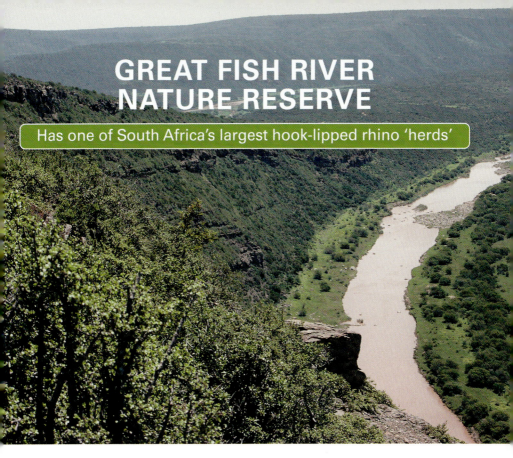

GREAT FISH RIVER NATURE RESERVE

Has one of South Africa's largest hook-lipped rhino 'herds'

Lie of the land

This Eastern Cape conservation area covers 45 500 ha comprising the contiguous 6 500 ha Andries Vosloo Kudu Reserve, the 15 500 ha Sam Knott Reserve and the 23 500 ha Double Drift Reserve. It is focused on the Great Fish River, which winds dramatically through it and in places has cut a deep gorge through the rock. The Keiskamma River forms the north-west boundary, and the Koonap and Kat rivers flow in from the north-east, reaching confluence with the Great Fish River in the north. Altitude ranges from 95 m above sea level in the riverbed to 561 m above sea level on the highest dividing ridge. Much of the area consists of steep river valleys with broken inter-basin ridges, with some open flattish areas.

LOCATION

Brief history

A number of Later Stone Age sites and San rock paintings are found in the vicinity. Khoekhoen pastoralists had settled here about 1 700 BP but by around 1 700 AD they had been driven away or assimilated by tribes arriving from the north. The most important of these tribes entering the Eastern Cape were the AmaXhosa and the AmaMfengu, whose three major controlling clans were the AmaNdlambe, AmaHlubu and the AmaGqunukwebe. Their hold over the area

Several rivers are associated with this reserve but the Great Fish is the principal watercourse.

Great Fish River Nature Reserve 173

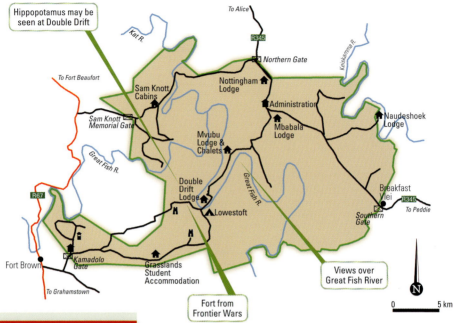

HIGHLIGHTS

- Dramatic scenery, especially overlooking the Great Fish River.
- One of South Africa's largest hook-lipped rhinoceros populations and a large population of 'disease-free' savanna buffalo.
- Significant plant diversity with a number of endemics.

Vegetation map

- Bisho thornveld
- Great Fish noorsveld
- Great Fish thicket

was broken with the arrival of white settlers in 1812, followed by Boers from the west and British settlers in 1820. Conflict continued through much of the 19th century between the Khoekhoen, largely allied to the local tribes, and the white settlers and militia, in what became known as the Frontier Wars. There is evidence of these wars and skirmishes in the form of graves, river crossings and the forts at Double Drift, Willshire and Botha's Post. The Great Fish River formed the disputed boundary between whites on the west bank and blacks in the east.

The Andries Vosloo Kudu Reserve was proclaimed in 1973 and the farm Lowestof was added in 1976. In 1982 the South African government purchased 10 farms which were later given to the then 'homeland' of Ciskei and proclaimed the L.L. Sebe Game Reserve. Sebe was overthrown in a coup in 1990 and the reserve was renamed Double Drift Reserve. The bequest of several farms by Sam Knott led to the formation of the Sam Knott Nature Reserve in 1987.

Geology and landscape

Grey-red mudstone and sandstone sedimentary strata of the Middleton (Adelaide) Formation belonging to the Beaufort Group (Karoo Supergroup) predominate throughout the area. Most of the exposed rock formations are sandstone but in the valleys the rivers have cut deeply into the softer mudstones. Soils are generally shallow and underlaid with shale banks, particularly in the western sector.

Vegetation

Much of the area is classified as Great Fish Thicket, a complex of 12 principal vegetation types. It is a subtropical thicket mosaic interspersed with areas of grassland and savanna. In good rain years, more grass is visible at higher altitudes. Only about 400 plant species from 80 families have been recorded but at least 100 more may be added over time. At least 27 invasive alien species are present, with some such as **jointed cactus** (*Opuntia aurantiaca*) reaching pest proportions in places. From west to east there is a gradual shift from tall, dense, largely thornless shrubs and low trees to short, thorny, succulent shrubland. These thickets are dense and extremely difficult to penetrate, except for the hook-lipped rhinoceros and savanna buffalo with their heavy bodies and thick hides. Prominent plants, especially on slopes, include several tree euphorbias such as the **honey euphorbia** (*Euphorbia tetragona*) that may exceed 10 m in height, and the **river euphorbia** (*Euphorbia triangularis*) that may reach 18 m. They have a toxic milky sap and like many of the plants here, come well armed with thorns. In limited areas, such as on the Grahamstown-Fort Beaufort road, you will see another euphorbia, the much shorter stemmed (to 2 m) **five-cornered euphorbia**, or **noorsdoring**, (*Euphorbia pentagona*). The **bitter aloe** (*Aloe ferox*) grows to about 2 m on a single stem and produces its showy orange-red flower spikes in June/July. **Climbing aloes** (*Aloe ciliaris*) wind their way through bushes and trees up to 6 m and their bright red, yellow-tipped flowers may stand out from the surrounding greens at any time of the year. The **porkbush**, or **spekboom**, (*Portulacaria afra*) is an important browsing plant for several game species including greater kudu and bushbuck and is common on the slopes. One of the largest trees here, especially along rivers and streams, is the long white-thorned **sweet thorn** (*Vachellia karroo*). When showing its red to pink blossom clusters in spring and summer the short **Karoo boer-bean** (*Schotia afra*) tree stands out in the dense thickets.

A number of historic sites can be found within the reserve, including this blockhouse at Fort Double Drift.

CLIMATE

This is a semi-arid area with variable annual rainfall. The annual average is 434 mm below 300 m, 620 mm above. There is a small tendency towards summer rainfall with peak falls in October and March, and winters are largely dry. Drought is not unusual. South-facing slopes are generally cooler and receive more precipitation in the form of rain and river fog. January maximum average temperature is approximately 30°C and the mean daily minimum in July is about 0°C. Several days of frost are recorded each winter.

Tree euphorbias grow in the reserve's subtropical thicket.

FACILITIES AND ACTIVITIES

- Four lodges in the eastern Double Drift sector, refurbished farmhouses and 2-bed chalets. Mvubu Lodge on the west bank has six 4-bed chalets. Mix of full-service and self-catering accommodation.
- Basic campsite (few facilities) on the west bank of the Great Fish River at the river ford.
- Guided hiking trails of 1–3 days; check whether these are functioning.
- Hide at dam within west bank sector.
- Network of gravel game-viewing roads in a variable state of repair; most can be traversed by means of a saloon car.
- Various other activities such as day and night game drives.
- Approximately midway between Grahamstown and King William's Town.

The Great Fish River reserve is one of the few conservation areas where hook-lipped rhinoceros are regularly seen.

Wildlife

Mammals

Although this conservation area was initially set aside to conserve the **greater kudu**, which is common here, it was soon expanded to protect all biota. The population of **hook-lipped rhinoceros**, now numbering more than 100, is one of the largest in the world. The more than 400 **savanna buffalo** are important for their 'disease-free' status; the founding population was introduced from Addo. **Hippopotamus** have been introduced in the Great Fish River but numbers are not accurately known. Apart from kudu, other antelope include **red hartebeest**, **common eland**, **springbok**, **blesbok**, **mountain reedbuck**, **steenbok** and **common duiker**. One ungulate that you cannot miss is the **common warthog**, introduced in the early days of the reserve from KwaZulu-Natal and thriving to the extent that it has to be regularly culled. Many animals have dispersed from the reserve on to surrounding farms, much to the chagrin of landowners. **Leopard** and **brown hyaena** are present but seldom seen, but **black-backed jackal** are common and frequently heard calling in the evening and early morning. The most commonly seen carnivores are three mongooses, the troop-living **suricate**, the group-living but solitary-foraging **yellow mongoose**, and the lone **small grey mongoose**. Most of the 19 rodent species are seldom seen, except the **four-striped grass mouse**, which you will see especially at picnic sites and at the Double Drift campground. **Springhares** have dug their burrows at the campground and can be seen with the help of a strong torch at night.

Birds

Several of the 247 bird species recorded are vagrants or just occasional visitors, but there are many residents and regular migrants. A population of **red-billed oxpeckers**, one of several in

Black-headed orioles can be identified by their loud calls.

the Eastern Cape, is located here. As usual some of the best birding is to be had around the lodges, camp and picnic grounds, but the hide in the western sector offers good aquatic birding. **African fish eagle** are commonly seen and heard along the Great Fish River, and **crowned eagle** are occasionally seen. The six species of owl include the **African scops owl** which is close to its southernmost range here.

Reptiles and amphibians

Surprisingly, no detailed surveys have been undertaken of the herpetofauna of the reserve. Based on records from surrounding areas and a few local ones, at least 44 reptiles and 16 different amphibians could occur. In the 1970s several **southern African pythons** and **giant bullfrogs** were released within the Andries Vosloo Kudu Reserve sector but their current status is unknown. Some controversy exists as to whether pythons occurred here in the past, and if so why they disappeared. The authors have seen **puff adder**, **Cape cobra**, **boomslang** and **spotted skaapsteker** here and at least a further 17 species could very well occur. **Marsh terrapin** and **leopard tortoise** are common. At least 20 lizard species probably occur, the most obvious being the **rock monitor** and **water monitor**.

Fish

Up to 24 fish species are known from the Great Fish, Koonap, Kat and Keiskamma rivers in or near the conservation area but of course a number will be seasonal or only occasional visitors. Several are exotic to these river systems, such as **sharp-tooth catfish** and **large-mouth bass**, both voracious predators.

WILDLIFE FACTS

- At least 69 mammal species, excluding several that have been introduced in the Double Drift sector that did not occur historically. The park's policy is to remove all species that did not previously occur in the area.
- One of South Africa's largest hook-lipped rhinoceros populations.
- About 247 species of birds, including some rare vagrants.
- No comprehensive listing, but perhaps 44 species of reptile and 16 amphibians occur.

Left: Bladder grasshoppers are seldom seen as their coloration serves to camouflage them. Below: After mating this male praying mantis provided his partner with a meal.

- Beware of dangerous game species, such as hippopotamus, hook-lipped rhinoceros and buffalo.
- No fuel or supplies available.

KWANDWE PRIVATE GAME RESERVE

Guided tours the order of the day

Lie of the land

This 22 000 ha privately owned game reserve, to the north-east of Grahamstown, straddles some 30 km of the length of the Great Fish River and is almost equally divided by it. The reserve's flatland, situated mainly along the floodplain, was once heavily cultivated and grazed by domestic livestock. With the cessation of agricultural practices this land is set to gradually recover from past abuse. Many of the grazing species reintroduced into the reserve can be found here along the waterway and on the floodplain. The remainder of the reserve is dominated by rugged and broken hill country that is generally densely vegetated by thicket. Kwandwe bears many similarities to the Great Fish River Nature Reserve a short distance to the east (see pages 173–177).

Kwandwe Game Reserve is well known for its abundance of greater kudu.

Brief history

Little has been recorded on the prehistory of Kwandwe but evidence indicates that at least Later Stone Age peoples lived in the area. Further research is likely to date the presence of humans in the area to the Earlier and Middle Stone Ages,

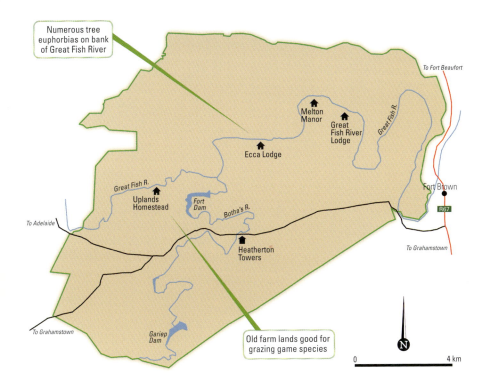

as in neighbouring areas. Khoekhoen pastoralists were present in the area from about 1 700 BP and by 1 700 AD black pastoralists and cultivators had largely assimilated them into their own societies. For further details see the chapter on the Great Fish River Nature Reserve (see pages 173–177). The reception building is a converted fortified farmhouse dating from the Frontier Wars of the 19th century.

HIGHLIGHTS

- Big Five reserve with elephant, both African rhinoceros species, lion, cheetah and wild dog.
- Luxurious accommodation.
- Game drives with ranger guide.
- Malaria-free, like all Eastern Cape parks and reserves.

The Great Fish River cuts through the game reserve and is its most dominant landscape feature.

Kwandwe Private Game Reserve   **179**

CLIMATE

The climate here is similar to that of the nearby Great Fish River Nature Reserve (see page 175). Only a few yearly records are available, indicating that annual rainfall ranges from 236 mm to 560 mm. January maximum temperatures have ranged from 28°C to 32°C while minimum temperatures range from 15°C to 18°C. July maximums are from 21°C to 25°C, and minimum temperatures are from 2°C to 5° C.

A few pairs of blue crane live seasonally in Kwandwe.

Geology and landscape

Rock formations and soils closely mirror those of the Great Fish River Nature Reserve (see page 174). The landscape is dominated by riverine floodplains, with rolling country and rugged broken areas stretching across the north of the reserve.

Vegetation

Much of the vegetation is Great Fish Thicket subdivided into 11 different zones. Many species are shared but may be dominant in one zone and not in another. Although **porkbush**, or **spekboom**, (*Portulacaria afra*) occurs in dense stands and thickets on steep slopes in the west and north, it is rather sparse in other areas and often mixed with a range of euphorbias and several woody species. Euphorbia zones can be broadly divided into the extensive areas with short species, locally called **noorsdoring** (*Euphorbia bothae*), and those dominated by tall, tree-like species that grow on steep slopes close to the Great Fish River in the north, including the **honey euphorbia** (*Euphorbia tetragona*) and **river euphorbia** (*Euphorbia triangularis*). There are also areas of bushclump savanna thicket,

Vegetation map

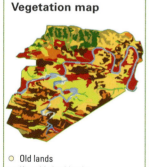

- ○ Old lands
- ○ Karroid shrublands
- ○ Short and tall euphorbia thicket
- ● Bushclump savanna
- ● *Portulacaria* thicket
- ● Bushclump karroid thicket
- ○ *Euphorbia portulacaria* mosaic
- ● Drainage line thicket
- ● Dry forest
- ○ Riverine thicket

Warthog are common prey for several of the larger predators.

karroid shrubland, and an area of about 750 ha of dry forest in the north with most trees in the 5 m to 10 m range. The **sweet thorn** (*Vachellia karroo*) dominates along much of the narrow riverine line.

Wildlife
Mammals
Some of the game species, such as **greater kudu, bushbuck** and **common duiker** were here when the reserve was established. Species that were reintroduced include **savanna elephant, savanna buffalo, hook-lipped rhinoceros, square-lipped rhinoceros, common hippopotamus, lion, cheetah, wild dog** and **serval**. Species that did not occur here in the past include **giraffe, common waterbuck** and **impala**. The smaller naturally occurring species here are similar to those found in the Great Fish River Nature Reserve (see page 176).

Birds
The 300 bird species include rarities and vagrants as well as residents or regularly occurring migrants. Bird life here is similar to that of the Great Fish River Nature Reserve (see pages 176–177).

Reptiles and amphibians
There may be 60 reptile and 18 amphibian species but no detailed surveys have been undertaken.

Fish
No detailed fish survey has been undertaken, but it is likely to be similar to the Great Fish River reserve account (see page 177).

FACILITIES AND ACTIVITIES
- Four luxury lodges, fully catered; two for exclusive party bookings.
- Day and night game-viewing drives in open vehicles.
- Not a 'free-movement' reserve, but requires bookings through &Beyond.

WILDLIFE FACTS
- Some 68 mammal species, including the reintroduced Big Five.
- About 300 birds including rarities and vagrants.
- No detailed reptile survey but the composition is similar to that of the Great Fish River reserve (see page 177).
- Estimated 18 possible amphibian species, nine confirmed.
- Fish species probably same as for the Great Fish River reserve (see page 177).
- Some 374 plant species, including 78 tree/bush species, 29 grasses and 11 aloe.

Red-backed shrikes are summer visitors to the area.

The spider fauna of the reserve is not well documented.

- As you will be 'in care' most of the time, risks are few. But be aware that dangerous game species, including lion and elephant, are around.

Kwandwe Private Game Reserve   **181**

WESTERN CAPE

The Western Cape's shores are washed by the cold waters of the Atlantic Ocean in the west and the warmer Indian Ocean to the south. Its northern boundaries fringe arid Namaqualand and the steep escarpment of the Upper Karoo. The narrow southern and south-western coastal plain is separated from the dry interior by a chain of parallel mountain ranges known as the Cape Folded Belt.

One of the province's major drawcards is that it is home to the Cape Floral Region, the smallest – and the richest – of the world's six floral kingdoms. The key feature of this Cape heathland, or fynbos, is that it only covers 0.04% of the world's land surface but has about 8 580 species of flowering plants, of which almost 70% are endemic.

Geologically the area covered by the Cape heathland can be divided into three main rock types. The lowest layer, the Malmesbury Shales, consists of mud sediments that were deposited under the ocean. Between 610 and 500 million years ago, great volcanic activity caused magma to break through to the surface, covering and intruding into the Malmesbury Shales. As the magma cooled and solidified it became the Cape Granite of today. The region rose gradually out of the ocean and, over about 50 million years, erosion and weathering created a level plain. Then the land mass sank again, and was covered by shallow water for about 200 million years. During this time marine and land-origin sediments were laid down.

Much of the western and central parts share a Mediterranean climate, with cool, wet winters and warm, dry summers. Strong south-easterly winds blow in summer and bracing north-westerlies in winter. Rainfall is more evenly spread throughout the year in the central and eastern coastal regions, while summer rainfall prevails in the extreme east. In the north-west and to the north of the coastal mountain chain, rainfall is more limited.

Cape Point lies at the southernmost tip of the Table Mountain National Park.

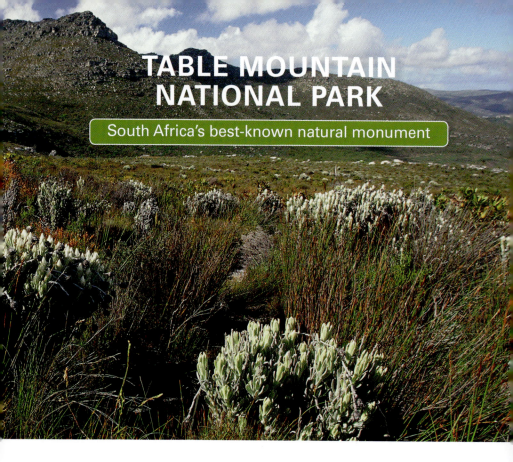

TABLE MOUNTAIN NATIONAL PARK

South Africa's best-known natural monument

Lie of the land

The park covers about 30 342 ha of the mountainous Cape Peninsula, with False Bay washing its eastern shores and the Atlantic Ocean its western flank. It includes land owned by SANParks as well as state and private land managed by them, and a marine protected area that covers an additional 975 km². The world-famous Table Mountain, ringed by Cape Town and its suburbs, lies at its northern edge, with a backbone of rugged mountain ridges and peaks extending to Cape Point, where the rocks disappear beneath the ocean – a distance of about 27 km. The park is about 5 km wide at its broadest point.

Brief history

Humans have occupied the Cape Peninsula from about 600 000 BP. There are several archaeological sites, but the best evidence is available on the Later Stone Age inhabitants and the San and Khoekhoen peoples from about 2 000 BP. The most obvious signs of San and Khoekhoen presence are the shell middens scattered above the high water mark. Several caves also show evidence of inhabitation, in the form of stone tools and potsherds. The San were hunter-gatherers and although the Khoekhoen also hunted and harvested wild plants, they kept livestock.

Table Mountain National Park conserves one of the world's richest plant hotspots, the Cape heathland, or fynbos.

184 Western Cape

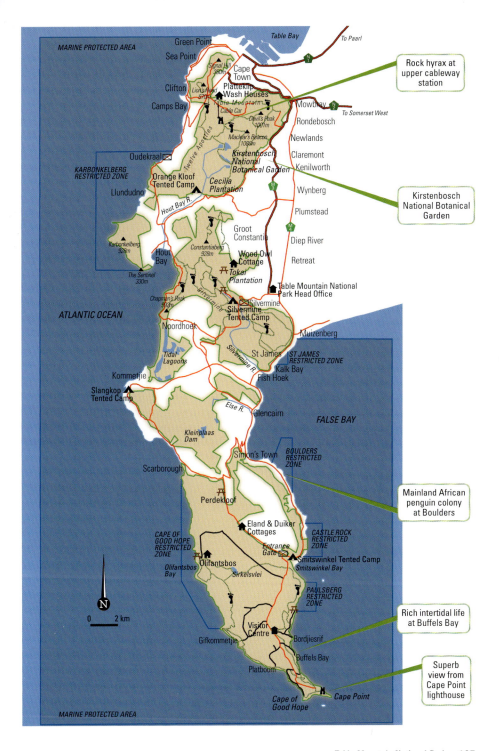

HIGHLIGHTS

- Dramatic mountain scenery and seascapes.
- Close to Cape Town.
- Massive diversity of plant species within Cape Floral Kingdom.
- Rich bird life and easily accessible mainland breeding colony of African penguin.
- Several game species reintroduced into the southern sector of the park.

Several small pristine beaches can be found along the rugged coastline of the Cape Peninsula.

There may have been 8 000 Khoekhoen in and around the Cape Peninsula when the first Europeans arrived. By the beginning of the 17th century it was reported that only about 100 of these people, calling themselves the Goringhaicona, were living on the Peninsula, while a larger group known as Goringhaiqua occupied areas inland. From the arrival of the Dutch East India Company and the first European residents in 1652 to about 1720, the original inhabitants were virtually wiped out by disease, starvation and forced labour.

The Khoekhoen name for Table Mountain and its rugged companions was Hoerikwaggo, which means 'sea mountain' or the 'mountain in the sea'. In 1939 the Cape of Good Hope Nature Reserve was established, and in 1958 all of Table Mountain above the 152 m contour was proclaimed as a national monument. In 1998 the Cape Peninsula National Park was proclaimed, and in 2004 it was renamed Table Mountain National Park.

Geology and landscape

Table Mountain National Park contains much rugged, mountainous country, while the coastline is a mixture of rocky areas and open, sheltered beaches in small bays. At Cape Point and Smitswinkel Bay, the mountains descend into the sea. In the southerly Cape of Good Hope section there are open, rolling plains. The Cape Peninsula consists of three major rock formations. The oldest of these, the Malmesbury Group, consists of dark grey mudstones and paler sandstones deposited as sediments by the Adamastor Ocean, the great body of water that preceded the Atlantic. About 540 million years BP this was followed by Cape Granite, volcanic material from deep in the earth, which underlies much of the Peninsula mountains. It can be seen in great boulder clusters at Boulders Beach near Simon's Town and along the shoreline below Chapman's Peak. This rock is relatively coarse-grained and usually light grey in colour. The third group, the Table Mountain Group sandstones, make up most of the Peninsula's mountains and were laid down as sediments from about

Table Mountain National Park is home to 112 erica species.

520 million years BP. During the break up of Gondwana about 130 million years BP, the Peninsula underwent block-faulting, which caused the break in the mountains across the Fish Hoek Valley.

Vegetation

The floral splendour of the Cape Peninsula is the jewel in the crown of this national park. The park is an extremely important conservation area that falls within the Cape Floral Kingdom, one of only six such plant kingdoms recognized worldwide. The four main groups of plants representative of this heathland, or fynbos, are the often showy proteas, the ericas, the reed-like restios and the bulbous geophytes. Although some heathland species are widespread in the Peninsula, many are very localized and may be found only in tiny areas. There are over 2 200 species of flowering plant in the Peninsula, and the vast majority are found in the park, while at least 90 species occur only here. For comparison, the entire plant diversity of Britain amounts to 1 492 species! The park contains 112 species of erica and many species of protea. It is also an exceptionally rich ground orchid area with at least 70 species in the genus *Disa* alone, including the splendid **red disa** (*Disa uniflora*). Some of the more noticeable species belong to the protea family and include the **tree pincushion**, or **kreupelhout,** (*Protea conocarpodendron*) which produces its numerous yellow flower heads from September to January. The **king protea** (*Protea cynaroides*) grows to just 2 m but produces showy flower heads up to 30 cm in diameter from summer into winter. More localized species will repay the effort required to locate them. One of the more spectacular of these species is the protea *Mimetes fimbriifolius* that grows to a height of about 4 m just to the south of Smitswinkel Bay on the False Bay coast, and flowers from August to November. Although many plant species blossom from late winter through to early summer, each month has its own floral selection. The vegetation zones can be broadly divided into the Peninsula

Vegetation map

- Cape Flats dune strandveld
- Peninsula granite fynbos
- Peninsula sandstone fynbos
- Cape Winelands shale fynbos
- Cape Flats sand fynbos
- Peninsula shale renosterveld
- Hangklip sand fynbos
- Southern Afrotemperate forest

Numerous hiking trails on Table Mountain offer spectacular views of the Cape Peninsula.

The red disa occurs along cliffs and seeps on Table Mountain.

Table Mountain National Park 187

CLIMATE

The area has a typical Mediterranean climate with a long, warm, dry summer, and a short, cool, wet winter. Some rain can be expected throughout the year, and the annual average rainfall is 515 mm; but some areas are much wetter than others. The Peninsula can be windy, and the south-easterly 'Cape Doctor' prevails in summer. In winter, the north-westerlies are associated with cold fronts that sweep in from the Atlantic Ocean, and can reach gale force. The temperature ranges from 16°C to 27°C in February, from 7°C to 18°C in July. Local temperatures vary because of the mountains and ocean. Table Mountain and other Peninsula mountains have a 'table cloth' cloud formed by condensation of moist air carried up the slopes by south-easterly winds. This moisture provides an important supplement to the rainfall.

Approximately 300 Chacma baboons live in the park.

sandstone fynbos, which covers much of the park, Cape Flats dune strandveld in a narrow strip along the west coast, and Hangklip sand fynbos in small patches in the south and across the Fish Hoek Valley. Other zones cover smaller areas, as do sheltered patches of Afromontane forest on east-facing slopes in the upper north-east. The Orange Kloof Forest above Hout Bay is one of the larger patches that remain from what may once have been more extensive stands. Most trees in these forests are evergreens 15 to 30 m tall; only 33 species have been recorded. These Peninsula forests include **real yellowwood** (*Podocarpus latifolius*), **ironwood** (*Olea capensis*), **hard pear** (*Olinia ventosa*), **Cape beach** (*Rapanea melanophloeos*) and **stinkwood** (*Ocotea bullata*). A visit to Kirstenbosch National Botanical Garden, with its many footpaths and trails, provides an excellent introduction to the plants of the Cape Floral Kingdom.

The shallow waters along the coastline also exhibit great plant diversity, and are home to a great many different seaweeds.

Wildlife
Mammals

The nutrient-poor heathland vegetation, growing on largely leached soils, has offered little attraction for large resident herbivores in the past. Nomadic species such as **common eland** and **red hartebeest** once roamed naturally across the area but were hunted out in the early years of settlement. These two species, as well as **bontebok** and **Cape mountain zebra**, can now be seen in the Cape of Good Hope sector in the south of the park. Historic records suggest that these latter two species were not endemic. **Common duiker**, **grey rhebok** and **steenbok** occur naturally in the park wherever habitat is suitable, and **Cape grysbok** is widespread. **Klipspringer**, small agile rock-dwelling antelope once locally extinct through competition with the alien Himalayan tahr and other factors, have been reintroduced to Table Mountain and the Cape of Good Hope since the tahr were

Rock hyrax are a regular sight at the upper cableway station.

188 Western Cape

almost eradicated. A commonly seen mammal is the **Chacma baboon**, with 10 troops totalling about 300 individuals found in the central and southern areas of the Peninsula. These primates are completely isolated by human development from baboons living in the mountains to the north of the Cape Flats. A small number of baboons and a very large number of humans is a recipe for conflict, and various strategies are being employed to try to limit the friction. Another species is the **rock hyrax**, commonly seen for example near the upper cableway station at the top of Table Mountain. Most rodents are shy and nocturnal, but the day-active and attractively marked **four-striped grass mouse** is regularly seen. These, along with other species such as the **Namaqua rock mouse**, are important pollinators of several fynbos flowers such as creeping forms of protea. In the 17th and early 18th centuries lion, leopard and spotted hyaena were Peninsula regulars but today the only carnivore you are likely to see is the **small grey mongoose**. Several other species occur, such as **caracal**, **Cape fox**, **water mongoose**, **Cape clawless otter** and **striped polecat**, but they are all primarily nocturnal and secretive. **Cape fur seals** are commonly seen around the coastline, although they rarely beach. Large numbers inhabit Seal Island in False Bay. At least three species of whale (mainly seasonal) and three dolphin species are commonly seen from vantage points in the park. **Southern right whale** is the most abundant large whale while in residence from May to October. **Dusky** and **bottle-nosed dolphins** are frequently seen around the park's coastline, and the **long-beaked common dolphin** may form schools thousands strong. Among the best cetacean viewpoints are Rooikrans, Boyes Drive between Kalk Bay and Muizenberg, the road between Boulders and Smitswinkel Bay, and above the Slangkop lighthouse.

Cape fur seals can be expected anywhere around the coastline.

Birds

With just over 300 bird species the park is a prime destination for birders, especially for those with a particular interest in oceanic and

Tented accommodation is available in the park's Silvermine sector.

FACILITIES AND ACTIVITIES

- Cape Town has a vast range of accommodation; accommodation in the park includes self-catering units at Cape Point, in the Tokai pine plantation, above Constantia Nek, and at the Platteklip Wash Houses above Oranjezicht, as well as tented camps at Smitswinkel Bay, Silvermine, Slangkop and Orangekloof
- Numerous mountain bike, walking and hiking trails, including the 4-night, 5-day Hoerikwaggo Hiking Trail (75 km).
- Cable car up Table Mountain.
- Many scenic drives (including Chapman's Peak), and game-viewing roads in the Cape Point sector.
- All the activities of a major city.

Sunbirds, here the orange-breasted, feed on the nectar of protea and other flowers.

There is a breeding colony of African penguins at Boulders.

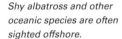

Shy albatross and other oceanic species are often sighted offshore.

coastal species. The waters around the Table Mountain National Park are considered among the best in the world for observing oceanic birds. One may choose sea-based viewing with a tour operator, or land-based, where some of the best locations are at Cape Point and off the Cape of Good Hope. There is generally great diversity at any time of year and the best viewing is said to be when strong winds are blowing. Species such as **shy albatross**, **black-browed albatross**, **Atlantic** and **Indian yellow-nosed albatross**, **white-chinned petrel**, **sooty shearwater**, **Wilson's storm-petrel** and **subantarctic skua** are present in all months, with a chance of spotting more than 30 species throughout the year. Local birds such as **Cape gannet**, **Cape cormorant** and **African penguin** are present year-round. Watching great skeins of Cape cormorant moving to and from the feeding grounds is a special experience. African penguin, Africa's only resident penguin, are best viewed at Boulders Beach in Simon's Town. A pioneer pair nested here in 1985; now approximately 1 000 pairs breed on the beach and in adjacent gardens. Road signs in the area warn of penguins crossing. The Kirstenbosch National Botanical Garden is excellent for a representative mix of heathland (fynbos) and forest birds. These include **Cape sugarbird**, **orange-breasted sunbird**, **southern double-collared sunbird**, **southern boubou** and **brimstone canary**. **Cape spurfowl** and **helmeted guineafowl** are seen widely in the park, with **grey-winged francolin** fairly common in parts. **Verreaux's eagle** is a resident, as is **forest buzzard** in a number of plantations and forests on the eastern flank, and the **peregrine falcon** is regularly sighted. A further 20 raptor species have been recorded, although some are secretive and seldom seen.

Reptiles and amphibians

Only a few of the 64 reptile species will be observed by the casual visitor. In warm weather the common **angulate tortoise** is frequently seen in the sandy areas, but the smaller **parrot-beaked padloper** is more elusive. To date 22 species of snake have been recorded, including five considered dangerous to humans; of these, the **Cape cobra** and **puff adder** are the most commonly seen. Very few of the lizard species show themselves readily, but the **southern rock agama** and the **black girdled lizard** oblige by sitting prominently on rocks.

Seventeen amphibian species are known but most are seldom seen, although several may be heard during the breeding season. One, the **Table Mountain ghost frog**, is known only from a few perennial streams running through forested gorges on the eastern slope of Table Mountain. The **western leopard toad** is the largest amphibian in the park and is considered to be endangered because of its very limited range. Another endangered frog that finds refuge in some of the darkwater ponds in the park is **Gill's platanna**, which is primarily aquatic but during rain may move several hundred metres between ponds.

Fish

Indigenous freshwater fish populations are limited, as several alien species are established here. Marine fish populations are diverse, in part because of the cold Benguela Current that pushes northwards along the western Atlantic Ocean coast, the warm Agulhas Current that sweeps down the east coast past sheltered False Bay, and their convergence zone around the Cape Peninsula. Several hundred marine fish species, including several important to the commercial fisheries, occur in these rich waters. False Bay is particularly important for the conservation of the **great white shark**.

Invertebrates

The park has a great diversity of insect species, including for example more than 3 000 different beetles, and a number of species that are

WILDLIFE FACTS

- Cape Peninsula is best known for its incredible diversity of fynbos species, boasting 2 285 flowering plants, of which at least 1 470 are found on Table Mountain alone.
- Some 58 land mammal species, including several large game species in the Cape Point sector, as well as Cape fur seal and 36 marine mammal species. Klipspringer reintroduced at Cape Point and Table Mountain since the near-eradication of the alien Himalayan tahr population.
- Of 303 bird species recorded, 16 are very rare vagrants and 29 are oceanics.
- Boulders African penguin population is readily accessible and well worth a visit.
- There are 64 reptile species but only a few of these, such as the angulate tortoise and southern rock agama, are regularly seen.
- At least 17 different frog and toad species, including some rarities.

The parrot-beaked tortoise is a Cape heathland, or fynbos, endemic.

Cape Peninsula moss frog.

Table Mountain National Park **191**

The park is an important refuge for the perlemoen, or abalone, which has been over-exploited elsewhere.

endemic to the Peninsula. Many of the beetles, butterflies and flies that occur here are important heathland pollinators, and one butterfly, the **Table Mountain beauty**, is the sole known pollinator of 15 species of red-flowered plants, including the red disa. Perhaps as many as 20% of the heathland plants rely on certain ant species to carry their seeds into the underground chambers, protecting them from seed-eating rodents and destruction by fire. The ant's reward is the nutritious coating that wholly or partly covers the seed.

The marine invertebrate diversity in the waters of the park is huge, as is evident from the many rock pools in the intertidal zone. There are rocky and sandy bottoms as well as great kelp beds on the west coast, and all form unique habitats for their own groups of species. The marine conservation areas of the park are important for many commercially exploitable species, including **west coast rock lobster** and **perlemoen**, which have been over-exploited in other areas.

At least 21 species of cave-dwelling invertebrates are found only in a few cave-systems on Table Mountain, including a **cricket** species, *Speleiacris tabulae*, and a **blind shrimp** species, *Spelaeogriphus lepidops*. There are four species of velvet worm, or peripatus – not worms at all but specialized arthropods that give birth to live, well-developed young. One example is the **white cave peripatus**.

The Table Mountain beauty is the sole pollinator of at least 15 plant species.

- If you are walking or hiking in the mountain areas be aware that weather changes can occur rapidly and with little warning, and be prepared for all conditions.
- Throughout the park Chacma baboon troops have become a nuisance. Never feed them or leave food unattended. They may open car doors and help themselves, or snatch food from humans, especially children. Never try to retrieve anything that has been snatched.

BONTEBOK NATIONAL PARK
Contributed greatly to conservation of the bontebok

Lie of the land

The 3 900 ha Bontebok National Park is South Africa's smallest park. It is surrounded by agricultural development, mainly cropland, and the south-western part largely lies in a basin. Altitude ranges from about 60 m to 200 m above sea level and much of the terrain is flat and open, but the basin is bordered by a rocky ridge. The Breede River, which forms 6 km of its southern boundary, is broad and for much of the year slow moving, with parts of the south bank formed by low cliffs. The rugged Langeberg Mountain range rises to the north; it is outside the park, but much of it is protected by a number of nature reserves, including Marloth, which stretches westwards from Swellendam, about 5 km south. The N2 highway lies between Swellendam and the park.

Brief history

All three Stone Age periods are represented in the area, and many stone tools, including very large Earlier Stone Age hand axes, are turned up by local farmers' ploughs. When the first Europeans arrived in what was to become Swellendam, the Khoekhoen group known as the Hessekwa was settled along the Breede and Sonderend rivers. San were also here, and reports from 1668 indicate that they regularly raided Hessekwa cattle. The camp in the park is named for the

The attractive Lang Elsie Rest Camp is located just above the Breede River.

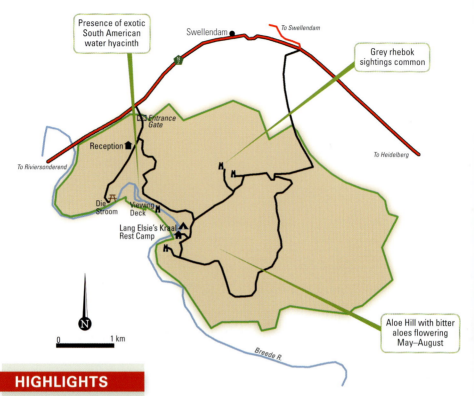

HIGHLIGHTS

- Magnificent backdrop of the Langeberg Mountains to the north.
- Freedom to walk on trails – no dangerous game around.
- One of the best locations for observing both grey rhebok and Cape grysbok.

Cape grysbok are secretive but quite commonly seen here.

original farm, or kraal, which took its name from Lang Elsie, a female Khoekhoen clan leader (*kaptein*) who apparently lived here from 1734 onwards. By that year the clan structure had broken down for several reasons, including the decimation of whole settlements following the outbreak of a smallpox epidemic.

By the early 19th century the local San had been largely hunted into extinction. Swellendam, the third oldest town in South Africa with much of historical interest, was founded in 1746. The bontebok probably once thrived along the coastal belt from Mossel Bay in the east to Caledon, Bredasdorp and Cape Agulhas in the west. By 1900 there were no longer any free-ranging bontebok; they survived only on a few farms where they had been protected by the landowners from the 1830s onwards. In the early 1920s the farms were sold and divided, and bontebok numbers fell.

In 1931 the first Bontebok National Park, comprising just 22 bontebok, was established on a portion of the farm Quarrie Bos; by 1939 there were 123 animals and several sub-populations were started on private farms and in nature reserves. However, the population again declined, and the present-day park was proclaimed in March 1961 with a starting population of 61 animals. Today there are more than 3 000 animals in various conservation areas; the park's population is maintained at around 200.

Aquatic water hyacinth, a South American alien, grows here.

The Breede River yellowwood favours sandy soils and can be found along rivers or streams.

Geology and landscape

As with the Langeberg range to the north, much of the exposed rock in the park consists of quartzites of the Table Mountain Group, with large areas of silcrete and conglomerates and shallow soils. The dominant features are the tall mountain range to the north and the river valley to the south, with the largely flat-bottomed, nearly circular valley towards the south-west.

Vegetation

Much of the park is dominated by what is known as Swellendam silcrete heathland, or fynbos, with alluvial (river floodplain) vegetation along the Breede River and minimally elsewhere. Vast swathes of this fynbos outside the park have been put to the plough, and the park contains one of the largest surviving pieces. The heathland is mostly of low to moderate height and includes a mix of protea species, such as the abundant **yellow bush** (*Leucadendron salignum*), which grows to a height of about 2 m. Two heathland structures can be easily recognized: areas where proteas and leucadendrons, or cone bushes, are dominant, and zones of mixed **renosterbos** (*Elytropappus rhinocerotis*). Some 470 plant species have been identified, including a number of heathland rarities.

The floodplain vegetation is generally short and consists of a mix of grasses, reeds and several tree species. Some tree species that grow here include **Breede River yellowwood** (*Podocarpus elongatus*), **Cape willow** (*Salix mucronata*), **wild olive** (*Olea europaea*) and **white milkwood** (*Sideroxylon inerme*). The white-thorned **sweet thorn** (*Vachellia karroo*) is most noticeable along the game-viewing road that runs along the south of the park near the river. In the river you will notice tangled masses of floating plants with swollen stems and pale violet clusters of flowers; this is the alien **water hyacinth**

CLIMATE

This is a winter rainfall area but rain can be expected throughout the year. The driest months are December and January, with 59% of falls between April and September. The annual average rainfall is 520 mm. Summer days are warm, around 28°C in January, and July temperatures remain over 5°C.

Vegetation map

- Swellendam silcrete fynbos
- Cape lowland alluvial vegetation

Bontebok National Park   **195**

FACILITIES AND ACTIVITIES

- Lang Elsie's Kraal Rest Camp has 10 self-catering chalets for 2–4 people.
- Caravan/camping sites at Lang Elsie.
- Three short hiking and walking trails (1.6, 3.3, 5.4 km).
- Mountain bike trail.
- Game-viewing road network of 25 km or more (gravel).
- Full range of services in Swellendam.

Some of the accomodation units look over the Breede River.

(*Eichhornia crassipes*). It was introduced here from the Americas as an ornamental plant in 1884 and has since become a major pest in water bodies in South Africa. Efforts at control have largely failed.

Wildlife
Mammals

The park was originally established to conserve the then endangered **bontebok**, but it is now managed to conserve all its biota, especially the vegetation. Small numbers of **Cape mountain zebra** and **red hartebeest** have been introduced, and **grey rhebok**, **Cape grysbok**, **common duiker** and **steenbok** occur naturally here. Of the 13 species of carnivore recorded in the park the largest is the **caracal**, but only the **small grey mongoose** is regularly seen, usually close to the river and around the camp. **Yellow mongoose** are day-active and so are sometimes sighted, mainly in more open areas away from the river. The resident **Cape fox** is occasionally seen, usually in the morning and late afternoon hours. There have also been rare sightings of the **African striped weasel.**

Birds

Some 201 species of bird have been recorded but several of these are rare vagrants, such as the kelp gull, Cape vulture and western osprey. On the open heathland the **southern black korhaan** is resident and **Denham's bustard** is sometimes seen. Watch out for the **black harrier**, a relatively common sight in these open areas, as well as **Cape clapper lark** and **Agulhas long-billed lark**. However, some of the best birding is in and around the camp and on the Aloe Hill Trail,

The park was originally established to protect the bontebok.

where it is enhanced by the proximity of the Breede River. Residents include **Cape robin-chat**, **bokmakierie**, **southern boubou**, **Cape spurfowl**, **red-winged starling**, **chestnut-vented tit-babbler** and **fork-tailed drongo**. Wherever there are aloes in flower, even in the camp, you are likely to see **Cape sugarbird**, **orange-breasted sunbird**, **malachite sunbird** and others. **Cape weavers** and **red-winged starlings** also frequent these sources of nectar. The **African paradise flycatcher** is a common summer breeding migrant.

Red-sided skinks are found in the vicinity of the river floodplain.

Reptiles and amphibians

Although few of the 28 species of reptile occurring in the park will be seen by the casual visitor, there are a few exceptions. **Angulate**, or **ploughshare**, **tortoises** are quite commonly seen along the sandy areas close to the river and in the camp, the smaller **parrot-beaked tortoise** more rarely. **Southern rock agama** are often seen in the rocky areas, especially in proximity to the river, as are **skinks** of at least three species. Snakes are seldom seen but walkers should be alert for the highly venomous **Cape cobra** and the **puff adder**; neither will attack unless provoked.

There are 10 known species of amphibians here; they are hard to spot, but at the right time of the year you are likely to hear the calls of the males of several species . In spring and summer, large numbers of **Ranger's toad** call from the Breede River. These toads are also often seen at night in the camp, foraging for insects.

Fish

With only 6 km of the Breede River running along the south of the park it is difficult to establish an accurate checklist of fish species. So far, twelve species, of which at least six are exotic to this river system, have been recorded locally. Two small endemic species, **Cape galaxias** and **Burchell's redfin**, have been recorded in the past but it is not clear whether they are still present.

Grey-winged francolin are present on higher ground.

WILDLIFE FACTS

- Initially established to conserve the endangered bontebok but now also important for floral diversity.
- Some 37 species of mammal, although several bat species are known from single reports.
- More than 200 bird species.
- 28 reptile and 10 amphibian species.

Bontebok National Park   **197**

AGULHAS NATIONAL PARK
South Africa's southernmost park

LOCATION

Lie of the land

This park covers 22 700 ha, including some outlying blocks of land. It lies at the southernmost tip of Africa; its southern boundary is formed by the confluence of the Atlantic and Indian oceans, though some argue that the true boundary between the oceans lies at Cape Point further to the west, as evidenced by some differences in marine organisms. Its south-eastern boundary adjoins the holiday town of L'Agulhas. The park is 72 km long and extends inland between 7 km and 25 km, stretching from Struisbaai in the east to near Pearly Beach in the west. The park incorporates approximately 45 km of sandy beaches and 60 km of rocky shoreline. The coastline is backed by sand dunes and limestone hills leading to rolling plains.

This stormy coastline around Africa's southernmost tip, at Agulhas, is the resting ground of many ships.

Brief history

The Agulhas area has a human prehistory and history stretching back more than a million years. Archaeological sites and stone tools date from the Earlier, Middle and Later Stone Ages. Later Stone Age sites from about 20 000 BP are found at De Walle, Hoek se Baai, Oubaai, Rasperpunt and Cape Agulhas. Limestone shelters, or overhangs, are located on cliffs overlooking Rasperpunt. Two main types of

198   Western Cape

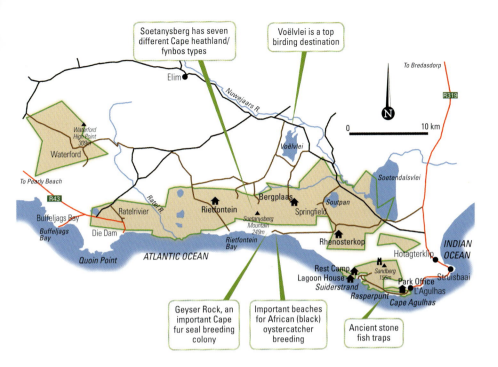

site are obvious: stone fish traps and shell 'kitchen' middens. The fish traps, known as *visvywers*, are large stone enclosures in the intertidal zone, probably built within the last 2 000 BP and maintained over the centuries. Good examples can be seen at L'Agulhas, Rasperpunt and Suiderstrand. 'Kitchen' middens are piles of mollusc shells above the high water mark, left over from food-gathering, possibly by Khoekhoen people.

Europeans entered the area in the early 1770s and by the early 19th century extensive farms had been established just inland. The town of Bredasdorp was established in 1838 by Michiel van Breda, a major landowner. On 1 March 1849 the Cape Agulhas lighthouse, now inside the eastern edge of the park, was inaugurated to guard this coast of treacherous reefs and severe gales.

The first small area of the national park was proclaimed in 1999, and much more land has since been added.

Geology and landscape

Looking northwards along the shoreline, you will see the remnant of a wave-cut platform that is largely covered by calcareous sands forming dunes and flats, with areas of shallow marine sandstones and limestones belonging to the Bredasdorp Group. Like much of the park area, this overlies the sandstones of the Table Mountain Group that

HIGHLIGHTS

- Cape Agulhas is the southernmost tip of the African continent.
- One of the richest areas of plant diversity for its size in the world.
- Excellent wetland, coastal and heathland (fynbos) birding.
- Numerous cultural heritage sites.

Agulhas lighthouse is in the east of the park.

Agulhas National Park **199**

A member of the protea family, Mimetes cucullatus, known as rooistompie, is prolific along the flats in this area.

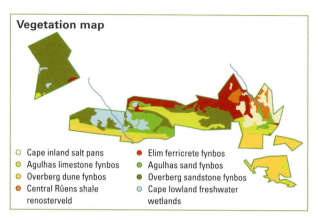

Vegetation map

○ Cape inland salt pans
○ Agulhas limestone fynbos
○ Overberg dune fynbos
● Central Rûens shale renosterveld
● Elim ferricrete fynbos
● Agulhas sand fynbos
● Overberg sandstone fynbos
○ Cape lowland freshwater wetlands

also form the Cape Folded mountains in the interior. Some of the low hills further inland consist of these same sandstones and some have cappings of limestone, an indication of higher sea levels in the past. Inland, the undulating plain is mainly made up of soils derived from Bokkeveld shales and Table Mountain sandstones. These are now among South Africa's most productive wheatlands. Many variations in soil structure and nutrients are found in the park, a major factor in its amazing plant diversity.

The landscape is greatly enriched by many small streams and other wetlands, such as (from west to east) the Groothagelkraal and Ratel streams, and the Melkbos, Vis, Waskraal and Sout pans.

Vegetation

Eleven distinct vegetation zones yield more than 40 subdivisions, each sharing a range of plants with its neighbours while having some that

These historic Strandloper fish traps are located near the lighthouse and eastern entrance of the park.

are unique to itself. The Agulhas Plain, large areas of which are now protected within the park, is one of the largest surviving storehouses of lowland heathland/fynbos and renosterveld in South Africa. There are probably close to 2 000 species of terrestrial plant. Lying roughly in the centre of the park, the Soetanysberg alone has seven different heathland types growing on its slopes and ridge, including four considered to be under serious threat in the rest of the Cape Floral Kingdom. Although most zones are forms of Cape heathland, a few such as the inland saltpans and the freshwater wetlands have their own plant species complexes. The most important heathland types here are characterized by the soil types in which they grow, such as Elim ferricrete fynbos, Agulhas limestone fynbos, Overberg sandstone fynbos and Rûens shale renosterveld. Overall it is a mix of short to medium-height heathland with a great diversity of proteas, ericas, daisy-type Asteraceae and reed-like restios. One of the most superb of all proteas, *Protea pudens*, grows very low to the ground and is limited to a small area on the Agulhas Plain. It produces its colourful bell-shaped flowers from May to September. Another creeping protea found here, *Protea aspera*, displays its yellowish flower heads from September to December. Rather more prominent is the tall (to 3.5 m) **Bot River protea** (*Protea compacta*), which offers its beautiful rich pinkish-red flower heads from April to July. Various species of **cone bush** (*Leucadendron*), another protea family member, abound here. SANParks is making concerted efforts to eradicate alien species, including **red eye**, or *rooikrans*, (*Acacia cyclops*) and **Port Jackson willow** (*Acacia saligna*), which form extensive stands of bushes on the plain and which once established, tend to overwhelm the indigenous species. There is also great diversity associated with the freshwater wetlands, with 53 species identified to date, and so far nine algae (seaweed) species are known along the coast but many more certainly occur.

CLIMATE

This is the windiest area in South Africa throughout the year. The westerly wind prevails in winter, the easterly in summer. Wind speeds of 35 km/h and more are common. It is a winter rainfall area, wettest between May and October. Annual rainfall measures between 400 mm and 600 mm, with the heaviest rains in the west. Heavy mist banks are common in autumn and winter. Annual average temperature is 15°C, with a mean daily maximum around 25°C to 27°C in January, and an average minimum of over 7°C in July. Both temperature and rainfall vary with distance from the coast, and this has encouraged plant diversity. Sea temperature ranges from 21°C in summer to 14 °C in winter.

Vegetation along the coastal strip has a low profile because of prevailing gale-force winds.

Agulhas National Park **201**

FACILITIES AND ACTIVITIES

- There are 15 chalets in the rest camp and several historic farmsteads have been upgraded for accommodation.
- Various camping and accommodation options in L'Agulhas and Struisbaai.
- Road network under development with upgrading of existing tracks, some accessible to 2x4 vehicles; also 4x4 trails.
- Walking, hiking and mountain bike trails.
- Fuel, supplies and other services in L'Agulhas and Struisbaai in the east and Gansbaai in the west. Bredasdorp, the nearest large town, is 35 km to the north and has most facilities.

Below: Kelp gulls, such as this one with its chicks, are common residents along the coast.
Right: Cape fur seals breed on Geyser Rock.

Wildlife
Mammals

The Agulhas Plain was never a big game area but certain nomadic species, such as **common eland** and **red hartebeest**, would certainly have spent time here. **Bontebok** were resident on the coastal plain, as are **common duiker**, **Cape grysbok**, **steenbok** and **grey rhebok** today. Few explorers and naturalists entered this area, so our historical knowledge of game species is limited. **Cape mountain zebra** may have lived in the hills. As this area is of critical botanical importance great care will have to be taken over which game species to reintroduce. There are occasional unconfirmed sightings of **leopard** in the area, but this realm belongs to the smaller carnivores. The Agulhas Plain is an important area for the **honey badger**, **Cape clawless otter** and **caracal**, but more commonly seen are the **small grey mongoose** and the **large grey**, or **Egyptian, mongoose**. The **otter**, seldom seen, forages in the freshwaters and along the coastline, where its tracks are visible on the beaches. On Geyser Rock, 3 km offshore, there is a breeding colony of **Cape fur seals** that produces several thousand pups each breeding season in early summer. Fur seals are commonly seen just offshore, and occasionally on mainland beaches and rocks. This is also an important area for **southern right whales**, and several species of dolphin are seen from time to time, especially in the more sheltered areas of the coast. Of the large number of rodent species here, several are found only in the Cape Floral Kingdom, such as **Cape dune mole-rat** (you will see their large mounds along the coastal strip), **Cape gerbil**, **Cape spiny mouse** and **Verreaux's mouse**. But the most visible is the day-active and very widespread **four-striped grass mouse**.

Birds

Both Dyer Island and Geyser Rock will be incorporated into the park through the marine protected component and are important breeding locations for **African penguin**, **Cape**, **crowned** and **bank**

202   Western Cape

The creeping pincushion is pollinated by small rodents.

WILDLIFE FACTS

- Some 65 species of mammal, including 21 rodents and 14 small carnivore species. Larger game, such as bontebok and common eland, will be introduced but maintained in low numbers.
- About 232 bird species with strong marine/coastal and wetland contingents and 133 terrestrial species.
- Only 24 reptile species reported but at least 22 more are expected to be added to this count.
- Some 15 amphibian species, with three classified as endangered.
- Despite extensive wetlands, only two indigenous fish species occur.
- Terrestrial, freshwater and marine invertebrate fauna is rich but poorly known.
- 1 750 plant species on record, 24% of which are regional endemics.

cormorants, as well as **kelp gulls**. The coastline is a particularly important breeding location for the threatened **African (black) oystercatcher**. During the summer, large numbers of Palearctic migrant waders are present on both the coastline and the freshwater wetlands, with counts exceeding 20 000 water birds at times. Large numbers gather to feed at Soetendalsvlei, Uilkraals River estuary and Voëlvlei. It is also a good location to watch for oceanic/pelagic birds, especially during or shortly after storms. Most of the bird species are terrestrial, and numerous **blue cranes** and smaller numbers of **Denham's bustard** breed on the inland plains. The heathland is home to **Cape sugarbird** and three species of sunbird, all important pollinators. In open areas watch for the **Agulhas long-billed lark**. **Cape spurfowl** and **grey-winged francolin** are fairly common, with the former mainly found on the coastal plain and the latter more in the uplands.

Reptiles and amphibians

Twenty-four reptile species have been recorded, and it is likely that more will be found. The abundant **angulate tortoise** favours sandy areas but is sighted throughout the park. The smaller **parrot-beaked tortoise** is less frequently seen. At least three sea turtle species probably occur in these waters, but only the **leatherback sea turtle** has been recorded, from beached youngsters carried southwards by the Agulhas Current. In some parts venomous snakes such as **Cape cobra**, **boomslang** and **puff adder** are common, although most species here are only mildly venomous or harmless. Of the park's 10 known species of lizard only two, the **southern rock agama** and the **Cape girdled lizard**, are commonly seen on rocky terrain in suitable weather.

The fiscal flycatcher swoops from its perch to catch insects on the ground.

Agulhas National Park **203**

The western leopard toad is an endangered species but finds sanctuary in the park.

There are 16 known species of amphibian, plus a possible species of moss frog. None is readily observed but the males may be heard calling during the breeding seasons. Three of the species found here, the **western leopard toad**, **Cape (Gill's) platanna** and the **micro frog**, have very limited ranges and are endangered.

Fish

Surprisingly, only two indigenous species of freshwater fish, the **Cape kurper** and **Cape galaxias**, are known, although four alien species occur within the Nuwejaars system to the east. Well over 100 marine species are already known, but further surveys should greatly increase this number. There are several shark species here, including the **great white shark**, probably attracted by the Cape fur seal population associated with Geyser Rock.

Invertebrates

Terrestrial, freshwater and marine invertebrate fauna are rich but poorly catalogued as yet. Three of the butterfly species in the park have very limited ranges and are endangered. The small *Argyrocupha malagrida maryae* is only known from Struisbaai and adjacent areas; one of the coppers, *Poecilimitis brooksi tearei*, has its westernmost range limit in the park, and one of the 'seaside' thestors, **Rossouw's skolly**, is found between Stanford and the west of the park, a very limited range. The marine environment is extremely important for its substantial populations of **perlemoen**, a valuable commercial shellfish that is seriously threatened by poaching.

Cape galaxias is one of only two indigenous freshwater fish species occurring in the park.

- Inshore currents and tides can be treacherous.
- Weather extremes are possible year-round; hikers should be prepared.
- Stick strictly to demarcated roads and trails as these are very sensitive ecosystems.

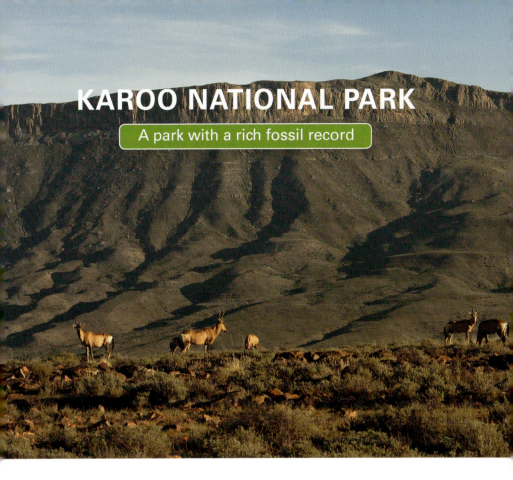

KAROO NATIONAL PARK
A park with a rich fossil record

Lie of the land
Karoo National Park, which exceeds 88 000 ha, is in the north-east of the Western Cape province, abutting the border with the Northern Cape province. It lies in the heart of the Great Karoo with the Nuweveld mountain range and escarpment forming an amphitheatre backdrop to the plains that make up the bulk of this conservation area. The escarpment cliffs rise to 1 912 m above sea level but the mountainous areas constitute just 5% of the park, whereas much of the flatland lies below 1 000 m, averaging 850 m above sea level. The plateau rises in two steps, the middle sector which extends from about 1 100 m and the northern upper plateau which extends beyond 1 750 m. The plains are scored by numerous, usually dry, watercourses that rise on the escarpment. On a clear day, far to the south, one can see the Swartberg Mountains.

LOCATION
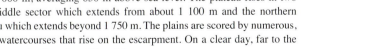

Brief history
The area centred on the park has an extremely rich fossil record and a short interpretive trail explains a little about this treasure house. Many of these fossils are found in sedimentary rocks of the Beaufort Group that were laid down about

Red hartebeest are one of many game species reintroduced into this rugged park.

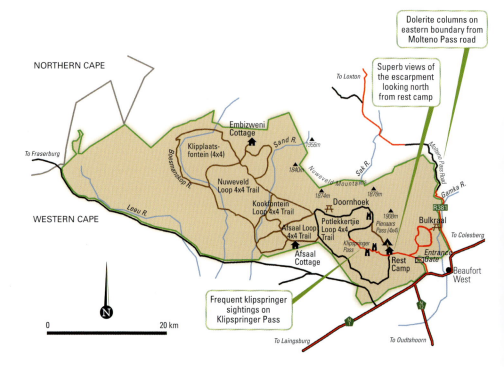

HIGHLIGHTS

- Spectacular escarpment scenery.
- Interesting mix of game species, including savanna buffalo and hook-lipped rhinoceros.
- One of the best locations to observe klipspringer and grey rhebok.
- Excellent arid area birding.
- Easy access.

250 000 000 BP as the Karoo Sea was silting up. Not much work on early humans has been undertaken here but certainly San people had been in the area for several thousand years, and Khoekhoen herders with their livestock probably settled as long ago as 2 000 BP.

These peoples were here when the first Europeans arrived in the early 18th century. The Gamka River is a Khoekhoen word for lion and at that time, Africa's largest cat was said to be abundant. However in March 1783 the explorer-naturalist Francois le Vaillant noted that because settlers had largely hunted out their antelope prey, lion had already become scarce and were now mainly to be found along the Nuweveld escarpment; yet they were still sometimes hunted hereabouts even as late as 1820. Other large predators at that time were cheetah, leopard, spotted hyaena and wild dog, none of which survive here today. In November 1778 Robert Jacob Gordon shot a hook-lipped rhinoceros apparently along the Gamka River, just 10 km outside present-day Beaufort West. Travellers observed herds of thousands of springbok throughout the early 1800s, and even up to 1920 springbok were encountered in herds hundreds strong.

Many remain on farms in the area, but the days of the great migrations are gone. The Karoo National Park was proclaimed in 1979 with commonage land donated by the town of Beaufort West and incorporating the farm Stolshoek. Since then the park has been greatly enlarged from its original 20 000 ha.

Rocks in the area are rich in fossils.

CLIMATE

Although this is mainly a summer rainfall area with 60 to 75% of rain in this season, falls may occur in winter, and are more likely in the east. Annual rainfall averages 250 mm but may vary from 175 mm to 406 mm across the park, and most rain falls on the high plateau, often during thunderstorms. It is a drought-prone area, with occasional flash floods following heavy rains. The upper areas of the great escarpment experience what is known as a cool steppe climate, while the lowland has a warm steppe climate. During the hot summers daytime maximum temperatures regularly exceed 32°C (42+°C on record), and during the cool to cold winters the mean minimum temperature is 3.5°C, with an average daily maximum of 18°C. The lowest minimum recorded on the upper plateau was -15°C. Mild to heavy frosts occur in winter, especially at higher altitudes, with occasional snowfalls on the peaks. Prevailing winds are south-westerly or east-south-east in summer, and north or north-westerly in winter. The growing season lasts just over seven months.

Geology and landscape

About 95% of the park consists of flat or undulating country, with low hills to the north (the middle plateau), but the steep cliffs of the Nuweveld Mountains dominate the park. Several seasonal rivers rise in or near the park. The Gamka, Sand, Boesmanskop and Leeu rivers drain to the south and feed into the Gamka. The headwaters of the Sak River rise on the north side of the escarpment and drain northwards. Many lesser seasonal streams cut into the southern plains, or pediment. Rocks here all belong to the Karoo Supergroup and include the Dwyka, Ecca and Beaufort formations. The Beaufort mudstones and sandstones overlie the Ecca Group. Jurassic age dolerite has extensively intruded into, and overlies, the Beaufort rock strata in the form of dykes and sheets. These are the concentrically scalloped intrusions that can be clearly seen forming the upper reaches of the middle and upper plateaux. These lava dolerite sills and sheets are up to 100 m thick in places, and the scarps form a palisade-like structure, in places forming into clusters of columns. One of the best examples of this can be seen on the initial climb up the public road to Loxton that skirts the eastern boundary of the park.

Vegetation

The vegetation can be divided into three major groups, associated with the three altitude levels: the upper and middle plateaux, and the plain. Botanists recognize at least 13 distinct types, with overlaps. On the upper plateau with its higher rainfall and harsher winters, fairly dense grassland dominates, with mainly **mountain wire grass** (*Merxmuellera disticha*) and a scattering of **resin bush** (*Euryops* spp.). This mix occasionally leads to fires from lightning strikes during storms. Permanent pools, fringed with **common reed** (*Phragmites australis*), are located along the headwaters of the Sak

Vegetation map

- Karoo escarpment grassland
- Upper Karoo hardeveld
- Gamka Karoo
- Western upper Karoo

River. Although mountain wire grass also grows on the highest reaches of the middle plateau, vegetation diversity here is greater and includes areas of **iron grass** (*Aristida diffusa*), while along watercourses there are dense thickets of **sweet thorn** (*Vachellia karroo*), **common spike-thorn** (*Maytenus heterophylla*), **parsley tree** (*Heteromorpha arborescens*), **dogwood** (*Rhamnus prinoides*), **camphor tree** (*Tarchonanthus camphoratus*) and several species of low bushes belonging to the genus *Rhus*. Other areas have a mix of typical low Karoo bushes (under 1 m) like those in the low-lying plains. On the plains, among other grasses, there is **foxtail buffalo grass** (*Cenchrus ciliaris*) and **thimble grass** (*Fingerhuthia africana*), with low growth such as **anchor Karoo** (*Pentzia incana*), a variety of Hermannia species, **sheep blue-bush** (*Monechma incanum*) and several species of **cotton bush** (*kapokbos*) (*Eriocephalus*). Along some watercourses there are stands of the white-thorned **sweet thorn**, **karee tree** (*Rhus lancea*), **lye bush** (*Salsola aphylla*) and several species of **wolf thorn** (*Lycium* spp.). Many areas of the park, especially in the plains, were badly overgrazed and eroded in the era of commercial farming. A slow recovery is in progress.

Wildlife
Mammals

Of the 67 species of mammal, several were reintroduced after the historic populations were hunted to extinction. Among these are **lion**, **hook-lipped rhinoceros**, **Cape mountain zebra**, **common eland**, **red hartebeest**, **southern oryx** (**gemsbok**), **brown hyaena** and **mountain reedbuck**. **Greater kudu** are now common and occur widely along watercourses outside the park. There are also **springbok**, **grey rhebok**, **common duiker** and **steenbok**, and the rock-dwelling **klipspringer** is fairly common. **Rock hyrax** (**dassies**)

Karoo violet in full bloom.

The snake aloe flowers in spring.   *A historic stone leopard trap testifies to the presence of this animal.*

Quagga-like plains zebra were removed from the park in 2016 to prevent them from breeding with Cape mountain zebra.

are common wherever there is suitable habitat in the rocky areas, as witnessed by extensive 'whitewashing' from their urine on the rocks. **Chacma baboons** occur throughout the escarpment and on the slopes, occasionally venturing onto the plains along the wooded watercourses. **Vervet monkeys** are mainly restricted to the river courses with stands of sweet thorn trees. Of the 18 rodent species you are only likely to see the **four-striped grass mouse**, especially around the campground; interestingly the **pygmy rock mouse**, present only in the highest reaches of the escarpment, is at the easternmost limit of its range here. Fifteen species of carnivore are known, and another, the **leopard**, possibly traverses the higher reaches of the park. **Lion** are regularly heard and sighted in the park. The visitor is most likely to see solitary **small grey mongoose** in areas of dense vegetation, **yellow mongoose** and **suricate** in more open terrain; **black-backed**

FACILITIES AND ACTIVITIES

- Some 38 units for accommodation, including 6-bed family cottages and 3-bed chalets and cottages; caravan/camping sites.
- Two rustic cottages situated outside the main rest camp for overnight stays.
- Restaurant and shop, but no fuel.
- Guided hiking trails; short nature trails (fossils, Karoo bushes) at Main Rest Camp.
- Accompanied game-viewing and night drives.
- More than 80 km of game-viewing roads, tarred and gravel, and four 4x4 trails.
- Located 3 km north-west of Beaufort West, which has a full range of services available.

The rest camp is set against the impressive backdrop of the Nuweveld Escarpment.

WILDLIFE FACTS

- Some 67 mammal species including reintroduced lion, hook-lipped rhinoceros, brown hyaena, Cape mountain zebra, mountain reedbuck and common eland.
- At least 220 species of bird, including particularly dense Verreaux's eagle population.
- Some 68 species of reptiles, including five tortoises and 11 amphibians; park is regarded as an extremely important biogeographic refuge.
- Just one species of fish, the chubbyhead barb, in headwaters of the north-flowing Sak River.
- About 864 plant species belonging to 93 families.

Steenbok are common on the open plains.

The white-backed mousebird is one of three mousebird species, all of which occur in the park.

jackal may be heard calling in early evening and morning hours. There is a fairly high density of **caracal** but these moderate-sized cats are very rarely seen.

Birds

The number of bird species that have been recorded here stands at 220, although this total includes vagrants and occasional visitors. The park is well known for its unusually dense population of **Verreaux's eagle**, with perhaps as many as 20 breeding pairs. The abundant hyrax make up much of this eagle's diet. In fact, with 23 raptors on the checklist, Karoo National Park is a bird of prey hotspot. **Booted eagles** are known to nest here and **black harrier** are commonly seen hunting on the escarpment. The cliffs are also nesting locales for such species as **African harrier-hawk**, **jackal buzzard** and **rock kestrel**. **Common ostrich** are usually seen on the plains, as are **kori** and **Ludwig's bustards**, and the **Karoo korhaan**. As usual, the camp is one of your best starting points for birding. Unfortunately, the bird hide in the camp is usually masked from the waterhole by dense vegetation but it is still worth having a look, and a dedicated birder should be able to mark off at least 30 species in the camp and especially the well-wooded campground. Species likely to be seen are **African red-eyed bulbul**, **Namaqua warbler**, **acacia pied barbet**, **dusky sunbird**, **pririt batis**, **fairy flycatcher**, **common cuckoo** and all three species of South African **mousebirds**. The tarred road up the Klipspringer Pass brings you within reach of mountain-dwellers such as **short-toed rock-thrush**, **ground woodpecker**, **long-billed** and **African rock pipits**, and **pale-winged starling**.

Reptiles and amphibians

No fewer than 68 reptiles, including six tortoises (five land tortoises; one terrapin), and 11 amphibian species have been recorded, the greatest diversity for any similar-sized area in the world. The sole aquatic tortoise is the **marsh terrapin**; the largest of the land-

At least 20 breeding pairs of Verreaux's eagle are active in the park.

The female ground agama lays her clutch of eggs in a hole she has dug in the ground. The eggs hatch after about two months.

dwellers is the **leopard tortoise**, which frequents mainly low-lying areas, especially around river courses. A few visit the campground lawns for easy, well-watered meals. The other four species are much smaller, habitat-specific and seldom seen. Of the 35 lizard species, eight are thick-toed geckos (*Chondrodactylus* & *Pachydactylus* spp.) but only **Bibron's thick-toed gecko** is likely to be encountered, both because of its relatively large size and because it frequents buildings in the camp, where it catches insects attracted to the lights. The sand-burrowing **common barking gecko** is not likely to be seen, but on warm evenings the males give their chirping bark from the mouths of their burrows. By far the largest lizard here is the **rock monitor** but it seems to favour the escarpment and is not often seen. Improbably for such an arid area, two species of chameleon occur, the ground living **Namaqua chameleon**, and the tree dwelling **Karoo dwarf chameleon**. One of the most commonly sighted lizards is the rock-dwelling **southern rock agama**. To date 18 snake species are known and although several are common, they are seldom seen. **Cape cobra** is found throughout the park at all altitudes, and the **horned adder** is particularly common in the plains and parts of the middle plateau. The calls of male amphibians may be heard after rain, but of the 11 species, the only one readily encountered is the **Karoo toad**, which hunts insects at night under the lights around buildings.

Fish

Just one small, shoaling fish species has been recorded here. The **chubbyhead barb** is found in reed-fringed pools near the source of the Sak River on the plateau.

- Since the reintroduction of lion in the park, walking on trails outside the main camp is no longer permitted unless hikers are accompanied by an armed ranger.
- Be prepared for extreme heat in summer and below-freezing temperatures in winter.

WEST COAST NATIONAL PARK

Protects greatest numbers of Palearctic waders

LOCATION

The Postberg section of the West Coast National Park is only open to visitors during the spring flowering season.

Lie of the land

West Coast National Park is bounded by the Atlantic Ocean for about 30 km, with Saldanha Bay in the north and the sheltered Langebaan Lagoon to the south. The park covers 40 233 ha, of which approximately 5 600 ha is taken up by the lagoon. The lagoon is separated from the ocean by a narrow spit of land (about 2 km wide and 15 km long) that terminates with Postberg and a closed military area. Most of the terrain is flat or slightly undulating, broken only by sand dunes along the coast, low ridges of limestone and calcrete, and low granite outcrops in the far north. The highest of these outcrops are Vlaeberg at 193 m above sea level and Konstabelkop at 189 m above sea level. Islands, including Marcus, Malgas and Jutten, are included in the park. The park is approximately 100 km north of Cape Town and just south of Saldanha, and it forms the northern core of the West Coast Biosphere Reserve.

Brief history

The calcrete areas near the dunes at Geelbek and the adjacent Elandsfontein are renowned for their mammalian fossil riches. Abundant fossils dating back to

212 Western Cape

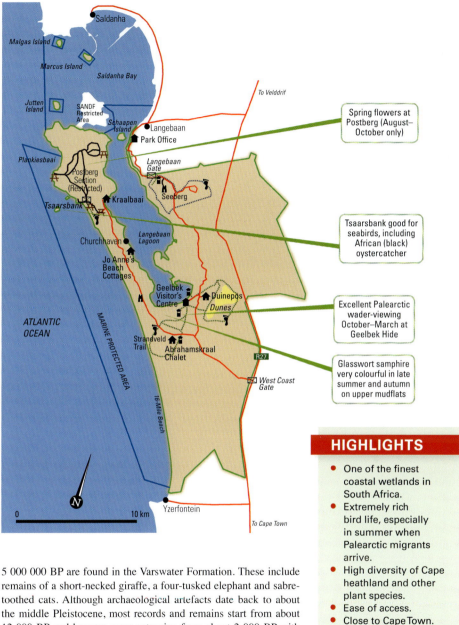

HIGHLIGHTS

- One of the finest coastal wetlands in South Africa.
- Extremely rich bird life, especially in summer when Palearctic migrants arrive.
- High diversity of Cape heathland and other plant species.
- Ease of access.
- Close to Cape Town.
- Very high diversity of marine organisms in both Saldanha Bay and Langebaan Lagoon.

5 000 000 BP are found in the Varswater Formation. These include remains of a short-necked giraffe, a four-tusked elephant and sabre-toothed cats. Although archaeological artefacts date back to about the middle Pleistocene, most records and remains start from about 12 000 BP and become more extensive from about 2 000 BP with the arrival of the stock-keeping Khoekhoen. The most visible relics are stone fish traps and large 'kitchen' middens made up of mollusc shells and other waste. An 117 000-year-old set of fossilized human footprints, now preserved in a museum, was found in the park, and since then a more extensive 'trackway' has been discovered.

The southern sector of the Langebaan Lagoon is dominated by succulent glasswort samphire.

At Oudepost 1 at Kraalbaai, the first known meeting took place between officials of the Dutch East India Company (VOC) and local Khoekhoen. Early European travellers to the region reported sightings of elephant, hook-lipped rhinoceros, common eland and red hartebeest. The Geelbek building on the Langebaan Lagoon is a restored farmhouse and now a heritage site.

In 1973 the Langebaan Lagoon was proclaimed a reserve, and the Langebaan National Park was established in 1985. In 1988 the name was changed to West Coast National Park. The park covers about 38 000 ha and the aim is to nearly double this extent in the future.

CLIMATE

The area experiences a mild, semi-arid Mediterranean climate. Most of the mean annual rainfall of 265 mm occurs during the winter months, but precipitation from fog supplements this, especially in summer and autumn. Wind is frequent, strong south-easterlies prevailing in the summer and north-westerlies in the winter. Monthly maximums range from 18.4°C to 27.5°C, with monthly minimums between 7°C and 15°C.

Geology and landscape

The Langebaan Lagoon is tidal and subtidal and mostly under 4 m in depth, and this and Saldanha Bay are the dominant landscape features. Much of the surrounding terrain is low-lying, consisting mainly of calcrete sheets and loose sands, with the occasional granite outcrop. The basement rocks are of the Malmesbury formation and were laid down as marine sediments some 700 million years BP. The ocean levels have advanced and receded repeatedly, at times reaching approximately the 150 m contour. The last advance occurred about 9 000 years BP, when the barrier dune line was breached between the granite headlands, and the present-day lagoon and bay were formed. The northern breach has remained open and allows oceanic water circulation, mainly in the north of the lagoon. Near the coast most of the ancient bedrock lies buried by up to 90 m of sand, or as much as 60 m underwater. Successive intrusions of molten volcanic rock have resulted in today's isolated exposed granite outcrops, mainly in the north of the park. These are granites, quartz monzonite and quartz porphyry of the Langebaan-Saldanha Pluton. The sandy soils, derived from marine deposits, contain a large proportion of calcareous material and some of the older sand dunes have become calcified into a sandy limestone through a process of water leaching. Near Geelbek these limestones reach a thickness of 88 m.

Vegetation

Most of the park is dominated by the vegetation of the Cape Floral Kingdom, that is Cape heathland or fynbos, and includes Saldanha flats sandveld in the north-east and south-east, and large expanses of Langebaan dune strandveld that surrounds much of the lagoon and extends into the Postberg. Also in Postberg there is Saldanha granite strandveld and to the south-east, areas of Hopefield sand fynbos. Each has its own unique species as well as some it shares with other groups. The vegetation around the lagoon is made up of dense shrubs up to 2 m, but most plants are lower, and include such species as **yellow daisy-bush** (or **geelknopbos**) (*Pteronia divaricata*), **sweet milkbush** (*Euphorbia burmannii*) and, after good winter rains, a magnificent showing of annual flowering plants. This draws many visitors to Postberg in spring. The Saldanha flats strandveld as well as the granite strandveld also offer these dramatic floral displays. Flats strandveld also has fairly abundant succulents, including *Tylecodon wallichii* and the **yellow milkbush** (*Euphorbia mauritanica*) with its pencil-like stems. In the Hopefield sand fynbos there are more 'typical' heathland species such as the protea *Leucospermum rodolentum* with small but numerous 'pincushion' flower heads and the **cone bushes** (*Leucadendron foedum* and *L. pubescens*). The strandveld vegetation types cover more than 24 000 ha of the park, with just over 6 000 ha of Hopefield sand fynbos. The rich flora has been split into more than 36 botanical communities. The aquatic flora is similarly diverse, with more than 200 species of green, brown and red algae (seaweed) in the bay and lagoon, and more than 50 species of plant associated with the lagoon's salt marshes, the most extensive in South Africa. Plant diversity and density is highest in the south of the lagoon, and species include **glasswort samphire** (*Sarcocornia perennis*), **cord grass** (*Spartina maritima*) and **common reed** (*Phragmites australis*).

Wildlife
Mammals

Historically many game species such as elephant, hook-lipped rhinoceros, common eland and lion roamed the area, but most were probably at least partly nomadic because of the low nutrient levels of the vegetation. **Common eland** and **red hartebeest** have been reintroduced, and **Cape grysbok**, **steenbok** and **common duiker** occur naturally. **Grey rhebok** has been reported but has not been recently confirmed. No fewer than 19 rodent species are recorded but only two day-active species may show themselves, the **four-striped grass mouse** and the **bush karoo rat**. The former forages around

Vegetation map

○ Cape inland salt pans
○ Cape seashore vegetation
● Langebaan dune strandveld
● Saldanha flats strandveld
● Saldanha granite strandveld
● Cape estuarine salt marshes
● Hopefield sand fynbos

The sour fig thrives in the coastal sands of the south-western Cape.

West Coast National Park **215**

FACILITIES AND ACTIVITIES

- Good choice of accommodation both in and adjacent to the park, including moored houseboats.
- Restaurant at Geelbek, several in Langebaan.
- Various aquatic activities, including boating in different forms, scuba diving and swimming, are all governed by a zoning system.
- Bird-watching – four hides on east side of Langebaan Lagoon.
- Hiking trails of 1–2 days; circular walks from Geelbek.
- Biking trails.
- Flower-viewing in Postberg section in season.
- Road network of about 80 km (50 km tarred) for game-viewing and bird-watching.
- Towns of Langebaan and Saldanha have a full range of services. All approach roads are tarred.

The Duinepos chalets in the park are privately run.

Although not a big game reserve, the park is home to eland.

picnic sites and is easy to identify by the clear black stripes on its back. Bush karoo rats are greyish-brown and much larger; they build stick nests at ground level that can measure more than 1 m across. In the barrier dunes close to the ocean they use mussel shells to 'tile' the roofs of their nests. There are 13 carnivore species but most are secretive and/or nocturnal, although **small grey mongoose**, **yellow mongoose** and **bat-eared fox** are quite commonly seen. The largest is the **caracal** which is quite common, like the **honey badger** and **black-backed jackal**. **Grant's golden mole** lives in the loose dune sands but often emerges at night to hunt on the surface, when it may fall prey to owls. **Cape fur seals** have for several years ceased to breed on the islands in Saldanha Bay, although they are frequently seen and are important predators of birds on these islands. **Southern right whales** are often seen from the north-west of the Langebaan Peninsula and it is now known that they have a feeding ground off the west coast; until recently it was thought that they fed only in the Antarctic. **Humpback whales** are sometimes observed travelling to and from their breeding grounds near the equator. Four **dolphin** species are commonly seen close inshore; they are the **dusky**, **common**, **Atlantic bottlenose**, and the little west coast endemic **Haviside's**, which travels in small schools.

Birds

This is one of the most important wintering grounds (October to March) for Palearctic waders in the Western Cape with about 26% of the total. You might record up to 20 species but you should certainly see at least half that number. Over a 20-year period the waders averaged 34 700 birds annually, of which 90% were Palearctic breeding species. A single species, the **curlew sandpiper**, constitutes about half

Large numbers of Cape gannet breed on offshore islands here.

WILDLIFE FACTS

- A total of 54 terrestrial mammals occur, as well as a wide range of marine mammals, including southern right whale and Haviside's dolphin.
- The 308 species occurring here make it a top birding destination, especially for Palearctic waders in summer.
- There are 33 reptile species, including substantial populations of angulate tortoises and two species of girdled lizard.
- Some eight species of amphibian.
- About 29 species of bony fish and five of cartilaginous fish (sharks and rays); probably many more as yet unrecorded in the bay and lagoon.
- More than 400 species of marine invertebrate in the Langebaan Lagoon alone.
- Over 200 species of marine algae in Saldanha Bay and Langebaan Lagoon; more than 500 species of terrestrial plant.

this number, and three more species account for another 27%. At times numbers may soar to more than 70 000. During the southern winter more than 10 000 'local' waders are present, including substantial numbers of both **greater** and **lesser flamingos**. The best wader-watching is on an outgoing tide as the waters are shallow and the mudflats become exposed. For optimal mud-flat birding, Geelbek is best from 4.5 hours after high tide or two hours after low tide in Table Bay; Seeberg is best 1.5 hours either side of high tide. High tide is also good as the waders are pushed in to shore to roost. Dedicated twitchers tout the hide at Geelbek as South Africa's best for waders, although all are good. The islands have large breeding colonies, including more than 50 000 pairs of **Cape gannet**, more than 24 000 pairs of **Cape cormorant** and smaller numbers of rare species such as **African penguin**, and **crowned** and **bank cormorants**. Large numbers of **kelp** and **Hartlaub's gulls** also breed on the islands, and the breeding colony of kelp gulls on Schaapen Island is the largest in South Africa. Besides the numerous aquatic or wetland species, the park has the highest density of **black harriers** in South Africa and there is a great diversity of sandveld birds. **Cape spurfowl** are common throughout but **grey-winged francolin** are more sparse and secretive. The Abrahamskraal waterhole in the south of the park is one of the few fresh water sources, and it attracts many bird species.

Reptiles

There are 33 reptile species in the park, but only a few are regularly seen. During mild and warm weather you will almost certainly see the common **angulate tortoise**. Although 17 species of snake are known they are seldom seen, except perhaps for a **Cape cobra**, **puff adder** or one of the **whip snakes** crossing a road or pathway. The very rare **southern adder**, first described as late as 1997, has lost much of its habitat to development and now finds refuge in the park. It is a small adder averaging

Great white pelican.

The Namaqua rain frog is nocturnal and seldom seen but its distinctive tracks are proof of its presence.

28 cm in length, but some specimens exceed 40 cm. Thirteen lizard species are known and at least three more will almost certainly be confirmed. The small and secretive burrowing species are commonly overlooked. Most visitors will have difficulty identifying fleet-footed species such as the slender **sand lizards**, but the larger species such as the **Cape girdled lizard** and the **southern rock agama** display themselves on the rocks.

Fish

Some 29 species of bony fish and five sharks and rays are recorded within the lagoon. One of the most abundant predators is the **lesser sandshark** that feeds on bottom-dwelling molluscs and crabs, which it crushes with its flattened 'pavement' teeth. Although fish diversity is much lower here than on the south coast, a number of commercially important species occur, and the lagoon is an important feeding ground and nursery for several of these.

Invertebrates

Little work has been done on the terrestrial invertebrates in the park, but the aquatic organisms are better known. More than 400 species have been identified but over 60% of the invertebrate biomass is made up by one tiny 4 mm-long gastropod, the **globular mud snail**. These snails are a vital food source for many animals, including such wading birds as the curlew sandpiper. The lagoon is the only known location for the **slipper limpet**, South Africa's most endangered mollusc. Unfortunately, several aliens have established themselves, probably imported by ship into Saldanha harbour. These include the **Mediterranean mussel**, which now outnumbers local mussel species, a species of periwinkle and of anemone, and the **European shore crab**, a ferocious predator that poses a serious threat to several local mollusc species.

Below: Access to bird hides is along boardwalks.
Right: A historic Cape Dutch farmstead now houses the Geelbek visitor centre, which incorporates a restaurant and an education centre.

- Caution should be exercised with any water-related activity.
- Activity zones should be carefully noted.

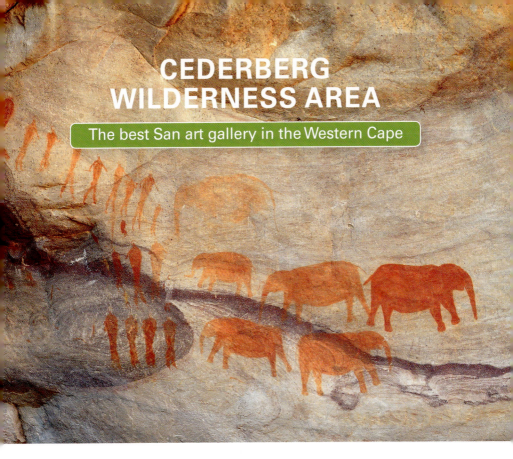

CEDERBERG WILDERNESS AREA
The best San art gallery in the Western Cape

Lie of the land
The core of the wilderness is formed by the Cederberg Mountains, with its highest peak the Sneeuberg rising to 2 027 m above sea level, with several other peaks topping 1 600 m above sea level. To the east the Matjiesrivier Nature Reserve extension spreads into the Tanqua Karoo. The main block of the Cederberg covers 71 000 ha, with the Matjiesrivier sector extending over some 12 000 ha. A group of cooperative conservancies bordering the wilderness area, covering over 492 000 ha, helps to form a buffer around the wilderness. A number of feeder streams of the Olifants River descend from the western flank of the watershed. The Cederberg is nearly the northernmost range of the Cape Folded Belt system and separates the Atlantic coastal plain from the arid interior plateau. It is located about 200 km north of Cape Town, with Clanwilliam close to its north-west and Citrusdal to its south-west point.

Brief history
The Cederberg range is the major San 'art gallery' in the Western Cape. There are several hundred rock painting sites in this and adjoining north-south mountain ranges. Only a few are well known and readily accessible. Many of the most

LOCATION

Some of the finest examples of San rock art in the Western Cape can be found in the Cederberg.

Cederberg Wilderness Area   219

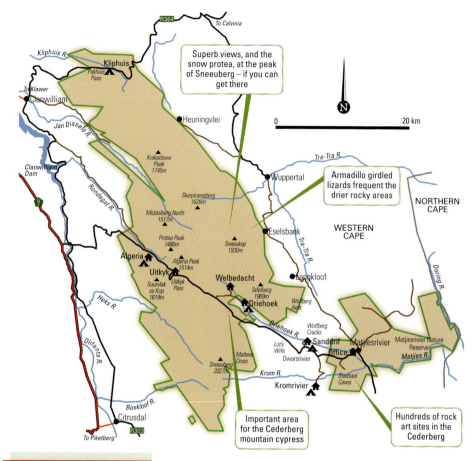

HIGHLIGHTS

- Spectacular scenery.
- Great diversity of plant species belonging to the Cape heathland, as well as succulents of the Tankwa Karoo within eastern Matjiesrivier.
- Considerable network of hiking trails, allowing access to many parts of the wilderness.
- Western Cape's greatest collection of San rock paintings.
- Good chance of seeing grey rhebok, klipspringer and Cape grysbok.

important sites lie on privately owned land within the greater conservancy complex. More than 125 sites are situated in the Bushman's Kloof Wilderness Reserve but, unfortunately, casual visits are discouraged. On the property Sevilla (Travellers Rest) there is one of southern Africa's finest San rock painting locations. These paintings vary in age, but the San were here before the arrival of the Khoekhoen people, perhaps more than 1 500 years BP.

It is claimed that the first Europeans to set eyes on the Cederberg were Bartolomeu Dias and his men who saw the range in 1488 from their ship, and named it the *Serra dos Reis* – 'the mountains of the three wise men of the East'. The Olifants River valley was settled by farmers as early as 1725 and Clanwilliam, one of the oldest towns in South Africa, was first named Jan Dissels Valley before being renamed in 1814 in honour of the Earl of Clanwilliam. On the west flank of the Cederberg range, elephant were once abundant; on 8 December 1660 Jan Dankoert and his party saw between 200 and 300 elephants on the slopes close to present-day Citrusdal. Just 100 years later it was reported that they had been hunted to extinction in the area. The Cederberg once had large stands of indigenous cedar trees but excessive harvesting brought this fine tree to the brink of extinction. Harvesting started at the end of the 18th century and at that time there were obviously some giants; one 'cut down in 1836 measured 36 feet in girth, whilst 1 000 feet of plank were sawn out of its giant arms.' In 1879, 7 250 cedars were felled to provide telegraph poles for the new 290 km line between Piketberg and Calvinia.

The Cederberg Wilderness was proclaimed in 1973 and is part of the Cape Floristic Kingdom World Heritage Site. The Matjiesrivier extension became a nature reserve in 1995. The reserves and large tracts of privately owned land lie within the jointly managed Greater Cederberg Conservation Area.

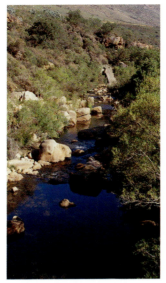

Streams, like this one near Algeria, flow throughout the area.

CLIMATE

This is a winter rainfall area with 70% of rain from May to August. West-facing slopes receive higher rainfall (averaging 450 mm) than east-facing ones. The Matjiesrivier sector averages 350 mm in the west, declining eastwards to just 200 mm. In the high-lying areas, fog also contributes to the precipitation levels and snowfalls are quite frequent during winter, with up to 10 days of frost. Average daily maximum temperature in February is about 29°C but 40°C has been recorded, whereas July average minimum is between 4°C and 5°C.

Geology and landscape

The mountain range, part of the Cape Folded Belt, is made up of hard sandstones belonging to the Table Mountain Group, producing

Over time, the Table Mountain sandstone has eroded to form a rock arch.

Vegetation map

- Cederberg sandstone fynbos
- Olifants sandstone fynbos
- Agter-Sederberg shrubland
- Swartruggens quartzite fynbos
- Swartruggens quartzite Karoo
- Northern inland shale band vegetation
- Western altimontane sandstone fynbos

acidic soils. It presents varying slopes, with bare rock and cliffs particularly on the west-facing aspects, and a more gentle aspect over parts of the east. Dramatically eroded landscapes can be seen at the top of the Pakhuis Pass. The Welbedacht Valley splits the Tafelberg and Sneeuberg ridges in the south. The Witteberg Group quartzite rocks extend to the Matjies River in the east, and the landscape is dominated by rocky ridges and plains.

Vegetation

The Cederberg range can be divided into two major heathland/fynbos types. The west-facing slopes, which receive a higher rainfall, support Olifants sandstone fynbos, while the eastern slopes are clothed with Cederberg sandstone fynbos. The rocky slopes, especially to the west, provide some protection against fire, and here one finds mainly relatively dense thicket growth and asteraceous ('daisy') vegetation with a mix of low tree species, such as **rockwood** (*Heeria argentea*), **wild peach** (*Kiggelaria africana*), **lance-leaved myrtle** (*Metrosideros angustifolia*) and **wagon tree** (*Protea nitida*). Here most protea species are found on the lower slopes, strongly mixed with reed-like restios, especially in areas with deeper sand cover. The eastern slopes often have a greater area under restios, dominated by low shrub in the driest parts. The wagon tree is a tall species with grey-green leaves and whitish-cream flower heads throughout the year. The soils become drier towards the east. Throughout the mountains,

The Clanwilliam cedar is highly endangered.

Grey rhebok regularly graze along the shale belt.

Western Cape

The snow protea is found on mountain tops in the Cederberg.

The smooth-leaf sugarbush grows 1 000 m above sea level.

FACILITIES AND ACTIVITIES

- Accommodation is limited, but there are two campgrounds: Algeria with 48 sites and Kliphuis on Pakhuis Pass with 10. Several guest farms and luxury lodges in the surrounds.
- Extensive network of hiking trails up to several days long, with overnight huts.
- Mountain bike trails.
- Rock climbing.
- Some of the finest San rock art sites in Africa.
- No fuel or supplies available in the wilderness area but Citrusdal and Clanwilliam have both.

except in exposed rock areas, there is a strong diversity of geophytes (bulbous plants), including no fewer than 62 species in the family Iridaceae. The Cederberg is also home to at least 52 Restionaceae species, 60 members of the protea family (Protaceae) and 53 species and subspecies of heath (Ericaceae). In all, there are well over 1 000 plant species. In the gorges on the drier slopes one finds the **wild olive** (*Oleae europaea*), **silky bark** (*Maytenus acuminata*) and **spoonwood** (*Hartogiella schinoides*). Of course there is the tree for which the mountains were named: the **Clanwilliam cedar**, or **mountain cypress**, (*Widdringtonia cedarbergensis*). It grows in the 'cedar zone' against cliffs and rocky areas above 1 000 m above sea level and despite many years of protection it struggles to survive. Another well-known, but inaccessible, species is the **snow protea**, or **snowball**, (*Protea cryophila*) that grows only above 1 750 m above sea level; the beautiful white and glossy red flower heads are at their best in February. Appropriately it grows on the peak of the Sneeuberg, seemingly surviving on bare rock. This is just one of 19 typical protea species in the mountains. Another important but limited vegetation type is a very narrow band (80 to 200 m wide) on shale rocks and soil, which includes a mix of shrubs and renosterbos with a strong component of grasses.

Prik se Werf is one of several cottages in the Cederberg Wilderness Area managed by CapeNature.

Wildlife
Mammals
At least 70 mammal species are known to occur within the greater Cederberg, including those species introduced on private land. Commonly seen are **Chacma baboon**, **rock hyrax**, and four species of small antelope. **Klipspringer** and **grey rhebok** are widespread, the former seen on rugged terrain while the rhebok favours less broken country but nevertheless is seen on steep slopes. In densely thicketed areas watch for **common duiker** and **Cape grysbok**, both common but tending to be secretive. This area is a **leopard** stronghold and although seldom seen, their calls may be heard and their tracks, urine scrapes and droppings betray their passage. In recent years they have started to expand their range eastwards away from the high mountains. A further 16 species of carnivore occur, of which the

WILDLIFE FACTS

- Some 70 mammal species, including a healthy population of leopard.
- Over 200 species of bird for the entire complex, but just 130 for the Cederberg proper.
- About 46 reptile species known; only seven species of amphibian confirmed.
- Of nine indigenous fish species in the Olifants River system, two are considered endangered and the remainder are under considerable threat.
- More than 1 000 species of plant in the wilderness area, including endangered Clanwilliam cedar.

The Cape eagle-owl has bright orange eyes.

day-active **small grey mongoose** is the most regularly seen. **Cape clawless otter** tracks indicate that they spend much time in low-lying areas, but they also hunt along the higher streams. Hikers at overnight huts may have nocturnal visits from the attractive, squirrel-like **spectacled dormouse**, wreaking destruction among rucksacks and food supplies. The **Cape rock sengi**, or **elephant shrew**, is a small day-active animal that waits among boulder clusters or near rock crevices to snatch up passing insects.

Birds

This is not a top birding destination but there are several species to look out for, including **ground woodpecker**, **Cape eagle-owl** (more often heard than seen), **black harrier**, **Cape rockjumper**, **Victorin's warbler**, **cinnamon-breasted warbler**, **orange-breasted sunbird**, **Cape sugarbird**, **protea seedeater** and **Cape siskin**. There is a good population of **Verreaux's eagle**, and **booted eagle** are often seen, with sightings of **martial eagle** mainly on the Matjiesrivier section. If you are not hiking, then excellent birding locations are the Algeria and Kliphuis campgrounds, the pass linking Algeria to the Matjiesrivier Nature Reserve and the Welbedacht Valley.

The Cape rock jumper is a fynbos endemic.

Reptiles and amphibians

There are 46 recorded reptile species, including 17 snakes; but these are seldom seen. A small snake, the **red adder**, was first collected and described in 1997 from the Cederberg but has since been found in the foothills to the east, and as far south as the Little Karoo. The only regularly seen snakes are **puff adders** at low altitudes, and the occasional **Cape cobra**. Several interesting lizards occur, including the heavily scaled and spined **armadillo girdled lizard**, which occupies the dry eastern regions and has the unique habit of curling up and biting its own tail, presenting any predator with a formidable array of spines. Unusually for lizards, these live in family groups in rock crevices. Five other armoured lizards occur in these mountains, including the **Cape** and **Karoo girdled lizards**, and the **graceful crag lizard**. The **small-scaled leaf-toed gecko** is only found at higher altitudes, where it shelters during the day in rock crevices or under the bark of Clanwilliam cedar trees. Only seven species of amphibian have been recorded, including the tiny **Tradouw's toad**, endemic to high rocky areas of the Cape Folded mountains.

Fish

The Olifants River and its tributaries rising on the western flanks of the Cederberg are home to the richest endemic fish fauna south

Several fish species here are endangered, including the sawfin.

The armadillo girdled lizard lives in family groups in rock crevices.

of the Zambezi River; but the fish are in serious trouble. Diversion, pollution and silting are having an impact, but it is the alien fish, such as the predatory **largemouth bass**, that are causing most damage. Two of the endemics, the **fiery redfin** and **Barnard's rock catfish**, are on the verge of extinction. Another six species are considered rare or vulnerable. The fish range in size from the 70 mm fiery redfin to the **Clanwilliam yellowfish** that can exceed 950 mm and 10 kg.

Many short streams feed into the Olifants River from the Cederberg mountains.

- Weather is unpredictable at any time of year and hikers should be prepared for extremes. During thunderstorms descend to lower ground; do not move around in fog or low cloud.
- Keep to the trails at all times; it is surprisingly easy to lose one's way.

Cederberg Wilderness Area **225**

DE HOOP NATURE RESERVE

An excellent viewing location for southern right whales

LOCATION

Lie of the land

Covering 60 000 ha (of which about 24 000 ha is marine reserve), De Hoop is one of CapeNature's largest and most popular reserves. The Indian Ocean laps its southern boundary, and the 14 km long, narrow De Hoop Vlei is within the reserve on its western flank. It is bordered to the north-east by the Breede River and its estuary. A line of white-sanded barrier dunes separates the ocean from the coastal plain, which rises gradually inland, lifting abruptly to a line of old vegetated dunes. In the east the Potberg ridge, an isolated outlier of the Cape Folded range, rises on the horizon. It is located about 260 km east of Cape Town. Swellendam lies due north of the reserve and Bredasdorp to the west.

The tidal pools at Koppie Alleen in De Hoop Nature Reserve are extremely rich in life forms.

Brief history

There is considerable evidence that early humans occupied the area of the present reserve, and that occupation probably spanned all three Stone Ages. The evidence includes potsherds, ochre (haematite), and stone flakes generated by

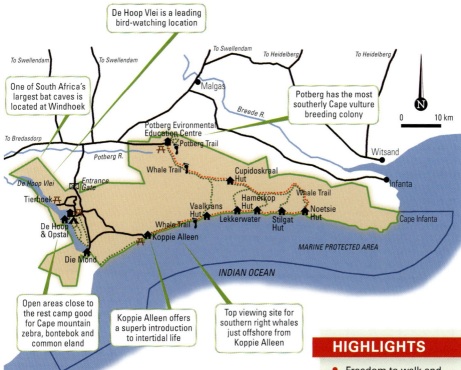

the manufacture of stone tools. Ostrich-shell beads found on ledges above De Hoop Vlei probably date back to 18 000 BP. An excavated site at Black Eagle Cave in the Potberg is from the Later Stone Age, but most visible relics date from about 2 000 BP and are found above the high water mark. The 'kitchen' middens consist of accumulations of mollusc shells, including those of abalone (perlemoen), seal bones and bird bones. Please remember that here and elsewhere in South Africa these artefacts are protected by law and may not be tampered with or removed.

The first European settlers arrived early in the 18th century, and Frederik de Jager was granted the local grazing rights in 1739 by the Dutch East India Company. By the early 1800s the whole district was being farmed. The Melkkamer farmstead in the reserve, built in 1907, has been refurbished and now serves as visitor accommodation. The original De Hoop farmstead and that at Potberg are both of considerable historical significance.

The farm De Hoop was bought by the conservation authorities in 1956, Windhoek was purchased in 1957, and the De Hoop Nature Reserve was proclaimed in that year. It was originally purchased for

HIGHLIGHTS

- Freedom to walk and move about without having to remain in a vehicle.
- Great diversity of Cape heathland, or fynbos, plants and excellent birding prospects.
- One of the best places in the Western Cape to observe rock pool life between tides.
- From May/June to November, Koppie Alleen is one of the best places in South Africa for watching southern right whales.
- The only place in the Western Cape, at Potberg, offering virtually guaranteed sightings of Cape vultures in flight.

De Hoop Nature Reserve 227

CLIMATE

The De Hoop area has a typical Mediterranean climate, with warm summers and mild winters. Mean daily maximum temperature for January/February is more than 25°C and average minimum for July is just under 7°C. Annual rainfall averages about 380 mm but this varies across the reserve and is highest on the upper levels of the Potberg (more than 500 mm annually). There is slightly more rain in autumn and winter, while December to February is drier. Sea fog and mountain mist also contribute to overall precipitation. Frost is very rare. East, west and south-east winds prevail during summer, westerlies and south-westerlies in winter. This is a windy area, and strong winds are common here.

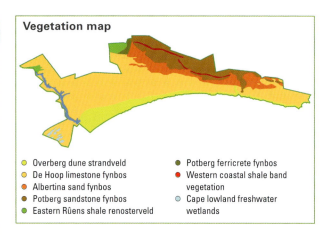

Vegetation map

- Overberg dune strandveld
- De Hoop limestone fynbos
- Albertina sand fynbos
- Potberg sandstone fynbos
- Eastern Rûens shale renosterveld
- Potberg ferricrete fynbos
- Western coastal shale band vegetation
- Cape lowland freshwater wetlands

the breeding of rare wildlife species but over the years its value as a biodiversity hotspot has been realized. The Potteberg Estate was added in 1978, the marine reserve was proclaimed in 1986, and further land was purchased in 1991.

Geology and landscape

Six major landscape features can be recognized at De Hoop. These are the coastline, the vegetated dune barrier, the bare and somewhat mobile dunes, the gradually rising coastal plain, a barrier of old, hard limestone dunes established at a higher ocean level, and the hard, coarse-grained sandstone of the Potberg in the east. The Potberg sandstones are an isolated outlier of the Table Mountain Group, whose closest cousins lie in the Langeberg range to the north. On the upper ridgeline of the Potberg is a very narrow band of shale

The coastal plain is carpeted with relatively short shrubs and bushes.

228 Western Cape

De Hoop is an important sanctuary for African (black) oystercatchers.

rock that forms clay soils, and other small areas of shale are found in the north-central part of the reserve. It is these extensive rich shale-derived soils that have allowed vast tracts north of De Hoop to be converted to productive agricultural land. The hard limestones of the old, leached sand dunes have in places been heavily eroded by acidic groundwater, thus forming caves and overhangs. These limestones cover much of the coastal plain between 'old' and 'new' dunes. The coastal dunes are continuously formed by windblown sands from seaward, seasonal prevailing winds moving them first one way and then the other. The De Hoop Vlei, fed by the Sout River, stretches for about 14 km along the western flank of the reserve.

Vegetation

The vegetation of De Hoop can be classified into five or six types according to preference. All belong within the Cape Floral Kingdom. De Hoop has at least 40 species that are only known to grow in this reserve and a further 108 species that are considered to be rare or threatened. The four main plant growth forms of Cape heathland occur, namely **proteas**, **ericas**, the reed-like **restios** and bulbous plants, or **geophytes**. Mountain heathland, or fynbos, is restricted to the Potberg, with sandplain heathland to the mountain's southeast. The most extensive heathland grows on the 'old' dunes and the plain that extends right across the reserve from west to east, and the sand dune heathland is located on and near the 'new' dunes just north of the high watermark. Each vegetation type is closely tied to a specific soil type. Tall trees are scarce, but on the limestone and especially in gullies near the vlei and along its shores, one sees the spreading, dark green, shiny-leaved **white milkwood** trees (*Sideroxylon inerme*). Typical species of the limestone plain and hills include **Muirs conebush** (*Leucadendron muirii*), and the late-winter flowering **meridian conebush** (*Leucadendron meridianum*), which

FACILITIES AND ACTIVITIES

- A wide range of accommodation including about 20 units with 4–10 beds, a 12-site campground and en-suite units in the Melkkamer farmstead. On the 5-day Whale Trail there are well-appointed overnight huts.
- Mountain bike trails, and hiking and walking trails from 1 km to five days.
- Restaurant at De Hoop.

Some accommodation units at De Hoop are located near the vlei.

- Bird-, game- and whale-watching.
- Limited game-viewing road network.
- De Hoop has no fuel and only very limited supplies but Swellendam and Bredasdorp have a range of services.
- The last 57 km from either town is on gravel roads.
- Access and internal roads are gravel and of variable condition.

De Hoop Nature Reserve 229

The Bredasdorp sugarbush is arguably one of the most striking of all the proteas.

grows to about 2 m; its many bright yellow leaves make it stand out from the rest. Other species include '**flower bush**', or '**blombossie**', (*Metalasia calcicola*), sometimes found in dense stands; as its species name implies, it only grows on limestone-derived soil. A showy protea is the **Bredasdorp sugarbush** (*Protea obtusifolia*), growing to 4 m and producing its large, creamy-white to deep-carmine flower heads from April to September. On the Potberg, common and tallish proteas include the **real sugarbush** (*Protea repens*) which may display its whitish-yellow flower heads throughout the year, and the **blue sugarbush** (*Protea neriifolia*) which yields its large, variably pink flower heads in spring and summer. Unfortunately, in areas of the Potberg and along the coastal dune fringes some of the trees and bushes are aliens. They have proved extremely difficult to control, in part because of massive seed production, and include **Port Jackson willow** (*Acacia saligna*) and **rooikrans**, or **red eye**, (*Acacia cyclops*). They were originally imported from Australia to contain the shifting sand dunes along the coast. The coastal dune system has many areas of bare sand but there are small, dense thickets of evergreen, hard-leaved shrubs and low bushes in moist hollows and wind-protected locations. Close to the coast, and in areas exposed to strong winds, the bush seldom exceeds 1 m and may form dense and continuous stands. This can be seen clearly near the car park at Koppie Alleen.

Wildlife
Mammals

De Hoop has important populations of **Cape mountain zebra** and these are easy to observe, as are the **common eland** and **bontebok**, both of which commonly feed and rest on the old lands and in the camp. **Grey rhebok**, **steenbok**, **Cape grysbok** and **common duiker** occur widely, but regular sightings of **klipspringer** are made only

Common eland frequent the grassy area near the rest camp.

Southern right whales are a main attraction at De Hoop between May and October each year.

at Potberg. Although **leopard** are known to traverse the reserve occasionally, the carnivores most frequently seen are the **yellow mongoose**, with several warrens in the old lands that have been in use for many years. Cape mountain zebra like to roll in the loose soil raised around these colonies. **Small grey mongoose** are frequently seen exploring around the edge of the vlei and patrolling the old stone walls for mice. **Large grey mongoose**, with their black-tipped tails, are occasionally seen, especially on the edge of the dunes, but all you are likely to see of the **water mongoose** is its tracks in the mud at the edge of the vlei. When the vlei has water it is a haunt of the large **Cape clawless otter** and with patience, one can sometimes watch a family party at play, especially south of the reserve headquarters. Their droppings are often found on the old slipway. **Rock hyrax** are common all along the rocky east bank of the vlei and around the camp. The large earth mounds you see scattered around in open areas are pushed by **Cape dune mole-rats**. Also, in the old open lands you will see small burrow entrances with fan-shaped spreads of loose sand: these are a sure sign that the **Cape gerbil**, a species restricted to the Cape heathlands, is in residence. In the evenings you will often see large numbers of small insect-eating bats hunting over the vlei, vlei edge and around camp. Many of these bats, up to 150 000 in summer, live in a large cave system in the Windhoek section of the reserve. Five bat species regularly roost in the cave, including **Schreiber's long-fingered bat** and **Geoffroy's horseshoe bat**. Before the cave was included in the reserve, local farmers used to 'harvest' large quantities of bat guano (droppings) for use as fertilizer. The bat cave is off limits to visitors. Many people visit De Hoop in winter and spring to watch the **southern right whales** that come close inshore, with cows giving birth and pairs mating. About 120 individual whales make the journey to De Hoop waters each year from their feeding grounds on the edge of the Antarctic

WILDLIFE FACTS

- Some 79 mammal species, including 13 cetaceans, one fur seal and one seal.
- Some 259 bird species – about 80% of the Western Cape inventory of birds – have been observed
- Of the 49 reptiles, 25 are snakes.
- 14 amphibian species found here.
- At least 250 species of marine fish, but only two freshwater species occur.
- 252 species of spider at last count.
- More than 40 species of plants are known to grow only at De Hoop.

De Hoop Nature Reserve   231

The Cape vulture breeding colony at Potberg in the north of the reserve is the most southerly in South Africa.

ice shelf. It is one of the best locations for watching these leviathans without sharing the sight with thousands of others. Some 13 cetacean species have been recorded in the marine sanctuary but most are only occasional visitors.

Birds

It is the 259 bird species that have been recorded here that draw most people. Potberg hosts the last breeding colony of the **Cape Vulture** in the Western Cape and visitors are not allowed to approach the nesting cliffs, although birds may be seen in flight. The Klipspringer Trail covers a 6 km circular route where there is a good chance of seeing, among others, **Cape rockjumper**, **orange-breasted sunbird**, **Cape siskin** and some vultures. The main camp is excellent for birds, including many **Cape spurfowl**, **helmeted guineafowl**, **bar-throated apalis**, **southern boubou**, Cape robin-chat and **Cape bulbul**. The trail along the eastern edge of the vlei with its thicket patches is also usually productive. When there is water in the vlei there are usually large numbers of birds, among them several duck species, grebes, waders and herons, including **black-crowned night herons** that roost in dense thickets along the vlei edge. Large numbers of swallows, martins and swifts are often seen hunting insects over the vlei, especially in the late afternoon. The coastline is good for several species of Palearctic waders in summer and **African (black) oystercatchers** are usually present throughout the year.

Reptiles and amphibians

The area is rich in reptiles with 49 species including 25 snake species. The three species of sea turtle are very rare vagrants; the **leopard tortoise**, one of three land tortoises, has been artificially introduced. The abundant **angulate tortoise** is commonly seen but favours areas with sandy substrate. Few snakes are seen but

The common egg-eater is one of 25 snake species found in the reserve.

this sector of the fauna is surprisingly rich and although four species, **puff adder**, **boomslang**, **Cape cobra** and **rinkhals**, are dangerous to humans, the majority are harmless and secretive. No fewer than five house snake species are known to occur. Surprisingly, only 16 species of lizard have been recorded to date, of which only four are commonly seen: the **southern rock agama**, **Cape girdled lizard**, **Cape crag lizard** and the smooth-scaled **Cape skink**. Among the rocks along the east bank of the vlei the **red-sided skink** is quite common. Few of the 14 amphibian species are likely to be encountered, although the **common platanna** is abundant when the vlei holds water, and forms an important component of the diet of Cape clawless otter and a number of aquatic birds such as cormorants and herons. **Ranger's** and **Karoo toads** sometimes forage around the camp buildings at night. Three species in the reserve are Cape heathland (fynbos) endemics, namely **western leopard toad**, **sand toad** and **Rose's rain frog**, and **Delalande's sand frog** is largely restricted to heathland.

Cape grassbirds are most frequently seen in the dense coastal scrub.

Fish

The marine fish life is quite rich; 250 species have been claimed but it is not clear whether this figure is based on actual collection and observation, or on extrapolation from the literature. Given the diversity of habitats, this total is certainly plausible. A diversity of klipfish and other small rock pool dwellers can be seen at Koppie Alleen. One of the two freshwater fish species present in the vlei is the **Cape kurper**, which is restricted to the Cape heathland biome.

Invertebrates

The large, clear rock pools along stretches of the reserve's coast, such as at Koppie Alleen, are the best conserved in the Western Cape. They are extremely rich in invertebrate life; at least 400 species have been recorded.

Below: The abundant marine life in the Koppie Alleen rock pools includes starfish (left) and Cape sea urchins (middle). Like other plough shells, smooth plough shells (right) rely on their sense of smell to detect carrion washed up on beaches.

> **!**
> - On the coast caution should be exercised as there are strong currents, and high waves may hit the rock pool areas unexpectedly.
> - Cape cobras and puff adders are common in some parts of the reserve.

NORTHERN CAPE

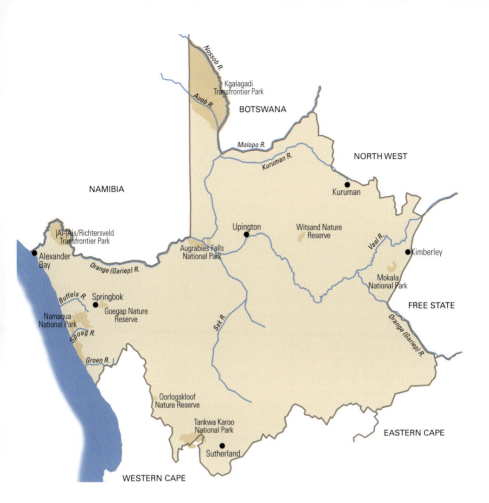

This is by far South Africa's largest and least populated province. In the north it shares its borders with Namibia, across the Orange (Gariep) River, and Botswana; to the east it borders on the provinces of North West and Free State, with Eastern Cape and Western Cape in the south. The cold Atlantic Ocean thunders against its western extremity. Despite its size, it is poorly endowed with conservation areas; but it does have five national parks, including the vast tract of the Kgalagadi Transfrontier Park that it shares with Botswana.

It is an arid land, with the Orange River separating the Kalahari Desert from the southern plains encompassed by Namaqualand, Bushmanland and the scrub-covered Karoo. Most of the province is flat but in the west the Kamiesberge and the famed 'klipkoppe' break the horizon; and in the south-west, the great cliffs of the Western Escarpment separate the inland plateau from the coastal plain.

When it rains, the Kalahari displays a variety of grassland and dwarf shrubland types. Some of the greatest plant diversity is found in the succulent Karoo to the west, one of South Africa's most important centres of plant endemism.

The province experiences extreme climatic conditions, from blistering heat during the summer months to sub-freezing temperatures on winter nights. The meagre rains fall mostly in summer in the east, and in winter in the west.

The Northern Cape is particularly rich in succulent plants, including tree-sized aloes.

Northern Cape   **235**

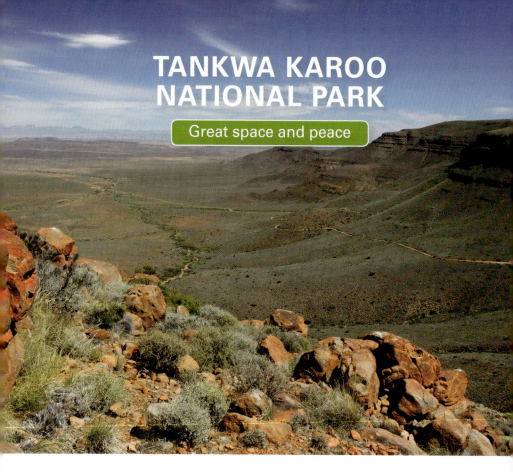

TANKWA KAROO NATIONAL PARK

Great space and peace

Lie of the land

The 151 928-ha Tankwa Karoo National Park is located in the western Karoo, some 250 km north-east of Cape Town and 90 km south of the Karoo town of Calvinia. Much of the terrain is flat, with isolated rock outcrops, but the park extends into the Roggeveld Mountains in the east. Altitudes range from under 300 m in the south-west to 1 568 m in the north-east.

Brief history

The peoples of the Earlier, Middle and Later Stone Ages occupied this area, and the hunter-gatherer San were still here when the first whites arrived. Few of the early explorer-naturalists seem to have passed directly through the area, although in 1774 Carl Thunberg recorded lions in the area between Calvinia and the Roggeveld. By the mid-18th century white farmers began to occupy the area, moving seasonally with their livestock, as did the game.

In the 19th century farm boundaries were established and properties were settled, but the low rainfall and overgrazing made them unviable. The park was proclaimed in 1986 and has greatly expanded to reach its present extent.

The Gannaga region lies in the north-east of the Tankwa Karoo National Park, with the Roggeveld Mountains as backdrop.

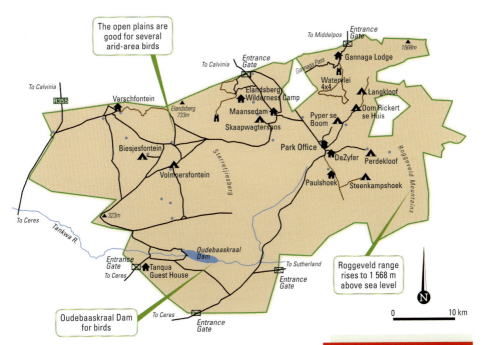

Geology and landscape

The rocks in the area are predominantly mudstone and sandstones, with some shales, from several different geological groups, such as the Beaufort Group, Karoo Sequence, Bokkeveld Group and Ecca Group. Jurassic Karoo dolerite dykes create outcrops and ridges at several locations within and around the park. Western and central areas of Tankwa are flat with a scattering of isolated outcrops, extending eastwards into the rugged Roggeveld Mountains. About 20 km of the Tankwa River is included in the south of the park, along with the Oudebaaskraal Dam.

Vegetation

The vegetation is characterized by low-growing shrubs, succulents and seasonal grasses. Tanqua Karoo vegetation dominates the flattish western part with a mix of low succulent shrubland, somewhat taller on the slopes of the isolated outcrops. After good seasonal rains many annuals put in an appearance. In the Tanqua Escarpment shrubland the tall, succulent **botterboom** (*Tylecodon paniculatus*) and the **milk bush** (*Euphorbia mauritanica*) are obvious. The Roggeveld in the eastern sector of the park contains shale renosterveld, named for the low bush known as **renosterbos** (*Elytropappus rhinocerotis*). The areas with dolerite outcrops are rich in geophytes, bulbous plants that only appear after good rains. Some areas have strong grass growth

HIGHLIGHTS

- Vast expanses with very few people.
- Lies within Biodiversity Hotspot of Succulent Karoo with rich plant diversity.
- Good arid-area birding.

Vegetation map

- ○ Low succulent seasonal grass
- ● Succulent shrubland
- ○ Medium height succulent shrubland
- ○ Highland mixed shrubland
- ● Shale renosterveld
- ○ Dolerite renosterveld

Tankwa Karoo National Park 237

CLIMATE

This area, one of the driest in the Karoo, receives most of its meagre rainfall in the winter months (May to August), though in some years up to 30% may fall in summer. Annual rainfall may average as little as 40 mm in some years in the west, but rises towards the Roggeveld Mountains, with an overall average for the area of just 80 mm. In exceptionally dry years the land takes on a moonscape-like appearance. In winter, temperatures are low (mean minimum of 5.6°C in July) and there may be 15 to 30 nights with frost, depending on the region. Mean maximum temperature in January is almost 36°C and highs may exceed 40°C.

after rain, including the white, or bushman, grasses (*Stipagrostis* spp.). Large areas in the west are referred to as rain-shadow desert, rather than semi-desert, because of the extremely low rainfall and frequent periods of prolonged drought. Large areas of the park, once commercial sheep farming country, have been heavily overgrazed and will take many years to recover. Nevertheless plant diversity, especially of succulents, is surprisingly high.

Wildlife
Mammals

Officially only 34 species are listed but at least 43 are present in the area. You are most likely to see the plains-dwelling **steenbok**, and **klipspringer** in the eastern hills. Other antelope include **grey rhebok** in the east, **greater kudu** and **springbok**. Recently **Cape mountain zebra**, **common eland**, **southern oryx** (**gemsbok**) and **red hartebeest** were reintroduced. There is a diversity of carnivores but you are only likely to observe the day-active **yellow mongoose** and **suricate**, and on cool overcast days the **bat-eared fox**, usually seen in small family parties. **Black-backed jackal** may be heard calling at night. The only primate in the park, mainly in the east, is the **Chacma baboon**, eking out a living by eating plant parts and seeking invertebrates and reptiles under rocks. The presence of **rock hyrax** (**dassie**) is betrayed by white urine marks on rock outcrops. Many rodent species are night-active but **four-striped grass mouse** and **Karoo bush rat** can be seen by day, and the latter's large surface stick-nests are obvious. Plans to reintroduce **cheetah** and **brown hyaena** are being investigated.

Birds

Currently 187 are listed, including a number of nomads, with the arid-area specials the main attraction for the keen birder. **Burchell's**

WILDLIFE FACTS

- About 34 mammal species; game numbers kept deliberately low.
- Plans afoot to reintroduce cheetah and hook-lipped rhinoceros.
- Some 187 species of bird, many of which are arid-area species.
- 38 reptiles, including ground-dwelling Namaqua chameleon.

The black-backed jackal is the principal predator in Tankwa.

Chalets in the park are modelled on typical farm labourers' dwellings found in the Karoo.

FACILITIES AND ACTIVITIES

- Elandsberg Wilderness Camp has five chalets; other accommodation options scattered in park; Perdekloof and Langkloof in east have formal campgrounds; six informal campsites.
- Walking is permitted.
- Internal road network fairly extensive.
- Access roads all gravel, of variable condition.
- Nearest fuel and supplies in Calvinia, 90 km away.
- Park cannot be entered directly from the Ceres-Calvinia road (R355), but can be reached by secondary roads from Sutherland, Middelpos and Calvinia.

courser breeds on the open plains. **Double-banded courser** and **Namaqua sandgrouse** are more frequently seen plains dwellers. The park has eight lark species, including the **Karoo long-billed lark**. Other notable species are **tractrac chat**, **Karoo chat**, **Karoo eremomela**, **rufous-eared warbler** and **fairy flycatcher**. It is worth exploring the sweet thorn-lined Tankwa riverbed and other streams. The Oudebaaskraal Dam on the Tankwa River attracts a remarkable diversity of water birds for such an arid area. In the east the Roggeveld has a number of species not found in the rest of the park. August to October is the best period for birding, but many species are present through the year.

Reptiles and amphibians

There are 38 known reptile species but more probably await discovery. Many species are secretive and nocturnal but a few, such as the **tent tortoise**, **Karoo sand snake**, **western rock skink**, **Karoo girdled lizard** and various rapidly moving sand lizards of the genus *Pedioplanis* are most frequently seen on warm days. At least five amphibian species defy the aridity but some only make themselves known after rain, when the males call to attract mates. The **Karoo toad** may be seen out hunting at night, even in winter, especially near buildings where there are lights to attract insects.

Invertebrates

The park probably has a rich scorpion and spider diversity.

!
- Extreme heat is possible in summer, so always carry water, use sunblock and wear a hat.
- Be alert for scorpions at night.

Unusually for the group, Namaqua chameleons live on the ground.

Parabuthus capensis is one of the most venomous of local scorpions.

Tankwa Karoo National Park **239**

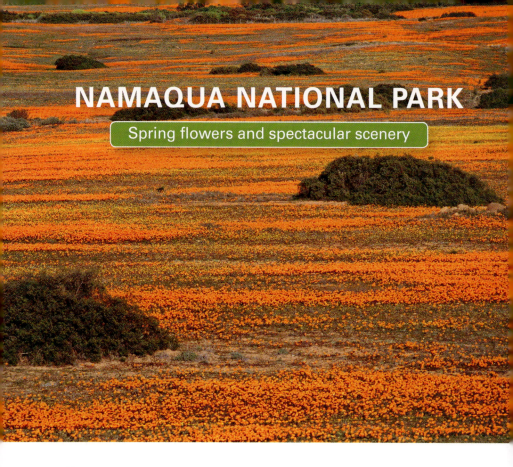

NAMAQUA NATIONAL PARK
Spring flowers and spectacular scenery

Lie of the land

This park is situated 21 km west of Kamieskroon, which lies 67 km south of Springbok on the N7, covering more than 150 000 ha west of the highway. The northern sector of the park encompasses predominantly rugged, spectacular Namaqua hill and mountain country, with the highest peaks about 900 m above sea level in the east, declining westward to Soebatsfontein and the coastal plain. A corridor links the north with the coastal section of the park running from the Spoeg River to the Groen River. The marine component of the park was recently established between these rivers. The coastal plain is flat with isolated rock outcrops.

Brief history

Most visitors come to the Namaqua National Park in spring to see the spectacular floral display in the park's Skilpad section.

Early peoples probably occupied this area but little archaeological work has been done here. Inhabitants would have been nomadic, moving between the high hill country and the coast to take advantage of seasonal food resources. The San and the first livestock-keeping people, the Khoekhoen, also lived here, probably as nomads. Their descendants still live in the region.

Jacobus Coetsé hunted elephant north of the Groen River in about 1680, and the explorers William Paterson and John Barrow recorded lion and elephant here

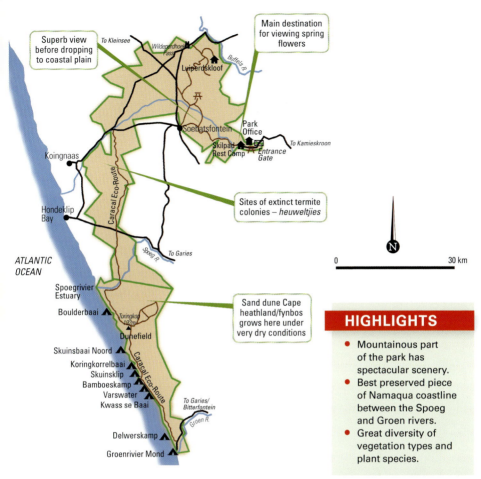

towards the end of the 18th century. The Kamiesberg, which includes the rugged mountains in the east of the park, translates as the *Lion Mountain*. Hartmann's mountain zebra may have survived in the Kamiesberg until at least 1915.

The park, originally the small Skilpad flower reserve run by WWF, was proclaimed as a national park in 1999 and continues to expand.

Geology and landscape

The park's most spectacular scenery is in the east, with its huge granite and gneiss domes and boulder outcrops dominating the skyline. These dramatic rock structures, commonly known as 'whale backs', belong to the Namaqua Metamorphic Province. The western and southern areas consist mainly of flat country, with some sand dunes closer to the coast, with the soils dominated by sand and sometimes gravel. Altitudes range from 0 m to 900 m above sea level.

Succulents are well adapted to arid conditions.

Adjacent to the park's northern boundary is the world's largest colony of Cape fur seals.

Vegetation map

- Rock outcrop (*klipkoppe*) scrubland
- Foothill shrubland
- Arid grassland
- Quartz succulent (vygie) veld
- Inland duneveld
- Kamiesberg mountain shrubland
- Coastal duneveld
- Strandveld
- Sand Cape heathland (fynbos)

Vegetation

Starting from the east in the hill country we find mainly bare slopes and areas of low shrubland (to just over 1 m), and plants have succulent, or very tiny, leaves. Around the lower rims of rock outcrops where more water runs off, the bushes are up to 3 m tall and have non-succulent leaves. The unique flora of the Namaqualand Heuweltjieveld grows on the ancient bases of extinct termite mounds and consists mainly of low shrubs and succulents. Small areas of Namaqualand Sand Fynbos (Cape Heathland) occur below 300 m on the coastal plain. Here the typical fynbos species, such as proteas, are adapted to particularly low rainfall, although they do lie in the Atlantic fog-belt. After good rains there are spectacular displays of flowering annuals and perennials. The famous Skilpad sector of the park, close to the entrance, is old cultivated land that plays host to pioneer flowering plants, mainly of the daisy (Asteraceae) family.

Wildlife

Mammals

In the past, elephant, eland and lion roamed the area, but now the inventory is more modest. There are **springbok** and **southern oryx** (**gemsbok**). **Klipspringer** are present in good numbers in the eastern hills, and **steenbok** are common on the western plains. **Grey rhebok**, **common duiker** and **Cape grysbok** are more scarce. **Hartmann's zebra** is a recent addition and there are plans to reintroduce other game species. **Rock hyrax** (**dassies**) are common, their white urine streaks and patches clearly visible in rocky areas. Also here are numerous but

In arid areas red hartebeest will travel great distances in search of grass. Depending on the season, they will also browse.

CLIMATE

This is a winter rainfall area (May to September) averaging 160 mm annually in the east, and just above 100 mm in the west. The area suffers cycles of drought, when under 100 mm may fall in a season. The coastal plain experiences frequent fog and mist in winter but also sometimes in summer, and this adds considerably to overall precipitation. Summer temperatures are higher in the interior with a mean maximum around 30°C. Winter is also colder in the high country, with an average minimum of 5°C.

elusive **Smith's red rock rabbits**; you may encounter their distinctive dung middens. Now that the park has coastal frontage, **Cape fur seals** join the list, but they are irregular land visitors. At least 23 species of whale and dolphin are known from inshore waters along this coast.

Birds

The official bird-list stands at 123 species but probably 70 will be added from the recently acquired coastline, such as **African (black) oystercatcher**, **white-fronted plover**, **kelp gull** and **swift tern**,

WILDLIFE FACTS

- About 46 mammals recorded but at least three more occur on coastal plain, and 23 marine mammals are known to occur.
- Some 123 bird species recorded to date but another 70 could be added with the incorporation of the coastal sector.
- Official reptile list of 28 species can be expected to increase
- Six amphibians recorded with another three expected to be added to this count.

Mountain wheatears are common in the rocky areas.

Namaqua National Park

The deciduous botterboom sheds its leaves in winter.

Ursinia cakilefolia thrives in Namaqualand's sandy terrain.

The quiver tree flowers from early to late winter.

FACILITIES AND ACTIVITIES

- Rest camp has four self-catering cottages; 3-bedroom guest cottage is accessible with 4x4 vehicle; rustic coastal campsites; fully catered luxury camping in dome tents in flower season.
- A 5 km circular route, suitable for all vehicles, for flower-viewing July–September.
- A 25 km scenic gravel road to Soebatsfontein, suitable for high-clearance vehicles.
- A 220 km road network, including the Caracal Eco-Route, for 4x4 only.
- Two short walking trails of about two hours each.
- Mountain bikes for hire.
- Kiosk has some basic supplies; no fuel available in park.
- Closest town Kamieskroon, with limited services; Springbok has full range of services.
- Access routes from N7 all gravel.

not to mention the host of Palearctic waders that descend on these shores during the northern winter. It is an excellent area for raptors, including **black harrier** and **pale chanting goshawk**. **Verreaux's eagle**, **jackal buzzard** and **Cape eagle-owl** nest in the rugged eastern parts of the park. The **southern black korhaan** and the **Karoo korhaan** may be seen in the open areas. Look out for **ground woodpecker** and **cinnamon-breasted warbler**, and **pale-winged** and **red-winged starlings**.

Reptiles and amphibians

Reptiles currently number 28, including eight snakes. The three tortoises include the very localized **speckled padloper**, the world's smallest species. The most commonly seen, especially on the coastal plain, is the large (20+ cm) **angulate tortoise**. Visible lizards are the **Karoo girdled lizard** and the **southern rock agama** that often perch on top of rocks. There is a good range of **sand lizards** (*Pedioplanis* spp.) and **skinks** (*Trachylepis* spp.) but these are difficult to separate to species level, and often take off at high speed when disturbed. Six amphibians have been recorded so far, with one of these, the burrowing **Namaqua rain frog**, living on the coastal sand plains. A further three are likely to be added to the species count.

Fish

No detailed inventory of the marine fish of this coastal sector has been compiled. Although diversity is lower than on the south coast, a number of species occur in great numbers, many of which are fished commercially. No freshwater fish species have been recorded.

- Many internal roads are rough and unmaintained.
- Be prepared for punctures and breakdowns, as adequate support is only available in Springbok.
- Always carry enough drinking water, especially during the hot summer months.

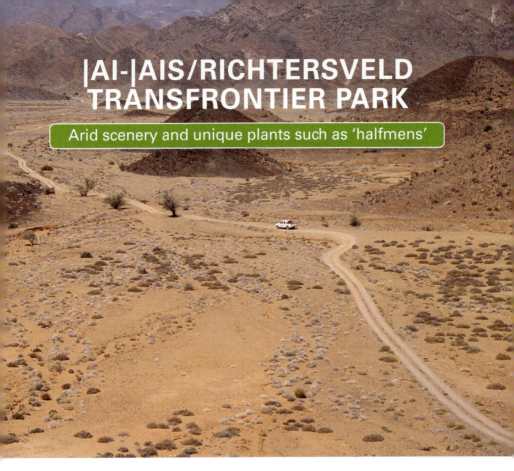

|AI-|AIS/RICHTERSVELD TRANSFRONTIER PARK

Arid scenery and unique plants such as 'halfmens'

Lie of the land

This park straddles the Namibia–South Africa border. It is located in the north-west corner of South Africa, in the Northern Cape province, 326 km from Springbok and 180 km north-east of Port Nolloth. The South African section, approximately 162 445 ha in size, was proclaimed in 1991 and the transfrontier park, covering a further 449 983 ha, was established in 2003. The park is focused on the Orange (Gariep) River, which makes a great northerly and then southerly sweep to pour its waters into the Atlantic Ocean. On its southern boundary is the Richtersveld Community Conservancy. Both areas consist of rugged mountain and broken hill country, interspersed with sand flats and washes, and gravel plains. Altitudes range from about 200 m to 1 363 m on the summit of Vandersterrberg.

Brief history

Archaeological evidence shows that humans have lived in the Richtersveld for at least 200 000 years. The three Stone Ages are represented but most artefacts relate to the Middle and Later eras, with the major deposits being located along the coast and outside the park. Modern humans, in the form of the hunter-gatherer

LOCATION

At first glance the |Ai-|Ais/Richtersveld park appears barren and empty, yet it is rich in plant and animal species, all adapted to desert living.

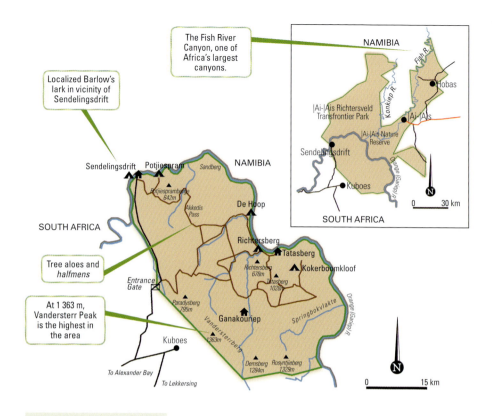

HIGHLIGHTS

- Spectacular and dramatic desert scenery; Fish River Canyon on the Namibian side.
- Extremely rich and diverse arid-area plant life.

San, lived in the area for several thousand years, and their bloodlines mingled with the Nama, a Khoekhoen group, who entered South Africa around 2 000 BP along with their fat-tailed sheep, goats and, later, cattle. Groups moved westwards along the Orange (Gariep) River as far as its estuary, some settling on the north bank (Great Namaqua) and others on the south (Little Namaqua). Scattered through the area are grave sites of Nama and San, and other rock structures, as well as rock engravings, or petroglyphs.

It appears from meagre records that the first whites made hunting (and raiding) excursions into the Richtersveld in the 1730s. In 1761 Robert Jacob Gordon, travelling through the Great and Little Namaquas, believed that only some 400 indigenous people survived at that time. After the early explorers came the missionaries, *trekboere* (nomadic white stock farmers) and finally the mineral prospectors from about the 1920s.

Geology and landscape

The |Ai-|Ais/Richtersveld complex has some of the most spectacular landscapes in southern Africa, with forbidding mountain chains, isolated volcanic plutons (such as the 1 028 m Tatasberg in the east of the park), the rugged backdrop to the Orange (Gariep) River and the massive water-carved canyon system of the Fish River in Namibia. Richtersveld is one of the finest geological 'classrooms' in the world. Most rocks are of volcanic origin and of many different types and were formed in several periods beginning some 2 000 million years BP. Various granites and quartzites are readily recognized. Among the numerous inter-montane sandy-bottomed washes one of the most spectacular is the Springbokvlakte to the south of the Tatasberg.

Vegetation

More than 10 major vegetation types in the Richtersveld share one common denominator: adaptation to an arid environment. An exception and a surprise are the narrow strips of Cape heathland (fynbos) along the highest reaches of several mountain chains, including ridges of the Vandersterrberg in the west of the park. However, it is species such as the *halfmens* (*Pachypodium namaquanum*) with its thorny trunk and leaf-cluster at its tip that visitors seek out, as well as the **quiver tree** (*Aloe dichotoma*) and the rare **giant tree aloe** (*Aloe pillansii*). Much of the west of the park falls within the Succulent Karoo Biome, the richest succulent plant region in the world, with more than one third of the world's total of these species. The greater Richtersveld falls within one of the five centres of endemism that have been recognized within the biome, the !Gariep Centre, and it has all of 350 endemic plant species. Much of the rest of the park falls within the Desert Biome. At the foot of the hills and along the sandy washes you will see some low tree species,

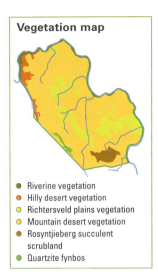

Vegetation map

- Riverine vegetation
- Hilly desert vegetation
- Richtersveld plains vegetation
- Mountain desert vegetation
- Rosyntjieberg succulent scrubland
- Quartzite fynbos

The Orange (Gariep) River separates the South African and Namibian sections of this transfrontier park.

The southern African ground squirrel lives in small colonies and is common in some areas of the park.

such as the white-trunked **shepherd's tree** (*Boscia albitrunca*), **Karoo boer-bean** (*Schotia afra*) and the **ebony tree** (*Euclea pseudobenus*), which takes its name from its hard black heartwood.

Wildlife
Mammals

Richtersveld is not a destination for seeing a lot of game but it can be very rewarding if you pay attention to those species that are present in this wilderness. Within historic times lion, hippopotamus, hook-lipped rhinoceros and elephant were present here. The largest species you are likely to see today is **Hartmann's mountain zebra**, mostly on the north side of the river. Small numbers of **southern oryx** (**gemsbok**) are present but the main concentrations are usually outside the park and closer to the coast. In the rocky and hilly country you may encounter **klipspringer** and **grey rhebok**, the former quite often in the hills fringing the Orange (Gariep) River. **Steenbok** and **springbok** are most commonly observed on the flats and along the sandy washes. **Vervet monkey** and **Chacma baboon** are found on the wooded banks of the river, though the latter are sometimes seen on the interior mountain ranges, especially after good rains. This is the only area in South Africa where you have a chance of seeing both the **southern African ground squirrel** and the **Damara ground squirrel**. Most other rodents are nocturnal but two exceptions, **Brant's** and **Littledale's whistling rats**, occur widely and draw attention with their sharp whistling calls. Although **leopard** and **brown hyaena** occur they are very rarely seen, but tracks can be found with some know-how. Carnivores that you may see include **black-backed jackal** (more likely to hear their characteristic call), **bat-eared fox**, **small grey** and **yellow mongooses** and the troop-living **suricate**. **Rock hyrax** (**dassies**) are common, especially in the hills fringing the river.

CLIMATE

This mountain desert has variable rainfall with annual averages ranging from as low as 45 mm, to slightly more than 200 mm on the very highest mountain ridges (above 1 100 m). Rain falls in a transition between summer and winter regimes, which is supplemented, particularly in the west, by the fogs locally known as *malmok* that roll in from the Atlantic Ocean. The west gets more rain in winter, the east in summer. This is also an area of temperature extremes, with some parts receiving frost in winter, whereas day shade temperatures of 50°C have been recorded in summer. Summers are warm to hot, whereas winter days are mild and very cold at night. The area experiences frequent strong south and south-west winds.

Quiver tree, or kokerboom.

Halfmens tree.

A klipspringer ram stands on alert on a rocky ridge.

Grey herons feed on aquatic animals found in the river.

Birds

To date 212 bird species have been recorded in the park, with a mix of arid-area species and those associated with the river and its woodlands. **African fish eagle** is a common sight, and sound, along the river, and **Verreaux's eagle** follows its principal prey, the rock hyrax. The world's largest bird, the **ostrich**, is seen on the plains and along the sandy washes. Birding along the river, along the water's edge and in the riverine vegetation, can be very rewarding. Here is the most westerly population of **goliath heron** in South Africa. There are several larks, including the very localized **Barlow's lark** usually seen in the vicinity of Sendelingsdrift. Both the **Cape** and **African pied wagtails** occur along the river. The only parrot in the arid west, the **rosy-faced lovebird**, is best watched for along the river.

Reptiles and amphibians

There are at least 75 species of reptiles within the transfrontier park, including five tortoises and 22 snake species. The **Nile monitor** hunts along the river banks and in the water. Many reptiles are secretive or nocturnal, but several can be easily spotted. Skinks often show themselves, including **Cape skink** on the riverbanks, **Kalahari tree skink** and **western rock skink**. The **Karoo girdled lizard** and the **southern rock** and **Anchieta's agamas** display themselves prominently on rocks. Ground-dwelling **Namaqua chameleons** are fairly common but their cryptic coloration means that they are often overlooked. Most geckos are night-active and seldom seen, including the **Richtersveld dwarf leaf-toed gecko**, so far known only from the park. A diurnal species is the tiny **Bradfield's dwarf gecko** that lives on the stems of tree aloes in the Richtersveld. **Common barking geckos** are rarely seen but at sunset you may well hear their characteristic call. Surprisingly, most of the nine species of amphibian that occur in the Richtersveld are not associated with the river, but with scattered springs and seasonal rain pools. The **paradise toad**,

FACILITIES AND ACTIVITIES

- Some 10 fully equipped units at Sendelingsdrift (park HQ); Tatasberg and Gannakouriep have four chalets each (wilderness camps); rustic camping grounds at several locations. Other accommodation at |Ai-|Ais on the Namibian side.
- About 200 km of roads on the South African side; many are rough and require high-clearance 2x4 or 4x4 vehicles. Some trails are for 4x4 only.
- Pontoon at Sendelingsdrift to cross international frontier.
- Mountain bike trails.
- Overnight hiking trail with facilities.
- Springbok and Port Nolloth have fuel stations and services.
- Road from Springbok to Port Nolloth is tarred, and from Port Nolloth to Alexander Bay surfaced; all other roads are gravel.

WILDLIFE FACTS

- 55 mammal species, including 10 bats. Largest species is Hartmann's mountain zebra, present on both sides of river.
- Very respectable 212 bird species, including both arid-area species and those able to adapt to the habitat along the Orange (Gariep) River.
- Richtersveld and |Ai-|Ais have exceptionally rich reptile fauna with at least 75 species.

Chalets at Tatasberg Wilderness Camp are partially made of reeds.

first described in 1996, was collected in springs draining from the Vandersterr Mountains in Paradise Kloof just to the north. It has since been collected in other localities inside and outside the park.

Fish

Some 15 species of fish occur in the stretch of the Orange (Gariep) River that divides the park. Many of these also extend northwards into the Fish River. The **Mozambique tilapia** and **carp** do not naturally occur here but have escaped from other areas. The two largest species are the **sharptooth catfish**, which can grow to more than 1 m in length and reach a weight of 30 kg, and the **large-mouth yellowfish**, which can attain 80 cm in length and 20 kg in weight. Most species have wide distributions but the small **Namaqua barb** only occurs in the lower Orange (Gariep) and some of the Fish River.

In the park, the African darter appears only along the river.

Invertebrates

The transfrontier park is a scorpion hotspot with many species that occupy virtually all available habitats. One large (up to 150 mm) species, *Hadogenes zumpti*, is only known from a very limited area along the lower Orange (Gariep) River, including the Richtersveld. Seven of the scorpions that occur here have potent venom and belong to the family Buthidae. In fact, the largest species in the world from this family, up to 180 mm, *Parabuthus villosus*, occurs throughout the park and, unusually, is day-active.

- There is extreme heat in summer; always carry sufficient drinking water.
- Never wander alone unless you inform somebody of your intended route, as a fall could be fatal, and it is a very easy area in which to get lost.
- It is wise to carry a second spare wheel for your vehicle.
- Scorpions occur, including a number with venom dangerous to humans, and closed shoes are advised when walking around at night; sleeping on the ground is unwise.

AUGRABIES FALLS NATIONAL PARK

Augrabies waterfall and leaping lizards

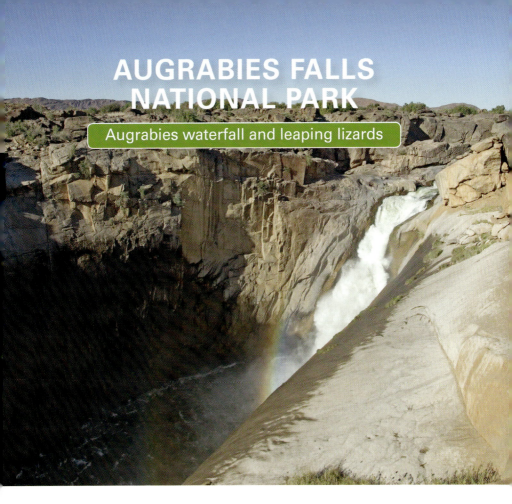

Lie of the land

The 51 000 ha Augrabies Falls park is one of the most popular conservation areas in the Northern Cape province, located 120 km west of Upington and 40 km north-west of Kakamas. The park is bordered in the north by the Orange (Gariep) River, and only the eastern, western and southern boundaries are fenced. It is focused on the Orange (Gariep) River, its waterfall and the 18 km long deep-cut ravine running from the falls westwards. The overall fall is 145 m, with a sheer 56 m drop over an eroded granite cliff. South of the river the land is fairly flat, ranging from 503 m to 704 m on Swartrandte Peak. Low, rounded outcrops are most visible closest to the river. To the north, and outside the park, the hills of Riemvasmaak are clearly visible.

Brief history

The Augrabies region shows evidence, such as stone tools, of the presence of humans throughout the Stone Ages. The Later Stone Age, which started around

LOCATION

The Augrabies waterfall, along with its adjoining ravine, is one of the most spectacular in South Africa.

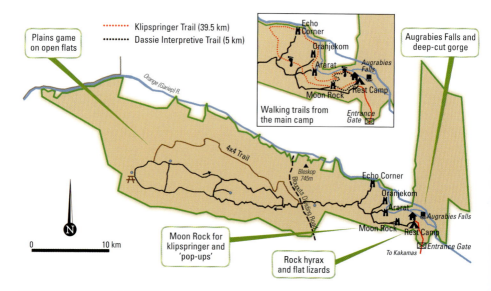

HIGHLIGHTS

- Some of the most spectacular arid-area scenery in the country.
- One of the world's most spectacular waterfalls.
- One of the best locations to view klipspringer; very good for rock hyrax.
- Numerous colourful Broadley's flat lizards around the falls.

Vegetation map

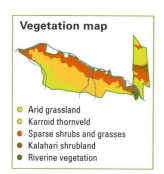

- Arid grassland
- Karroid thornveld
- Sparse shrubs and grasses
- Kalahari shrubland
- Riverine vegetation

22 000 BP, saw more finely made stone tools, as well as pottery. The Khoekhoen, who first introduced domestic livestock into much of southern Africa, migrated into the region about 2 000 BP, and their descendants made first contact with the Europeans. Many different clans neighboured the Orange (Gariep) River.

Hendrik Wikar is claimed to be the first white man to have set eyes on the mighty Augrabies Falls, on the 6th October 1778, but it is likely that others were there before him. The following year Robert J. Gordon recorded 50 elephant, 12 giraffe, five hook-lipped rhinoceros, 13 greater kudu, a herd of plains zebra, as well as hippopotamus in the river. The first Europeans, mainly hunters, found the riverbanks densely populated by mainly Khoekhoen peoples. Within the park there are also grave sites, simple rock cairns, believed to date to less than 1 000 BP, but many such sites reveal no evidence of burials and must have served some other purpose. Oddly, no rock paintings or engravings have been found in the park, although there are pictographs and paintings north of the river in the Perdepoort, Riemvasmaak. When the first whites travelled in this area the Namnykoa clan occupied Paarden Island north of the falls, and the Anoe Eijs (Bright Kraal people) lived near the falls. The first white settlers were already moving into the area by the mid-18th century and by the end of that century bands of Bastaards, Khoe, Oorlams, San and renegade whites were raiding farms as far south of their river strongholds as the Calvinia district. The so-called Koranna wars here, more skirmish than all-out conflict, ended when the Korannas under Klaas Pofadder, Klaas Lukas and Donker Malgas were defeated and dispersed by a colonial force in 1879.

Augrabies is derived from a Khoekhoen word, *Aukoerebis*, which means 'the place of great noise' and refers to the crashing sound of the water cascading down the falls.

These so-called 'pop-ups' are geological features unique to this part of the country.

Geology and landscape

Two granite-gneiss rock types dominate the geology of the park: Augrabies granite in the central area is surrounded by Riemvasmaak gneiss. Above the falls, the water-worn granites form rounded outcrops and free-standing boulders.

If you examine the gneissic rocks in the rest camp you will note that they are made up of a mix of quartz, feldspar and black biotite flakes. In several places in the park you will notice narrow white lines in the granites; these are intrusions of quartz. Outside the western boundary of the park there is a rose quartz quarry. The low, rounded, granite-gneiss outcrops, such as the huge dome of Moon Rock, show exfoliation where outer layers 'peel', almost like the layers of an onion, as a result of temperature extremes and other forces. An interesting feature on Moon Rock and other outcrops is the 'pop-ups', which apparently occur nowhere else in South Africa. Internal forces distort the outer 'peel' of rock and cause it to form domes, or to crack and form raised 'tent-like' structures. The *Swartrante* (Black Hills) in the western part of the park are made up of volcanic metamorphic rock with no quartz content. This rock is made up largely of ferro-magnesium and calcium-rich feldspar that usually has a 'coating' of desert varnish, typical of this type of rock in arid environments.

Vegetation

One can recognize three main vegetation types in the park. Among the hills and low mountains along the Orange (Gariep) River there is Lower Gariep Broken Veld, with very sparse plant growth dominated by low shrubs, perennial grasses and herbs, and numerous annuals following the first rains. Trees are few and far between but that giant aloe, the **kokerboom** (*Aloe dichotoma*), is obvious, as is the

CLIMATE

This is an arid area marked by temperature extremes, especially in winter. Daytime temperatures during the summer, in January or February, have been known to reach 46°C, with rock surface temperatures soaring to 70°C. Annual average temperatures range from 11°C minimum to 27°C maximum. Winter nights can drop below freezing. Autumn and spring temperatures are pleasant and mild. Most rain falls in thunderstorms from January to April, averaging just 130 mm each year. Periodic flooding of the area above the waterfall results from heavy rainfall in the upper catchment of the Orange (Gariep) River.

The wolftoon shrub, also known as the Namaqua porkbush, has tiny succulent leaves that grow in clusters on the branches.

black thorn (*Senegalia mellifera*) which produces large numbers of round, cream-coloured flowers with the onset of the spring rains. The western Augrabies region consists of undulating, rocky plains, with open shrubland and scatterings of low thickets of black thorn known as Blouputs Karroid Thornveld. Look out for the pale-trunked **shepherd's tree** (*Boscia albitrunca*) and **stink-bush** (*Boscia foetida*), which takes its name from the unpleasant smell emitted when the wood is sawn. The remainder of the park's vegetation is Bushmanland Arid Grassland on the plains, mainly sparse grassland dominated by the so-called white grasses (*Stipagrostis* spp.). After good rains there are displays of annually flowering plants.

Look out for **sweet thorn** (*Vachellia karroo*) and the tall, wide-spreading **camel thorn** (*Vachellia erioloba*), with its grey, velvety, kidney-shaped pods. The pods of both species are eagerly sought after by game during the dry months. **Namaqua fig-trees** (*Ficus cordata*), also known as 'rock-breakers', with their almost white bark and shiny green leaves, are mainly found in the broken-rock country along the river. Several occur close to the camp. The fruits are prized by baboons, vervet monkeys, hyrax and several bird species. The abundant Broadley's flat-lizard also wait below the trees to snatch up fallen figs. Sit quietly near one of these trees and watch the parade.

Wildlife
Mammals

The park has 48 mammals, including several reintroduced game species. Hook-lipped rhinoceros were reintroduced north of the river, but then were removed with the deproclamation of Riemvasmaak. There are populations of **springbok**, **southern oryx (gemsbok)**, **common eland**, **red hartebeest**, **greater kudu**, **Hartmann's mountain zebra** and **giraffe**. **Steenbok** are common on the open sand-flats and **klipspringer** are frequently seen in the rocky areas. In

Small numbers of reintroduced giraffe roam this unlikely environment.

Klipspringer are regular visitors at the rest camp.

fact, this is one of the best locations in southern Africa to spend time with this agile rock-dweller, as one does not have to wander far off the beaten track. A single klipspringer family has occupied the area near the camp for generations. These families are highly territorial so you have a good chance of seeing them if you are patient. Moon Rock has resident klipspringer as does the approach to the viewpoint over the gorge, Oranjekom.

Rock hyrax (**dassie**) are common, frequent the rocks around the camp, and are easy to approach and observe. This presents a unique opportunity to learn more about the behaviour of these fascinating creatures. **Southern ground squirrels** also frequent the camp area. Another day-active rodent is the squirrel-like, uniformly coloured, **dassie rat**, which lives in rock crevices but can be seen sunning itself in the cooler hours. Watch quietly and you will see how it dashes from shelter, nips off a green leaf or piece of succulent and runs back and eats it in the shade. **Chacma baboons** and **vervet monkeys** also roam around the cottages and campground but unfortunately have taken to snatching food from visitors.

There are 17 carnivore species in Augrabies but most are seldom seen. The most frequently sighted are the day-active mongoose species, **small grey**, **slender** and **yellow mongooses**, and that well-known group-dweller, the **suricate**. On a guided night-drive you have a good chance of adding others to the list, such as **small-spotted genet**. **Black-backed jackal** may be heard calling in the evening and early morning. The large carnivores, the **leopard** and perhaps the **brown hyaena**, are very rarely seen.

At least seven species of bat inhabit the park. At sunset, numerous insect-eating bats leave the shelter of crevices along the canyon walls and disperse to hunt into the night.

Birds

Despite the aridity 216 species of bird have been recorded. The camp environs offer excellent bird-watching, with such species as **acacia**

FACILITIES AND ACTIVITIES

- Chalets and bungalows (59 units); caravan/camping facilities, including electricity points.
- Hiking trails and walks.
- Mountain bike trails.
- Canoe trail.
- 4x4 trail.
- Guided night drives.
- Self-drive game-viewing and bird-watching.
- Licensed à la carte restaurant, coffee shop and shop with basic supplies.
- Diesel and petrol available.
- Range of services available at closest town, Kakamas, 40 km distant.
- Road from Upington and Kakamas is tarred.

The rest camp is located within a short walking distance of the waterfall and ravine.

WILDLIFE FACTS

- At least 48 mammal species occur within the park, including several, such as klipspringer, that are easy to observe.
- To date 216 species of bird recorded, including strong complement of raptors and arid-area adapted species such as larks (10) and Namaqua and double-banded sandgrouse.
- Some 45 reptiles, including 18 snakes.

A small population of Hartmann's mountain zebra is mainly seen in the west of the park.

pied barbet, golden-tailed woodpecker, Namaqua warbler, black-chested prinia, Pririt batis, dusky sunbird and the Orange River white-eye. This is also a good area to look for the short-toed rock-thrush.

African fish eagle are often seen along the river, and Verreaux's eagle is commonly sighted hunting hyrax in the neighbouring hill country. This raptor may also be seen along the gorge walls, where binoculars may also reveal peregrine falcon as well as pale-winged starling and speckled pigeon, both of which nest in this spectacular setting. Black stork also sometimes nest on the cliffs, and large mixed flocks of swifts and swallows hawking for insects are often visible from the gorge and the falls.

Several lark species may be seen on the open grasslands, although some, like Stark's lark, tend to be nomadic. Other typical arid-area species that may be nomadic because of the nature of this habitat include Ludwig's bustard, northern black korhaan, Namaqua sandgrouse, double-banded and Burchell's coursers. Rosy-faced lovebirds migrate locally and may not always be present.

Reptiles and amphibians

Many of the 45 reptile species are secretive, and some night-active, but there are exceptions. Along the rim of the gorge and especially on the rocks above the falls, Broadley's flat-lizard congregate in summer, the brightly coloured males outnumbered by the dowdier females. They feed on the swarming blackflies, snatching them from the rocks or in mid-air, and dash to snatch up the ripe Namaqua rock-figs as they drop. Throughout the rocky areas, the dominant blue-headed southern rock agama males seek out a vantage point and warn off rivals with their distinctive bobbing display. The largest lizard in South Africa is the Nile, or water, monitor, reaching a length of over 2 m. It frequents the river but also the side-streams near the camp. The night-active Bibron's gecko may be seen at the

The red markings on its skin distinguishes the marbled rubber frog from other amphibian species.

The park offers great sightings of predatory birds including lanner falcon (left), red-necked falcon and southern white-faced owl (right)

campground hunting insects attracted to the lights. The 18 snakes are seldom seen; the venomous species, including **puff adder**, **Cape cobra** and **black spitting cobra**, should be left alone if sighted.

Despite the dry conditions a total of 11 amphibian species have been recorded. A few are bound to permanent water but many shelter underground until the onset of the rains.

Fish

The river harbours 12 fish species. In the gorge pools, with binoculars you may pick out the broad mouths of feeding **sharptooth catfish**, which grow to 1.4 m in length and can weigh more than 30 kg.

Invertebrates

An insect hard to ignore, especially from September to April, is the tiny swarming **blackfly** (*Simulium* sp.). This blood-sucker does not transmit diseases to humans in this area, unlike elsewhere in Africa. Insect-repellents should keep them at bay. They help nourish swifts, swallows and Broadley's flat lizards, among others.

There are several scorpion species, though they are seldom seen, and usually at night. As many as six belong to the genus *Parabuthus*, with small pincers and thick tail, and carry potent venom dangerous to humans. *Parabuthus villosus*, up to 180 mm in length, is the largest member of the genus in the world, and unusually it is mainly active in the day. Shoes are definitely advisable.

- Although this is not within the malarial area and there are no recent known cases there is a small risk of malaria infection during the summer months.
- It is extremely hot in summer. Always carry drinking water, use sunscreen and wear a hat.
- Exercise great caution at the edge of the ravine and waterfall as the rocks are slippery and deaths have occurred.

KGALAGADI TRANSFRONTIER PARK

Arid-area game and bird life

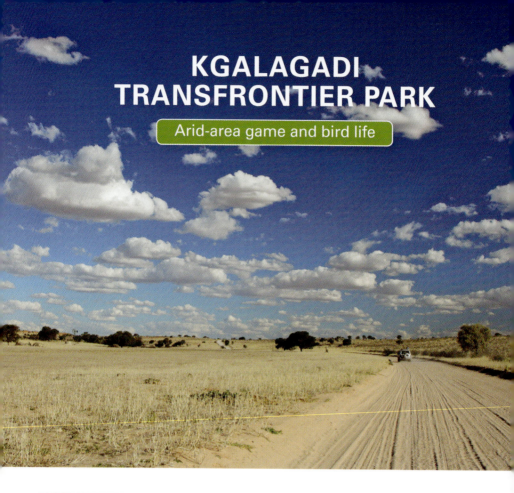

Lie of the land

In May 2000 South Africa's Kalahari Gemsbok National Park (proclaimed in 1931) and Botswana's adjoining Gemsbok National Park (proclaimed in 1938) were combined to form the first transfrontier park in Africa, the Kgalagadi Transfrontier Park, covering some 3.6 million ha. Located in the extreme north of the Northern Cape province, it is bordered in the west by Namibia. It lies in the south of the great Kalahari Basin and is dominated by the Auob and Nossob riverbeds in the west. Apart from some low calcrete outcroppings the park is dominated by low sand dunes and sandy plains beyond the Nossob to the east.

Most roads within Kgalagadi are of variable condition, so be prepared for corrugations and sandy tracks.

Brief history

The Kalahari is closely associated with the San, hunter-gatherers who eked out a living from this vast sand wilderness. These Later Stone Age people were here from perhaps 20 000 BP, and the first livestock herders, the Khoekhoen, arrived around 2 000 BP. The Kgalagadi arrived later and it is from their word for saltpans, or 'great thirstland' – Makgadikgadi – that the Kalahari was named.

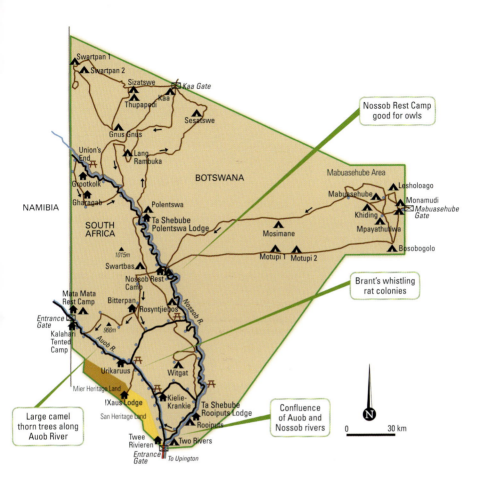

The first whites to arrive in the area were traders. In 1891 the British colonial authorities annexed this area to Bechuanaland (present-day Botswana). After World War I the area was subdivided and awarded to veterans, but the farms were unviable. The farmers became hunters, joined by biltong (dried meat) hunters from elsewhere, and game numbers declined dramatically.

The initial conservation area was extended in 1935 when land purchased along the south bank of the Auob River was incorporated into the Kalahari Gemsbok National Park.

Geology and landscape

In the South African sector the landscape is dominated by the Nossob (meaning 'dark clay') and the Auob ('bitter water') riverbeds. Both rivers rise in the Anas Mountains near Windhoek, Namibia, and flow south-east, reaching confluence just 6 km north of the main camp at Twee Rivieren. These are true rivers of sand as they flow only briefly,

HIGHLIGHTS

- Some of the best predator-viewing in South Africa, partly because of the open terrain.
- Waterhole park – patient watching at a drinking point is often more effective than driving around.
- Very good birding at waterholes and in three main camps.
- Unfenced wilderness camps.

Kgalagadi Transfrontier Park 259

CLIMATE

Between the months of October and April, 120 mm to 220 mm rain falls in the park, mostly in the form of thunderstorms. Winters are usually very dry. Seasonal temperatures are extreme, ranging at Mata-Mata from 40°C in December to -6.8°C in June. Frost is common during the winter.

The Cape fox is one of three dog species in the Kgalagadi park.

after exceptional rains. The Auob cuts a deep-sided narrow valley 100 m to 500 m wide, whereas the Nossob is a mainly shallow, sandy trough. Between the riverbeds and into Botswana the landscape is dominated by low, linear sand dunes of aeolian origin, underlain by silcretes and calcretes belonging to the Cenozoic Kalahari Group. Exposed white calcretes can be seen at some of the picnic sites and in the camps.

Vegetation

One can easily distinguish riverine vegetation and the duneveld dominated by seasonal grasses. The so-called Gordonia Duneveld, comprising much of the dune area – only 3 m to 8 m above the plains – on the South African side, is dominated by grasses, particularly **bushman grass** (*Stipagrostis amabilis*), and a scattering of shrubs, as well as **black thorn** (*Senegalia mellifera*) and the distinctive **grey camel thorn** (*Vachellia haematoxylon*). Along the beds of

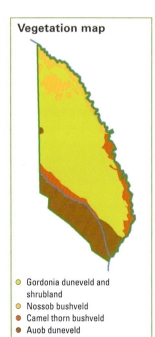

Vegetation map

- Gordonia duneveld and shrubland
- Nossob bushveld
- Camel thorn bushveld
- Auob duneveld

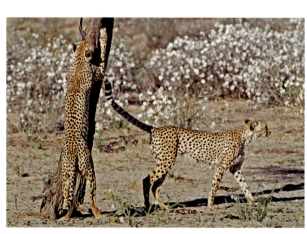

Cheetah mark their range by urine spraying and tree scratching.

260　Northern Cape

Some 400 spotted hyaenas range throughout the park.

the Auob and Nossob rivers, and in all three main camps, you will again encounter the grey camel thorn, and the park's largest tree, the spreading **camel thorn** (*Vachellia erioloba*) with its distinctive grey, kidney-shaped pods. Between the camp at Nossob and the northern tip of the transfrontier park you will find the **worm-bark false-thorn** (*Albizia anthelmintica*), a small tree with larger leaves than the acacias that produce flat, brown pods. The white-trunked **shepherd's tree** (*Boscia albitrunca*) is sparsely scattered through the park, like the distinctive **candle thorn** (*Vachellia hebeclada*), a low bush, with erect grey pods that resemble candles.

Wildlife
Mammals
Some 62 mammals inhabit the greater park, including several game species. There are about 450 **lion**, 200 **cheetah** and 150 **leopard**, and you have a better chance of spotting these cats here than even in Kruger. There are some 600 **brown hyaena**, and under 400 **spotted hyaena**. Small carnivores are also well represented, the most frequently seen being **black-backed jackal**, **bat-eared fox**, **yellow mongoose** and the communal **suricate**. All three main camps have resident populations of yellow mongoose and **southern African ground squirrel**. Especially in Nossob, the **acacia rat** may be found by torchlight, feeding on seed pods and leaves in the trees. Antelope are well represented, with particularly large numbers of **springbok** along the riverbeds, as well as **southern oryx (gemsbok)**, **red hartebeest** and **blue wildebeest**. Numbers vary greatly according to rainfall and the abundance of grazing but the dry season brings the greatest game concentrations along the riverbeds. **Common eland** in particular are highly nomadic and sightings are often a matter of luck. Giraffe have been reintroduced and are usually seen near Mata-Mata. Large colonies of **Brant's whistling rat** inhabit especially the outer edges of the lower dune road linking the two principal riverbeds. Here too are the numerous earth mounds of the **Damara mole-rat**, a colonial species with a complex social system.

FACILITIES AND ACTIVITIES

- Main rest camps, Twee Rivieren, Mata-Mata and Nossob, each have a range of accommodation options and a campground; six wilderness camps; two new lodges on the Botswana side.
- Twee Rivieren, Mata-Mata and Nossob have a small range of basics; Twee Rivieren has a restaurant. All have fuel stations and swimming pools. Only Twee Rivieren has cell phone reception.
- Several 4x4 trails (one guided overnight); accompanied night and game-viewing drives.
- Park lies about 265 km north of Upington. Tarred road joins the town to the park's southernmost camp, Twee Rivieren. The eastern route from Vanzylsrus is gravel and in bad condition.
- The park can be entered at Mata-Mata Rest Camp from Namibia via Keetmanshoop (280 km). There are three gates on the Botswana side. Remember to take passports along if entering or leaving via the Namibia or Botswana gates.
- Only Upington and Keetmanshoop have a range of services.

Kgalagadi Transfrontier Park 261

Summer rains, which mostly fall during thunderstorms, bring new vegetation growth for gemsbok.

Birds

At least 275 bird species are regularly recorded in the park, with an additional 72 species recorded as rare visitors, or vagrants. The estimated 16 000 **ostrich**, like many of the game species, are rather nomadic. The raptor diversity is impressive, with 34 resident or migrant species. They range in size from the diminutive **pygmy falcon** to the large **lappet-faced vulture**. The former may be spotted near the giant nest structures of the **sociable weaver**, whose colonies attain a density of 80 birds per square kilometre along the Nossob River. Several species of owl live and hunt in and around the camps. You should certainly hear **southern white-faced scops owl**, **African scops owl** and **pearl-spotted owlet**, and a bit of effort will reward you with sightings. Around the waterholes you may see such raptors as **lanner falcon**, **gabar goshawk** and **red-necked falcons** (best

> ### WILDLIFE FACTS
> - At least 62 mammal species, including Africa's three big cats.
> - No fewer than 275 bird species recorded but 72 are rare visitors or vagrants.
> - Of 48 reptile species present, only a few are readily observed.
> - All seven amphibian species spend months underground between the rains.

The bateleur is one of 34 raptor species recorded in the park.

Northern Cape

The self-catering Kieliekrankie Wilderness Camp is located near Twee Rivieren.

along Nossob). Travel north from Nossob Rest Camp to see more bushveld species, such as **southern yellow-billed hornbill** and **lilac-breasted roller**. One of South Africa's most finely plumaged birds, the **crimson-breasted shrike**, is fairly common and a regular in the camps. This is the best place in the country to watch the **kori bustard** and its bustard cousins the **northern black korhaan** and **red-crested korhaan**.

Reptiles and amphibians

A few of the 48 reptile species stand out, though in winter reptile activity is greatly reduced. The **ground agama** is commonly seen perched in a bush, or even on a road sign, along the dune roads. On warm evenings around sunset you will almost certainly hear the **common barking gecko**, and the tiny **Bradfield's dwarf gecko** can be seen by day hunting insects on trees at picnic sites and in the camps. In the camp lights at Twee Rivieren watch for **Bibron's thick-toed gecko** hunting insects. The **Kalahari tree skink** appears at virtually every picnic site and in the camps. The 17 snake species are seldom spotted. **Cape cobra**, especially the yellow variety, is occasionally seen around the large nests of the sociable weaver. At least six amphibian species survive the long dry season by burrowing underground and emerging after good rains.

On high alert during the day, ground agamas retreat speedily at the hint of danger.

- Malaria is possible after heavy summer rains and fatal cases have occurred.
- Summer day temperatures can be uncomfortably hot and winter nights very cold.
- Scorpions are common and you should wear closed shoes if walking around the camps at night.

MOKALA NATIONAL PARK
Open semi-arid parkland with good game-viewing

Lie of the land
Mokala, the Tswana name for the camel thorn, lies 78 km south-west of the Northern Cape's provincial capital Kimberley and west of the N12 that links Kimberley and Cape Town. Its current extent is 27 571 ha, which includes Wildehondepan in the west and Knoffelfontein on the Riet River in the east. Expansion plans continue. Numerous rocky hills are interspersed with open wooded plains; the Riet River forms part of the northern boundary.

Large tracts of grassland dominate much of Mokala National Park.

Brief history
Numerous San petroglyphs and paintings can be found here. This area played a pivotal role in the 2nd Anglo-Boer War, and several battles took place nearby.

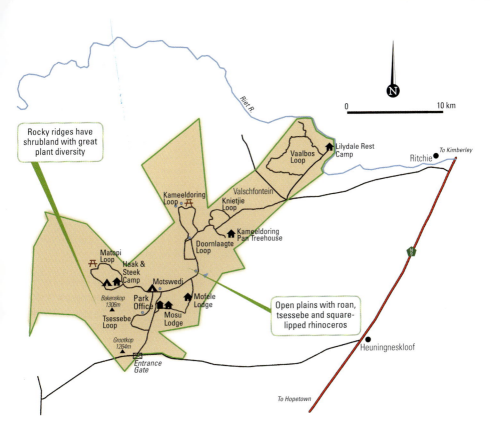

Geology and landscape

The numerous rock ridges and outcrops are surrounded by plains. The highest point is Bakenskop at 1 306 m above sea level. The hills and outcrops are a mix of Ecca and Dwyka sediments, with Karoo dolerites covering layers of sandstone and mudstone, and the lowlands are mainly covered with calcrete-rich sandy soils. Whitish chunks of calcrete are visible in many locations.

HIGHLIGHTS

- Both species of rhinoceros, savanna buffalo, tsessebe and roan antelope.
- Good birding but bird-list not complete.

Vegetation

The plains, dominated by open grassland (including recovering agricultural land) and Kimberley thornveld woodland, harbour such species as **camel thorn** (*Vachellia erioloba*), **umbrella thorn** (*Vachellia tortilis*), **sweet thorn** (*Vachellia karroo*), **black thorn** (*Senegalia mellifera*) and **shepherd's tree** (*Boscia albitrunca*), the latter easily recognized by its pale grey-white bark. The Kimberley thornveld can be further subdivided; the hilly country, Vaalbos rocky shrubland, generally has a greater diversity of

The thornveld harbours several Senegalia *and* Vachellia *species, including camel thorn.*

Vegetation map

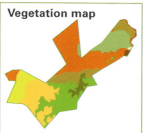

- *Schmidtia pappophoroides* and *Vachellia erioloba* open grassland
- *Vachellia erioloba* and *V. tortilis* open woodland
- *Senegalia mellifera* and *Vachellia tortilis* open woodland
- *Senegalia mellifera* and *Vachellia erioloba* open to closed woodland
- *Stipagrostis* sp. forbland
- *Searsia pendulina* woodland and riparian vegetation
- *Cynodon dactyolon* and *Ziziphus mucronata* open woodland
- *Rhigozum obovatum* and *Senegalia mellifera* open shrubland
- *Schimidtia pappophoroides* and *Vachellia erioloba* sparse woodland
- *Searsia lancea* woodland

CLIMATE

This area has mainly summer rainfall, from December to February, averaging 400 mm per year, usually accompanied by thunderstorms. In summer, midday temperatures range from 33° C to 36°C but can exceed 40°C, especially in January. June to August daytime maxima average 22°C, while nighttime temperatures frequently drop to below zero.

Greater kudu are frequently encountered in the park; here two bulls test each other.

The small spotted cat is nocturnal and elusive.

evergreen bush and tree species, including the **black thorn**, **yellow pomegranate** (*Rhigozum obovatum*), **common guarri** (*Euclea undulata*) and **buffalo thorn** (*Ziziphus rivularis*). Some additional species and zones will be added to the list as the park expands.

Wildlife
Mammals

At least 50 mammal species are here but a further 18 are known from the area. Rare game species have been reintroduced, including **square-lipped** and **hook-lipped rhinoceros**, **roan antelope** and **tsessebe**. A few of the species introduced before proclamation of the national park, such as **impala**, **common waterbuck** and **nyala**, are being removed and relocated. **Plains zebra**, **giraffe**, **savanna buffalo**, **red hartebeest**, **common eland**, **greater kudu**, **black wildebeest**, **steenbok** and **common duiker** also occur. On the plains you should see **bat-eared fox**, **yellow mongoose**, **slender mongoose**

Accommodation options at Mokala are varied and include lodges and a campground.

FACILITIES AND ACTIVITIES

- Three lodges with multiple accommodation options, including cottages and rooms; rustic cottage; rustic campground and camping sites; bird hide; treetop chalet overlooking a waterhole. Luxury private campsites and wilderness camps are planned.
- Restaurant and bar at main camp.
- Conference centre.
- Guided game drives. Guided horse and mountain bike trails are planned.
- Network of game-viewing roads, all gravel.

and **southern African ground squirrel**. **Springhares** can be seen at night in the grounds of Mosu Lodge.

Birds

At 139 species the list is already quite respectable and growing. The wooded hill behind Mosu Lodge and the rustic campground offer good bird-watching. A number of species approach their southern range limit in the park, including **pearl-spotted owlet**, **pygmy falcon**, **brubru**, **crimson-breasted shrike**, **golden-tailed woodpecker**, **southern yellow-billed hornbill**, **black-faced** and **violet-eared waxbills**.

Reptiles and amphibians

Distribution records suggest that at least 47 reptile species as well as 13 amphibian species can be expected within the reserve.

The Kalahari scrub robin prefers thickets and bushy areas.

The kori bustard is the largest of the bustards.

WILDLIFE FACTS

- Mammal list stands at 50 but at least a further 18 small species known to be in the greater area are likely to be added to this count.
- New and developing park yet bird-list already has 139 species.
- Amphibian and reptile surveys not yet undertaken.

- High temperatures in summer can be debilitating.
- Beware of dangerous game, such as rhinoceros and buffalo.

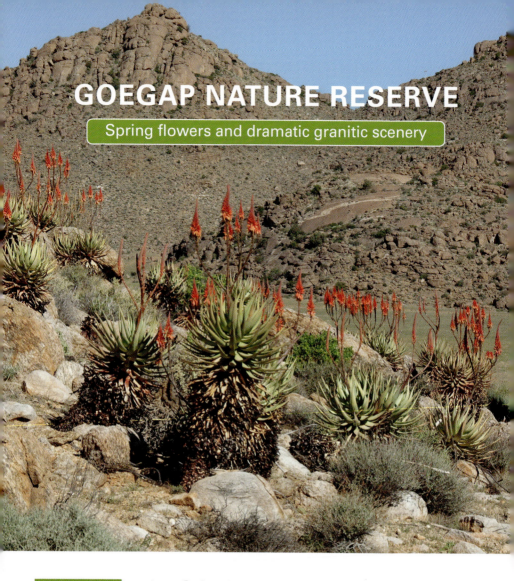

GOEGAP NATURE RESERVE
Spring flowers and dramatic granitic scenery

LOCATION

Goegap is a reserve with striking scenery and great floral diversity.

Lie of the land
The 14 864 ha provincial nature reserve of Goegap lies in the far north-west of the province, 15 km east of the town of Springbok. Here Namaqualand starts to blend with the great plains of Bushmanland to the east. The highest point is the Carolusberg at 1 344 m above sea level.

Brief history
Very little archaeological work has been undertaken in this area but it is certain that our early ancestors occupied parts of it, if perhaps only seasonally, before the arrival of the San. The San were already present in the area by the time the

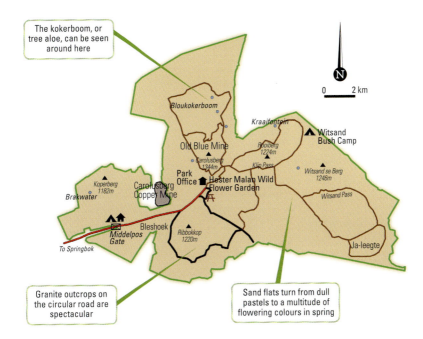

Khoekhoen livestock herders arrived about 1 500 BP. By the time the first Europeans reached the area, a Khoekhoen group called the Namaqua was already settled here.

On Carolusberg in October 1685, Governor Simon van der Stel and his party extracted copper ore, but commercial exploitation had to wait until the mid 1800s. In the 1860s richer deposits were discovered elsewhere, more specifically at Okiep and Nababeep. On the left-hand side, close to the entrance of the reserve, is the massive waste heap of the now closed Carolusberg copper mine; an eyesore that is unfortunately likely to remain in place for many years.

The original Hester Malan Nature Reserve was taken over by the provincial conservation authorities in 1960. It was formally proclaimed in 1966. In 1990 the enlarged reserve was renamed the Goegap Nature Reserve, a Nama word that means waterhole.

HIGHLIGHTS

- Dramatic granite outcrops.
- Good for succulents all year; impressive flower displays in spring after good rain.
- Freedom to walk and explore the reserve.

Geology and landscape

The same granites and gneisses that form domes and boulder clusters rising above the surrounding plain also underlie the valleys with their deep covering of sand. This patchwork of impressive outcrops and inselbergs, interspersed with sand-covered valleys, makes it one of the Northern Cape province's most attractive reserves. This is the Namaqualand Blomveld habitat, so named because following good rains these valleys are carpeted with both succulent and non-succulent flowers.

Wolftoon bush in bloom.

Goegap Nature Reserve 269

Vegetation map

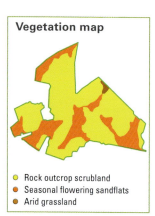

- Rock outcrop scrubland
- Seasonal flowering sandflats
- Arid grassland

Goegap Nature Reserve in spring is a blaze of colour.

CLIMATE

Here 80 mm to 160 mm (average 150 mm) of rain falls in winter, from May to September, but periods of drought are common. Summers are hot with an average maximum of 30°C in January, though temperatures can reach 40°C and the record is 48°C. Winters are cold with an average minimum of 5°C in July and a few nights of frost.

Vegetation

Plant growth on the rock outcrops is sparse but diverse. Most plant species attain less than 1 m, but the **tree aloe**, or **quiver tree**, (*Aloe dichotoma*) is an exception. Taller bushes grow at the bases of the outcrops, watered by run-off rain. There are many succulents, both in bush and creeping form, and small-leaved karroid bushes. In the sandy valleys there is a strong complement of bulbous plants, or geophytes. Almost 600 species of plant have been recorded, many of them short-lived spring/summer annuals.

Wildlife
Mammals
Hartmann's mountain zebra, **southern oryx (gemsbok)**, **common eland** and **springbok** have been reintroduced in small numbers.

Southern oryx, or gemsbok.

Springbok prefer open plains to rocky outcrops.

270 Northern Cape

Outside of breeding season, the rock kestrel is usually solitary.

A booted eagle appears here in its pale phase.

FACILITIES AND ACTIVITIES

- Camping as well as lodge facilities.
- Some internal gravel roads for game- and flower-viewing (17 km).
- 4x4 routes.
- Mountain bike route.
- Two short walking trails.
- Horse trails for those riders who bring their own mounts.
- Includes Hester Malan Wild Flower Garden.
- No fuel or supplies in the reserve but Springbok has a range of facilities.

Steenbok can be seen on the sand plains, and **klipspringer** in the hills. The 10 carnivore species are rarely sighted, except for **yellow mongoose**, **small grey mongoose**, **suricate** and **bat-eared fox**. **Rock hyrax** (**dassie**) and the day-active **dassie rat** are common in the hills. Dassie rats can also be spotted in the large quiver tree-bedecked rock garden to the south of the office complex – on cold mornings they may be seen basking in the sun and in the hot hours sheltering in the shade of rock crevices. The fleet of foot **western rock sengi**, or **elephant shrew**, can also be seen in this area. **Round-eared sengi** may be seen darting around on the sand flats, and their cousins the western rock sengi occupy the hills, where they sit in the shade and make short dashes to snatch up insects.

Birds

There are a few bird species of interest among the modest 106 recorded here. Both **Cape eagle-owl** and **spotted eagle-owl** occur and it is a good area for diurnal raptors, such as **jackal buzzard**, **black-chested snake eagle**, **Verreaux's eagle**, **booted eagle** and **secretarybird**. A good selection of larks includes **thick-billed**, **Karoo** and **Karoo long-billed larks** in the sand areas. Watch for **cinnamon-breasted warbler** on the rocky slopes.

Reptiles

Only 25 species are recorded but surveys in surrounding areas suggest a total of around 43. Residents include **tent tortoise**, **rhombic skaapsteker**, **coral snake**, **Cape cobra**, **horned adder**, **common barking gecko**, **Bibron's thick-toed gecko** and **western rock skink**.

WILDLIFE FACTS

- The 46 mammal species include Hartmann's mountain zebra, southern oryx (gemsbok) and springbok.
- Good location for watching klipspringer, sengi and dassie rat.
- Only 106 bird species recorded but several interesting residents.
- Up to 43 reptile species may live here but so far only about half confirmed.
- One toad and two frogs, with five more likely to be added to this count.

- Summer days can be very hot and winter nights may drop below freezing.

Goegap Nature Reserve 271

WITSAND NATURE RESERVE
An isolated sand dune system rich in life

Lie of the land

Witsand covers 3 500 ha. It lies 80 km south-west of Postmasburg and 59 km north-east of Groblershoop. The reserve is centred on the sand dunes, surrounded by level country approximately 1 200 m above sea level. The Langberg range just outside the eastern boundary forms a rugged backdrop.

Brief history

Because of its permanent water sources the area has been occupied since before 40 000 BP, as evidenced by stone tools and other archaeological artefacts found here. Several prehistoric sites exist in the Witsand reserve, and while wandering in the sand dunes you will encounter tool-working areas. These are protected and nothing may be removed.

More stone tools and potsherds indicate that the Korana people occupied the area from the 17th century to the 19th century. There is also evidence that the Tswana were here until about the end of the 18th century. The only inhabitants by the late 19th century were small groups of San who had probably been here for several hundred years.

To the east of the Witsand dune system lies the Langberg range, separated by a plain covered with scrub and trees.

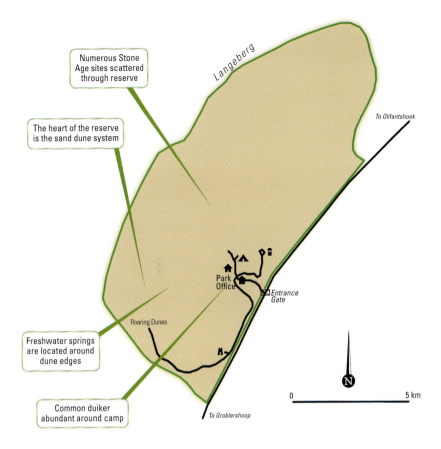

By the end of the 19th century white farmers and traders had settled along the fringes of the Langberg. A rebel Boer force under General Kemp took a stand here against government troops in 1914, and remnants of the stone walls they erected can still be seen in the high dunes. The reserve was proclaimed in 1994.

Geology and landscape

Witsand lies on the southern fringe of the Kalahari and the white sands, originating some 65 million years BP, have an average depth of 70 m. Coarse grains on the surface are interspersed with silts and clays. The dune patch, 9 km long and averaging 4 km in width, is rich in oxides that leach out over time and discolour some of the sand. These windblown and changing sand dunes are confined by alternating north-west and east-south-east winds. Small outcrops of ferricrete in the yellow sands area testify to wetter conditions prevailing during the Upper Pleistocene period. The basin holds vast quantities of fresh water thanks to the heavy clays and fine silt that

HIGHLIGHTS

- Spectacular sand dunes against the backdrop of the Langberg Mountains.
- Freedom to walk in the reserve.
- Bird hide at waterhole allows for excellent birding and is well known for viewing Namaqua and Burchell's sandgrouse at close quarters.

Vegetation map

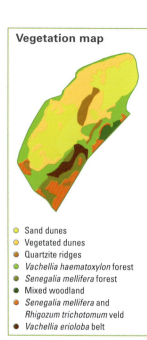

- Sand dunes
- Vegetated dunes
- Quartzite ridges
- *Vachellia haematoxylon* forest
- *Senegalia mellifera* forest
- Mixed woodland
- *Senegalia mellifera* and *Rhigozum trichotomum* veld
- *Vachellia erioloba* belt

Numerous springs are located around the dune bases.

serve as a gigantic sponge, and several small water bodies are present on the surface. The famous roaring sand, or 'brulsand', is caused by intense friction as the fine, even grains of sand are rubbed together, releasing trapped air. Sometimes the sound is more of a monotonous hum than a roar. The quartzites and shales of the adjacent Langberg range, dated at 1 900 to 2 050 million BP, belong to the Olifantshoek Supergroup and also underlie the Witsand.

Vegetation

The plains around the dune system are dominated by Karroid Kalahari Bushveld and Orange River Nama Karoo, with elements of Kalahari Mountain Bushveld. The most obvious trees are the **camel thorn** (*Vachellia erioloba*), **grey camel thorn** (*Vachellia haematoxylon*), and the shorter **candle thorn** (*Vachellia hebeclada*) with the erect grey-brown pods that give this bush its name. The white-grey trunked **shepherd's tree** (*Boscia albitrunca*) stands out, as does the

CLIMATE

Rain starts falling here in late October, but the principal rains are from February to March, making it a summer rainfall regime. The usual amount of rain is from 150 mm to 300 mm. Summer temperatures average 28°C but may reach 40°C, while winter daytime averages 20°C. Freezing temperatures are possible. The most pleasant months are April/May and October/November.

The sand dunes dominate this reserve.

Northern Cape

sweet thorn (*Vachellia karroo*) with its impressive (15+ cm) white thorns. Numerous annual and perennial grasses occur, including the so-called white, or bushman, grasses (*Stipagrostis* spp.), important to grazing mammals. There are numerous dwarf shrubs, bulbous plants, annuals and perennials.

Wildlife
Mammals

For such a small reserve, the list of 43 mammals is quite impressive and includes a number of reintroduced species, such as **red hartebeest**, **southern oryx (gemsbok)** and **springbok**. **Greater kudu** have naturally repopulated this protected area. **Steenbok** and **common duiker** are widespread, and the latter are particularly approachable in the accommodation area. Of the 12 carnivore species, you are most likely to see the day-active **suricate** and the **yellow** and **slender mongooses**. On cool days you may spot a **bat-eared fox**. Easily visible rodents are the **southern ground squirrel** and **four-striped grass mouse**. Many species are nocturnal but the sand dunes offer a wonderful tracking opportunity. On one visit the authors recorded no fewer than 23 mammal species on the basis of their tracks, droppings and feeding signs. The reserve harbours six rare mammals, **southern African hedgehog**, **pangolin**, **aardwolf**, **honey badger (ratel)**, **small spotted cat** and **aardvark**.

Birds

The latest bird tally stands at 171 species, of which many are arid-area adapted. Bird watching is good around the accommodation. This is the only reserve that has developed a bird hide at a waterhole specifically for viewing sandgrouse, but of course it is useful for other species too. The principal species are the **Namaqua** and **Burchell's sandgrouse** but **double-banded** also occasionally visit, with best viewing in winter. Besides the expected arid-area species, such as **sociable weaver**, **pygmy falcon**, **Burchell's** and **double-**

FACILITIES AND ACTIVITIES

- Accommodation in well-appointed bungalows and chalets, with air conditioning; caravan/camping sites.
- Walking trails.
- Mountain biking.
- 4x4 trails (fee payable).
- Swimming pools.
- Limited road network.
- No fuel in the reserve.
- Tarred R64 linking Upington with Kimberley runs south of the reserve, with gravel road turn-off 49 km east of Groblershoop. Distance on gravel is 42 km, with alternative 78 km route running south, 5 km west of Olifantshoek.
- Gravel roads are infrequently graded and may be in poor condition.
- Bergenaar's Pass is very steep and is not suitable for caravans and heavy trailers.

Common duiker usually occur singly.

Nests of white-browed sparrow-weavers.

Witsand Nature Reserve

The bird hide allows excellent viewing of sandgrouse, especially the Namaqua and Burchell's.

banded coursers, seven lark species, **crimson-breasted shrike** and **white-browed sparrow-weaver**, there are many woodland species. These include **southern yellow-billed** and **grey hornbills**, **green-winged ptylia** and **violet-eared waxbill**. This is also home to no fewer than six owl species, including our largest, the **giant eagle-owl**, and smallest, the **pearl-spotted owlet**.

Reptiles

Like many arid areas, Witsand has many reptile species, including three tortoises, 13 snakes and 23 lizards. More await discovery. Many of the reptiles are secretive and fast moving so offer little opportunity for close study, but there are exceptions. Of the seven skink species here, the larger **Cape** and **striped skinks** are commonly seen around the camp, as are the **ground** and **Anchieta's agamas**. The large **Bibron's gecko** hunts for insects around the chalet lights at night. The male **common barking gecko** is heard on summer nights.

Invertebrates

Witsand has a rich and little-studied invertebrate fauna. Two very interesting spiders occur in the dune area. The **dancing white lady** escapes predators by impressive leaps. It rests up in burrows during the day, emerging at night to hunt. The **buckspoor spider** (*Seothyra* sp.) may occur at high densities and takes its name from the silk laid over the entrance to its burrow, its shape similar to an antelope track There is a rich scorpion fauna, including several *Parabuthus* species dangerous to humans, with small pincers and robust tails. There are more butterfly species on Witsand than occur in the whole of the United Kingdom, including one endemic.

WILDLIFE FACTS

- At least 43 mammal species, including reintroduced game, and several rarities.
- 171 species of bird including 21 raptors.
- About 39 reptiles and five amphibian species, including South Africa's largest, the giant bullfrog.
- Excellent animal tracking in dunes and around numerous water bodies.

Common barking geckos live singly in burrows dug in the sand.

- There is extreme heat in summer, and temperature falls below freezing at night in winter.
- Avoid walking in the dunes during thunderstorms.
- Be alert for scorpions (wear closed shoes at night), ticks (tampans may carry tick-bite fever), and paper wasps (in summer).

OORLOGSKLOOF NATURE RESERVE

Spectacular scenery in a Cape heathland setting

Lie of the land

The 4 776 ha Oorlogskloof reserve, established in 1983, is located at the western edge of the Karoo on the escarpment. It is located on a deeply incised plateau focused on the canyon of the Oorlogskloof River in the east, which forms its eastern boundary. In the north is the Saaikloof River of Keiserfontein and to the south the Saaikloof River from the Klein Koebee. The ridge line to the west of the reserve boundary is called the Bokkeveldberge, and beyond one has superb views across the botanically important Knersvlakte. The unspoilt wilderness character of the reserve presents the opportunity for nature lovers to enjoy a unique wilderness experience. The highest point (Arrie se Punt) is 915 m above sea level, and the canyon bottom is at about 538 m. The canyon is up to 500 m wide and 80 m to 200 m deep.

Brief history

Because of the permanent water, the San may have been here for more than 5 000 years and remained up to about 1740. Certainly they were here when the

The Knersvlakte, lies below the Oorlogskloof Nature Reserve, and has impressive floral displays in the spring.

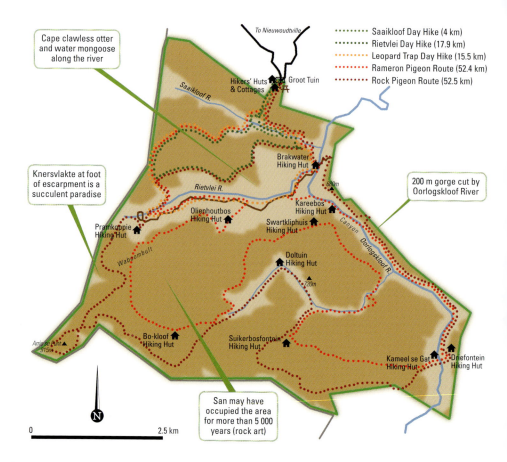

HIGHLIGHTS

- Dramatic scenery and mix of four distinct vegetation types.
- Rich bird life.
- Some 23 rock painting locations in the area.
- Not as overcrowded as other popular hiking routes.

Khoekhoen herders arrived around 1 500 BP, although the latter favoured the plains for grazing their animals. Evidence of these peoples remains in the numerous sites with rock paintings.

By 1739 the area below the escarpment, the Knersvlakte, was being grazed by nomadic Khoekhoen stock-farmers and their white counterparts, the trekboers. The colonists had to compete with the local peoples for water, grazing, land and livestock; when trade failed theft occured. The rivalry climaxed in September, when a white commando attacked a Khoekhoen settlement near the present-day reserve, killing 13 people and 'confiscating' much of the livestock. As a gesture of truce, they returned some of the stock. The canyon became known as Oorlogskloof (war ravine).

Geology and landscape

The landscape is dominated by the canyon systems formed by the Oorlogskloof River that rises in the Roggeveld Mountains near Calvinia, the Rietvlei and Saaikloof streams, the plateau through

Spectacular cliffs flank the Oorlogskloof River.

which they cut and the Bokkeveld Escarpment to the west. From the escarpment one looks westward over the flat, arid Knersvlakte. The rocks are sandstone and quartzites of the Table Mountain Group but in the deeper cuts you can see the softer limestones and shales.

Vegetation

Although dominated by Cape heathland (fynbos), known here as Bokkeveld sandstone fynbos, there are intrusions of western mountain Karoo scrub. Most species are low-growing but there are a few exceptions, such as the large tree protea known as the **waboom** ('**wagon tree**') (*Protea nitida*), whose hard wood was used to fashion wagon-wheel rims and brake-blocks. Other obvious bushes and small trees include the **laurel sugarbush** (*Protea laurifolia*),

CLIMATE

This is a winter rainfall area, with most rain falling from May to August. Rainfall is 160 mm to 415 mm, averaging 290 mm. The Oorlogskloof River flows from May to November, leaving standing pools for the rest of the year. Mean extremes range from almost 31°C in February to 4°C in July. A few winter mornings are frosty.

The reserve's grey renosterbos grows mainly on Vanrhynsdorp shale.

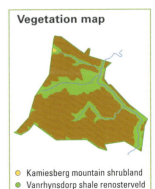

Vegetation map

○ Kamiesberg mountain shrubland
○ Vanrhynsdorp shale renosterveld
● Bokkeveld sandstone fynbos (Cape heathland)

Oorlogskloof Nature Reserve **279**

Although most people visit the area to witness the floral spectacle that comes with spring, time spent searching out the smaller blooms will be as rewarding.

Flower heads of Brunsvigia minor *appear after the winter rains.*

wild olive (*Olea europaea*) and **Cape willow** (*Salix mucronata*). There are also scattered stands of exotic trees, a legacy of the area's farming history. The low, grey shrub **renosterbos** (*Elytropappus rhinocerotis*), demarcating the Vanrhynsdorp shale renosterveld vegetation type, is found particularly in the canyon and gorges. The whole Nieuwoudtville area is well known for the great diversity of plants, and particularly geophytes, which flower in spring following good winter rains. On the western side of Saaikloof is a small portion of Kamiesberg mountain shrubland.

Wildlife
Mammals

African wild cats are solitary.

Hewitt's red rock rabbit is predominantly nocturnal.

At least 42 mammal species are thought to inhabit the reserve. **Cape mountain zebra** have been introduced and populations of **common duiker** and **Cape grysbok** occur naturally. **Chacma baboon** and **rock hyrax** (**dassies**) are common, as is the **small grey mongoose**, but many other species are secretive and night active. **Leopard** move along the escarpment at times but **caracal** and **African wild cat** are residents. If you disturb a **Cape rock sengi** (**elephant shrew**) it will disappear into a rock crevice. Wait quietly at least 10 m away, and it should re-emerge within a few minutes. Two very tiny nocturnal denizens of these crevices are the little-known **pygmy rock mouse** and **Barbour's rock mouse**. Up to five small rodent and sengi species may share a single crevice. Along the river and streams you may see the distinctive tracks of the **water mongoose** and the **Cape clawless otter**, but sightings are very rare.

Birds

Some 173 bird species have been recorded in the area. There is a good complement of raptors in the reserve that includes the hyrax-hunting **Verreaux's eagle**, the occasional **African fish eagle** along the Oorlogskloof River, **booted eagle**, **lanner falcon** and **black harrier**. Both **grey-winged francolin** and **Cape spurfowl** occur, and along the river you may see **African black duck**. **Black stork** are occasional visitors and **ground woodpeckers** are resident, as are

The three-banded plover is a resident wader.

FACILITIES AND ACTIVITIES

- About 151.7 km of hiking trails, from three short circular day hikes (Saaikloof 5.2 km, Leopard Trap 15.5 km and Rietvlei 17.9 km) to two trails of 52 km each (Rock and Rameron Pigeon trails) that take 4–7 days.
- Four cottages and hikers' huts with ablution block near entrance gate; log cabins along trails with long-drop toilets and solar power; camping site.
- Nieuwoudtville, 18 km to the north-east, has fuel and supplies.

species associated with Cape heathland, such as **Cape sugarbird** and **southern double-collared sunbird**.

Reptiles and amphibians

There are at least 37 reptiles, including the very localized **speckled padloper**, the smallest tortoise species in the world. The heavily armoured and spined **Armadillo girdled lizard** frustrates predators by biting its own tail to form an impregnable loop. You are most likely to see the **Karoo girdled lizard** and the **southern rock agama** because the males sit prominently on rocks; the agama male's head wagging display makes it even more visible. Just eight amphibians are known in the area.

Fish

Four fish species have been collected in the Oorlogskloof River, **Clanwilliam yellowfish**, **sawfin**, **Clanwilliam sandfish** and the small **chubbyhead barb**.

The red-spotted lily weevil feeds on the leaves of the ground lily.

The armadillo girdled lizard is seen here in a defensive posture.

WILDLIFE FACTS

- 42 species of mammal, including Cape clawless otter along the Oorlogskloof River.
- Some 173 bird species in the area.
- At least 37 reptile species and eight amphibian species.

- Beware of slippery and loose rocks, particularly after rain.
- It can be dangerous crossing the Oorlogskloof River in flood.
- Summer temperatures can be high; carry sufficient water, although this is available at several points.
- Watch out for snakes, especially Cape cobra, black-necked spitting cobra and puff adder.

IDENTIFICATION GUIDE

BIRDS

Common ostrich

Little grebe

African penguin

Cape gannet

White-breasted cormorant

Cape cormorant

Reed cormorant

African darter

Western cattle egret

Little egret

Great egret

Hamerkop

Grey heron

Black-headed heron

Goliath heron

Birds

Squacco heron

Green-backed heron

Black-crowned night heron

Great white pelican

Lesser flamingo

Greater flamingo

African spoonbill

Hadeda ibis

Glossy ibis

African sacred ibis

Southern bald ibis

African openbill

Black stork

Saddle-billed stork

Marabou stork

Woolly-necked stork

 Abdim's stork
 White stork
 Yellow-billed stork
 Fulvous whistling duck

 White-faced whistling duck
 Egyptian goose
 South African shelduck
 Cape shoveler

 Knob-billed duck
 Yellow-billed duck
 Spur-winged goose
 Cape teal

 Red-billed teal
 Southern pochard
 Secretarybird
 Black kite

Birds

Yellow-billed kite

Black-shouldered kite

Bearded vulture

Lappet-faced vulture

Cape vulture

White-backed vulture

Black-chested snake eagle

Bateleur

African harrier-hawk

Pale chanting goshawk

Steppe buzzard

Jackal buzzard

Martial eagle

Tawny eagle

Verreaux's eagle

Booted eagle

Long-crested eagle

African fish eagle

Rock kestrel

Greater kestrel

Pygmy falcon

Lanner falcon

Helmeted guineafowl

Crested guineafowl

Grey-winged francolin

Crested francolin

Natal spurfowl

Cape spurfowl

Swainson's spurfowl

Black crake

Red-knobbed coot

Birds 287

 Common moorhen
 African swamphen
 Northern black korhaan
 Red-crested korhaan

 Kori bustard
 Blue crane
 Wattled crane
 Grey crowned crane

 African (black) oystercatcher
 African jacana
 Water thick-knee
 Spotted thick-knee

 Temminck's courser
 Double-banded courser
 Kittlitz's plover
 White-fronted plover

Three-banded plover

Blacksmith lapwing

African wattled lapwing

Crowned lapwing

Black-winged stilt

Pied avocet

Grey-headed gull

Kelp gull

Hartlaub's gull

Swift tern

African green pigeon

Rock dove

Speckled pigeon

Namaqua dove

Red-eyed dove

Laughing dove

Birds 289

Emerald-spotted wood dove

African mourning dove

Cape turtle dove

Namaqua sandgrouse

Yellow-throated sandgrouse

Double-banded sandgrouse

Meyer's parrot

Cape parrot

Purple-crested turaco

Knysna turaco

Grey go-away-bird

Burchell's coucal

Western barn owl

Verreaux's eagle-owl

Cape eagle-owl

Spotted eagle-owl

290 Birds

Southern white-faced owl

Pearl-spotted owlet

White-backed mousebird

African hoopoe

Green wood-hoopoe

Brown-hooded kingfisher

Woodland kingfisher

Giant kingfisher

Pied kingfisher

European roller

Lilac-breasted roller

Swallow-tailed bee-eater

Southern carmine bee-eater

Little bee-eater

White-fronted bee-eater

Southern ground-hornbill

Birds   291

Southern red-billed hornbill

Southern yellow-billed hornbill

Crowned hornbill

African grey hornbill

Trumpeter hornbill

Acacia pied barbet

Black-collared barbet

Crested barbet

Bennett's woodpecker

Cardinal woodpecker

Barn swallow

Rock martin

Wire-tailed swallow

Red-breasted swallow

Yellow-throated longclaw

Cape wagtail

Fork-tailed drongo

Black-headed oriole

Cape crow

Pied crow

White-necked raven

African red-eyed bulbul

Arrow-marked babbler

Southern pied babbler

Cape rock-thrush

Sentinel rock-thrush

Groundscraper thrush

Karoo thrush

Cape robin-chat

White-browed robin-chat

Familiar chat

Ant-eating chat

Birds 293

Capped wheatear

Fiscal flycatcher

African paradise flycatcher

Cape batis

Magpie shrike

Bokmakierie

Yellow-billed oxpecker

Southern boubou

Common starling

Pied starling

Red-winged starling

Pale-winged starling

Wattled starling

Burchell's starling

Greater blue-eared starling

Cape white-eye

Cape sugarbird

Orange-breasted sunbird

Malachite sunbird

Black-headed canary

Cape sparrow

Red-billed buffalo weaver

Sociable weaver

White-browed sparrow-weaver

Cape weaver

Red-headed weaver

Lesser masked weaver

Thick-billed weaver

Southern red bishop

Long-tailed widowbird

Pin-tailed whydah

Birds 295

MAMMALS

Vervet monkey

Sykes's monkey

Chacma baboon

Wahlberg's epauletted fruit-bat

Round-eared sengi

Western rock sengi

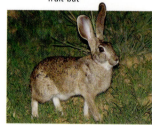
Scrub hare

Springhare

Southern African ground squirrel

Tree squirrel

Cape porcupine

Dassie rat

Four-striped grass mouse

Acacia rat

Littledale's whistling rat

Bush Karoo rat

Wild dog

Cape fox

Bat-eared fox

Black-backed jackal

Honey badger

Striped polecat

Banded mongoose

Small grey mongoose

Dwarf mongoose

Yellow mongoose

Slender mongoose

Suricate

Small-spotted genet

South African large-spotted genet

Spotted hyaena

Mammals

Brown hyaena

Aardwolf

Cheetah

Caracal

African wild cat

Small spotted cat

Serval

Lion

Leopard

Cape fur seal

Aardvark

Rock hyrax

Savanna (African) elephant

Hippopotamus

Cape mountain zebra

Plains zebra | Hook-lipped rhinoceros | Square-lipped rhinoceros

Common warthog | Giraffe | Savanna (African) buffalo

Common eland | Greater kudu | Nyala

Bushbuck | Roan antelope | Sable antelope

Southern oryx (gemsbok) | Waterbuck | Mountain reedbuck

Mammals 299

Common reedbuck

Black wildebeest

Blue wildebeest

Red hartebeest

Bontebok

Blesbok

Tsessebe

Impala

Springbok

Klipspringer

Steenbok

Cape grysbok

Sharpe's grysbok

Blue duiker

Common duiker

AMPHIBIANS

Karoo toad

Flat-backed toad

Red toad

Raucous toad

Banded rubber frog

African bullfrog

Cape river frog

Southern foam nest frog

Natal tree frog

Greater leaf-folding frog

REPTILES

Nile crocodile

Southern African python

Brown house snake

Common egg-eater

Herald snake

Spotted skaapsteker

Karoo whip snake

Mozambique spitting cobra

Snouted cobra

Cape cobra

Green mamba

Black mamba

Puff adder

Horned adder

Leopard tortoise

Angulate tortoise

Kalahari tent tortoise

Karoo tent tortoise

Karoo padloper

Parrot-beaked padloper

Speke's hinged tortoise

Marsh terrapin

Speckled thick-toed gecko

Bibron's thick-toed gecko

Moreau's tropical house gecko

Water monitor

Rock monitor

Reptiles 303

Flap-neck chameleon

Namaqua chameleon

Cape dwarf chameleon

Southern rock agama male

Southern ground agama female

Southern tree agama

Eastern striped skink

Cape skink

Western rock skink

Broadley's flat lizard male

Giant plated lizard

Cape girdled lizard

Western sandveld lizard

FLOWERS

Crane flower *Strelitzia reginae*

Mother-in-law's tongue
Sansevieria aethiopica

Tree orchid
Cyrtorchis arcuata

Plumbago
Plumbago auriculata

Devil's-thorn
Tribulus terrestris

Watsonia
Watsonia sp.

Grand duchess sorrel
Oxalis purpurea

Wine cup *Babiana minuta*

Red disa *Disa uniflora*

Blood lily
Scadoxus puniceus

Kalkoentjie
Gladiolus alatus

Blue waterlily
Nymphaea nouchali

White arum lily
Zantedeschia aethiopica

Jackalsmouth *Hoodia bainii*

Bitter aloe *Aloe ferox*

Strand aloe *Aloe thraskii*

Mitre aloe *Aloe mitriformis*

Coral aloe *Aloe striata*

Krans aloe *Aloe arborescens*

Cannon aloe *Aloe claviflora*

Red-hot poker *Kniphofia* sp.

Scarlet coccinea *Coccinea palmata*

Heather *Erica hebecalyx*

Heather *Erica inflata*

Ursinia sp.

Cape gazania *Gazania rigida*

Common gazania *Gazania krebsiana*

Impala lily *Adenium multiflorum*

306 Flowers

Yellow milkbush
Euphorbia mauritanica

Perskussing
Lapeirousia oreogena

Flame lily *Gloriosa superba*

Karoo violet
Aptosimum indivisum

Fireball lily
Scadoxus multiflorus

Bushman's poison
Boophone disticha

March lily *Brunsvigia* sp.

Pride-of-De Kaap
Bauhinia galpinii

Devil's-thorn
Tribulus zeyheri

Karoo rhigozum
Rhigozum obovatum

Wagon tree protea
Protea nitida

Blue sugarbush
Protea neriifolia

Real sugarbush
Protea repens

Common sugarbush *Protea caffra*

Flowers

TREES

Chinese lanterns *Nymania capensis*

Baobab *Adansonia digitata*

Broom cluster fig *Ficus sur*

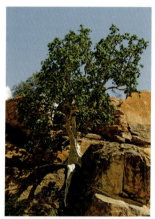
Large-leaved rock fig
Ficus abutilifolia

Sycamore fig *Ficus sycomorus*

Sickle bush flower
Dichrostachys cinerea

Sausage tree *Kigelia africana*

Common coral tree
Erythrina lysistemon

Halfmens
Pachypodium namaquanum

Weeping wattle
Peltophorum africanum

Sweet thorn *Vachellia karroo*

Fever tree *Vachellia xanthophloea*

Umbrella thorn *Vachellia tortilis*

Left: Grey camel thorn *Vachellia haematoxylon*
Right: Camel thorn *Vachellia erioloba*

False umbrella thorn *Vachellia luederitzii*

Flame thorn *Senegalia ataxacantha*

Flat-crown *Albizia adianthifolia*

Trees 309

 Zululand cycad *Encephalartos ferox*

 Karoo num-num *Carissa haematocarpa*

 Cape ash *Ekebergia capensis*

 Porkbush *Portulacaria afra*

 Karoo boer-bean *Schotia afra*

 Common cabbage tree *Cussonia spicata*

 Natal wild banana *Strelitzia nicolai*

 White milkwood *Sideroxylon inerme*

 Shepherd's tree *Boscia albitrunca*

Wild date palm *Phoenix reclinata*

Lala palm *Hyphaene coriacea*

Black monkey-orange *Strychnos madagascariensis*

Green monkey-orange *Strychnos spinosa*

Silky-haired pincushion *Leucospermum vestitum*

King protea *Protea cynaroides*

Wagon tree protea *Protea nitida*

Real sugarbush *Protea repens*

Blue sugarbush *Protea neriifolia*

Trees 311

Marula *Sclerocarya birrea*

Silver cluster-leaf *Terminalia sericea*

Lowveld cluster-leaf *Terminalia prunioides*

Mopane *Colophospermum mopane*

Forest fever tree *Anthocleista grandiflora*

Toad tree *Tabernaemontana elegans*

Natal mahogany *Trichilia emetica*

Nyala tree *Xanthocercis zambesiaca*

Leadwood *Combretum imberbe*

Red bushwillow *Combretum apiculatum*

Sjambok pod *Cassia abbreviata*

Transvaal beech *Faurea saligna*

Cape chestnut *Calodendrum capense*

False olive *Buddleja saligna*

Common tree euphorbia
Euphorbia ingens

Botterboom *Tylecodon paniculatus*

Quiver tree *Aloe dichotoma*

Trees 313

Suggested further reading

Mammals
Brett, M. 2010. *Touring South Africa's National Parks*. Struik Travel & Heritage, Cape Town.
Skinner, J.D. & Chimimba, C.T. 2005. *The Mammals of the Southern African Subregion*. Cambridge University Press, Cambridge.
Stuart, C. & Stuart, M. 2015. *Field Guide to the Mammals of Southern Africa*. Struik Nature, Cape Town.
Stuart, C. & Stuart, M. 2017. *Field Guide to the Larger Mammals of Africa*. Struik Nature, Cape Town.
Stuart, C. & Stuart, M. 2013. *A Field Guide to the Tracks and Signs of Southern and East African Wildlife*. Struik Publishers, Cape Town.

Birds
Chittenden, H. 2007. *Roberts' Bird Guide*. John Voelcker Bird Book Fund, Cape Town.
Cohen, C., Spottiswoode, C. & Roussouw, J. 2006. *Southern African Birdfinder*. Struik Nature, Cape Town.
Hockey, P., Dean, W. & Ryan, P. (eds). 2005. *Roberts' Birds of Southern Africa*. 7th ed. John Voelcker Bird Book Fund, Cape Town.
Newman, K. 2010. *Newman's Birds of Southern Africa*. Struik Nature, Cape Town.
Sinclair, I. & Ryan, P. 2009. *Complete Photographic Field Guide – Birds of Southern Africa*. Struik Nature, Cape Town.
Sinclair, I. & Ryan, P. 2010. *Birds of Africa South of the Sahara*. 2nd ed. Struik Nature, Cape Town.
Sinclair, I., Hockey, P., Tarboton, W. & Ryan, P. 2011. *SASOL Birds of Southern Africa*. 4th ed. Struik Nature, Cape Town.
Van Perlo, B. 1999. *Collins Illustrated Checklist – Birds of Southern Africa*. HarperCollins, London.

Reptiles & Amphibians
Alexander, G. & Marais, J. 2008. *A Guide to the Reptiles of Southern Africa*. Struik Nature, Cape Town.
Branch, B. 1998. *Field Guide to Snakes and Other Reptiles of Southern Africa*. Struik Publishers, Cape Town.
Branch, B. 2008. *Tortoises, Terrapins and Turtles of Africa*. Struik Nature, Cape Town.
Du Preez, L. & Carruthers, V. 2017. *Frogs of Southern Africa: A Complete Guide*. Struik Nature, Cape Town.
Tolley, K. & Burger, M. 2007. *Chameleons of Southern Africa*. Struik Nature, Cape Town.

Freshwater Fish
Skelton, P. 2001. *A Complete Guide to the Freshwater Fishes of Southern Africa*. Struik Publishers, Cape Town.

Marine
Branch, G., Branch, M. & Griffiths, C. 2017. *Two Oceans: A Guide to the Marine Life of Southern Africa*. Struik Nature, Cape Town.

Insects
Picker, M., Griffiths, C. & Weaving, A. 2003. *Field Guide to Insects of South Africa*. Struik Nature, Cape Town.
Woodhall, S. 2005. *Field Guide to Butterflies of South Africa*. Struik Nature, Cape Town.

Plants & Vegetation
Bezuidenhout, H. & Bradshaw, P. 2011. Unpublished Broad Vegetation Map of Mokala National Park. Conservation Services: Scientific Services, SANParks, Kimberley.

Bradshaw, P. 2010. *National Protected Area Expansion Strategy 2008.* (Protected areas boundaries.) South African National Parks and South African National Biodiversity Institute, Pretoria. Available at: http://bgis.sanbi.org/protectedareas/sanparks.asp [December 2010].

Manning, J. 2007. *Field Guide to Fynbos.* Struik Nature, Cape Town.

Manning, J. 2009. *Field Guide to Wild Flowers.* Struik Nature, Cape Town.

Moll, E. 2011. *What's That Tree? A Starter's Guide to Trees of Southern Africa.* Struik Nature, Cape Town.

Mucina, L. & Rutherford, M.C. (eds). 2006. The Vegetation of South Africa, Lesotho & Swaziland. *Strelitzia* 19. South African National Biodiversity Institute, Pretoria. Available at: http://bgis.sanbi.org/vegmap/map.asp [December 2010].

Palgrave, K. 2002. *Trees of Southern Africa.* 3rd ed. Struik Publishers, Cape Town.

Smith, G. & Crouch, N. 2009. *Guide to Succulents of Southern Africa.* Struik Nature, Cape Town.

Van Wyk, B. & Van Wyk, P. 2013. *Field Guide to Trees of Southern Africa.* Struik Nature, Cape Town.

[The Botanical Society in association with the South African National Biodiversity Institute has published an excellent series, *South African Wild Flower Guide*, covering most regions in the country.]

Geology

Norman, N. & Whitfield, G. 2006. *Geological Journeys – A Traveller's Guide to South Africa's Rocks & Landforms.* Struik Nature, Cape Town.

Useful contacts

South African National Parks (SANParks):
PO Box 787, Pretoria 0001
Tel (administration): 012 428 9111
www.sanparks.org

Limpopo – Limpopo Tourism & Parks:
PO Box 2814, Polokwane 0700
Tel: 015 293 3600 / 0860 730 730
www.golimpopo.com/parks.html

Mpumalanga – Mpumalanga Tourism & Parks:
Private Bag X11338, Mbombela (Nelspruit) 1200
Tel: 013 759 5300
www.mpumalanga.com

Gauteng – Gauteng Tourism Authority:
No.1 Central Place, Cnr of Henry Nxumalo and Jeppe Streets, Newtown, Johannesburg
Tel: 011 639 1600
www.gauteng.net

North West – North West Parks:
PO Box 4488, Mmabatho 2735
Tel: 018 397 1500
www.parksnorthwest.co.za

KwaZulu-Natal – Ezemvelo KZN Wildlife:
PO Box 13053, Cascades 3202
Tel: 033 845 1000 / 033 845 1999
www.kznwildlife.com

Eastern Cape – Eastern Cape Parks:
PO Box 11235, Southernwood, East London 5200
Tel: 043 705 4400
www.ecparks.co.za

Western Cape – CapeNature:
Private Bag X29, Gatesville 7765
Tel: 021 483 1090 / 483 0000
www.capenature.co.za

Northern Cape – Northern Cape Tourism Authority:
Private Bag X5017, Kimberley 8300
Tel: 053 833 1434 / 053 832 2657
www.northerncape.org.za

Free State – Free State Nature Conservation:
PO Box 517, Bloemfontein, 9300
Tel: 051 400 9527
www.fsnatcon.co.za

Photographic credits

All pictures copyright Chris and Mathilde Stuart with the exception of the following:

Front cover Stacey Farrell; **back cover** top centre &Beyond; top right Nigel Dennis/IOA; **spine** Walter Knirr/IOA; **half-title page** Gerald Hinde; **title page** Nigel Dennis/IOA; **contents page** bottom Johan Marais; **p8** Gallo Images; **p22** bottom Lanz von Hörsten; **p23** bottom right John Carlyon; **p37** bottom left John Carlyon; **p37** bottom right Nigel Dennis/IOA; **p38** top Johan Marais; **p42** top Nigel Dennis/IOA; **p44** top Nigel Dennis/IOA; **p44** bottom Steve Woodhall/IOA; **p45** Warwick Tarboton; **p48** top Friends of Nylsvley www.nylsvley.co.za; **p49** top Leonard Hoffmann/IOA; **p52** Hein von Hörsten/IOA; **p54** top Nigel Dennis/Africa Imagery; **p54** bottom Ariadne Van Zandbergen; **p55** top left and bottom Hein von Hörsten; **p56** left Ariadne Van Zandbergen; **p56** right Jéan du Plessis; **p60** bottom right Ariadne Van Zandbergen; **p65** bottom right Roger de la Harpe/IOA; **p66** top Nigel Dennis/IOA; **p67** Ezemvelo KZN Wildlife; **p68** top Albert Froneman; **p68** bottom Ezemvelo KZN Wildlife; **p69** left Alan Weaving; **p69** right John Carlyon; **p70** top A Channing; **p70** bottom Nigel Dennis/IOA; **p71** Shaen Adey/IOA; **p72** Peter and Beverly Pickford/IOA; **p73** top Peter and Beverly Pickford/IOA; **p74** top right John Carlyon; **p75** Ariadne Van Zandbergen; **p78** top John Carlyon **p79** middle right John Carlyon; **p79** bottom Nigel Dennis/IOA; **p80** Albert Froneman; **p82** top Albert Froneman; **p82** bottom right Roger de la Harpe/Africa Imagery; **p83** Nigel Dennis/IOA; **p86** both Nigel Dennis/IOA; **p88** top Albert Froneman/IOA; **p88** bottom Leonard Hoffmann/IOA; **p94** top Johan Marais; **p95** Roger de la Harpe/Africa Imagery; **p97** both Cormac McCreesh; **p99** top Shaen Adey/IOA; **p99** bottom right Caroline Culbert/Wilderness Safaris; **p100** top Nigel Dennis/IOA; **p100** bottom left John Carlyon; **p100** bottom middle Alan Weaving; **p101** bottom Roger de la Harpe/IOA; **p107** bottom right Johan Marais; **p108** &Beyond; **p110** top &Beyond; **p111** top right &Beyond; **p112** Lex Hes; **p113** Ariadne Van Zandbergen; **p115** top Albert Froneman/IOA; **p120** top Nigel Dennis/IOA; **p120** bottom Albert Froneman/IOA; **p121** top Peter and Beverly Pickford/IOA; **p121** bottom Leonard Hoffmann/IOA; **p122** Jéan du Plessis; **p126** Nigel Dennis/IOA; **p127** bottom Nigel Dennis/IOA; **p128** left Nigel Dennis/IOA; **p129** top Jéan du Plessis; **p129** Albert Froneman/IOA; **p142** Rod Haestier/IOA; **p143** top John Carlyon; **p144** top Leonard Hoffmann/IOA; **p144** bottom A Channing; **p153** bottom right Albert Froneman/IOA; **p155** Shaen Adey/IOA; **p158** Nigel Dennis/IOA; **p159** top right Peter and Beverly Pickford/IOA; **p159** bottom Leonard Hoffmann/IOA; **p167** Colour Library/IOA; **p169** Hein von Hörsten/IOA; **p170** right Gerald Hinde; **p172** top left Nigel Dennis/IOA; **p172** bottom Jéan du Plessis; **p176** bottom Penny Meakin; **p182** Hein von Hörsten/IOA; **p184** Nigel Dennis/IOA; **p186** top Walter Knirr/IOA; **p186** bottom Erhardt Thiel/IOA; **p187** left Shaen Adey/IOA; **p187** Walter Knirr/IOA; **p188** top Shaen Adey/IOA; **p189** top Peter and Beverly Pickford/IOA; **p189** bottom Bright Brown courtesy SANParks; **p190** top left Albert Froneman/IOA; **p190** bottom Penny Meakin; **p191** right A Channing; **p192** bottom Steve Woodhall/IOA; **p196** top SANParks; **p204** top A Channing; **p210** left Gerald Hinde; **p212** Gerhard Dreyer/IOA; **p216** top Keith Young; **p217** top Peter and Beverly Pickford; **p218** top A Channing; **p223** right CapeNature; **p224** left Peter and Beverly Pickford/IOA; **p225** bottom H Dürk; **p231** Jéan du Plessis; **p232** top John Carlyon; **p236** Karoo Images; **p239** top Karoo Images; **p239** middle Leonard Hoffmann/IOA; **p243** bottom John Carlyon; **p245** Karoo Images; **p247** John Carlyon; **p250** top Karoo Images; **p258** Karoo Images; **p260** both Alan Weaving; **p261** Alan Weaving; **p262** bottom Alan Weaving; **p266** top A Sliwa; **p270** top Karoo Images; **p271** left Alan Weaving; **p272** Karoo Images; **p274** bottom Karoo Images; **p288** bottom right John Carlyon; **p294** top, third from left John Carlyon; **p297** bottom left John Carlyon; **p298** top left MGL Mills; **p298** second row right A Sliwa

IOA = Images of Africa www.imagesofafrica.co.za

316

Index

Page numbers in *italic* refer to photographs

4x4 trails 36, 78, 87, 151, 158, 164, 170, 202, 209, 249, 255, 271, 275
  guided 20, 261

A
aardvark *298*
aardwolf *298*
abalone *192*
acacia
  red-pod *88*
Adamastor Ocean 186
adder
  horned *303*
  puff *159, 302*
agama
  ground *211, 263*
  southern rock *304*
  southern tree *79, 304*
Agulhas lighthouse *199*
|Ai-|Ais/Richtersveld park *245*
albatross *190*
Alexandria coastal dunefield *150*
Alexandria Forest 147, 149, 153
Alexandria Formation 149
aloe *169, 234*
  bitter, *Aloe ferox* 194, *306*
  cannon, *Aloe claviflora 306*
  coral, *Aloe striata 306*
  giant tree, *Aloe pillansii* 246, 247
  krans, *Aloe arborescens 306*
  snake *208*
  strand, *Aloe thraskii 306*
Amphitheatre *71, 72*
antelope
  roan 46, 265, *299*
  sable 17, *31, 34, 299*
  suni 104, 109, 113
ants 192
  army *18*
Arab traders 97
archaeological sites 26, 27, 95, 130, 138, 184, 213, 245, 272
  Black Eagle Cave 227
  Border Cave 95
  guided walk 20
  human skeletal remains 137

Iron Age 18, 27, 33, 40, 57, 75, 97, 116, 131
Iron Age Batswana settlements 52
Iron Age dwellings *132*
  Klasies River site 137
  ochre (haematite) 226
Stone Age 18, 40, 57, 75, 97, 116, 146, 173, 273
  stone tools 137, 155, 161, 193, 198, 252
  Thulamela 18
  tool-working areas 272
armadillo girdled lizard *225.*
  See also lizard
arum lily, *Zantedeschia aethiopica 305*
ash, Cape, *Ekebergia capensis 310*
Augrabies waterfall *251, 252*

B
baboon *74, 172, 188, 189, 296*
badger, honey *297*
banana, Natal wild, *Strelitzia nicolai 310*
baobab, *Adansonia digitata 19, 28, 308*
barbets, white-eared *120*
Barrier of Spears *64*
basaltic rocks 19, 108
basalt plain 66
bat boxes *25*
bat cave 227
bateleur *262*
batis, Cape *74, 153*
bat, Wahlberg's epauletted fruit- 17, *296*
Beaufort formations 157, 174, 205, 207, 237
beech, Transvaal, *Faurea saligna 313*
berry, bush-tick *138*
birding 27, 32, 53, 72, 76, 85, 90, 104, 113, 117, 156, 162, 227, 259, 265
  aquatic 45, 48, 53, 177
  arid-area 206, 237
  bearded vulture hide 65, 69
  endemics and rarities 65
  forest 81, 83, 138
  freshwater wetland 46
  fynbos 199, 227
  Geelbek Hide *213*
  guided walks 104, 119
  hide, Maloutswa 30, 31

hide, Mankwe Dam *55*
hides 30, 48, 55, 76, 94, 153, 154, 216, 218, 273
  mud-flat 217
  oceanic birds 190
  Palearctic migrant waders 203, 213, 217
  seabird breeding islands 149
  seabirds 213
  Voëlvlei 199
  wetland, coastal and fynbos 199
blesbok *129, 300*
blood lily, *Scadoxus puniceus 305*
bluebottles *145*
boer-bean, Karoo, *Schotia afra 148, 310*
Bokkeveld shales 200, 237
bontebok *196, 300*
botterboom, *Tylecodon paniculatus 244, 313*
Boulders, African penguin colony at 185, 190
Bredasdorp Group, marine sandstones and limestones 199
Brunsvigia minor 280
buffalo *6, 17, 90, 91, 299*
bullfrog, African *301*
bushbaby *43*
bushbuck 17, *20, 299*
Bushman's poison, *Boophone disticha 307*
bushveld igneous complex 35
bushwillow, red, *Combretum apiculatum 54, 313*
bustard, kori *267*
butterfly
  gold-banded forester *102*
  ragged skipper *44*
  Table Mountain beauty *192*
  variable mimic *102*

C
cabbage tree, *Cussonia spicata 310*
camel thorn
  Vachellia erioloba 265, 309
  grey, *Vachellia haematoxylon 309*
canoeing trails 141
Cape Floral Kingdom 201. *See also* Cape heathland; fynbos

Cape Floral Region 183
Cape Folded mountains 138, 148, 167, 170, 183, 200, 219, 221, 224, 226
Cape Granite 183, 186
Cape heathland 184, 215, 241, 279. *See also* fynbos
Cape Point lighthouse *182*
caracal *171, 298*
cat
  African wild *280, 298*
  small spotted *266, 298*
Cathedral Peak 64, 65, 68, 70
cedar, Clanwilliam *222*
Cederberg range 219, 220, 222
chameleon
  Cape dwarf *304*
  flap-neck *94, 304*
  Namaqua *239, 304*
Champagne Castle 64, 68
chats, familiar *86*
cheetah 17, *22, 148, 165, 260, 298*
chestnut, Cape, *Calodendrum capense 313*
Chinese lantern lillies, *Nymania capensis 66, 308*
Christmas bells *66*
Clarens sandstone 66, 125, 126
cobra
  Cape *302*
  Mozambique spitting *302*
  snouted *6, 56, 302*
coccinea, scarlet, *Coccinea palmata 306*
coral reef 96, *97*
coral tree, *Erythrina lysistemon 308*
coucal *100*
crabs, ghost *102*
crane, blue *180*
crane flower, *Strelitzia reginae 305*
crocodile *24, 27, 104, 107, 117, 302*
  information centre 96
cycad
  Drakensberg, *Encephalartos ghellinckii 72, 73*
  Zululand, *Encephalartos ferox 310*
cypress
  Cederberg mountain 220
  mountain 168

317

D

darter, African *250*
dassies. *See* hyrax
devil's-thorn
   Tribulus terrestris 305
   Tribulus zeyheri 307
disa, red, *Disa uniflora 187,*
   305
dog, wild *37*, 58, 148, *297*
dolerite 40, 59, 67, 72, 76, 85,
   131, 156, 163, 206, 207, 237
   columns *134*, 157
   dome hills 162
dolomitic tufa 58, 59
dolphin *142*, 189
dragonfly, dropwing *49*
Drakensberg basalt 125
Drakensberg range 63, 64,
   135
duck, white-backed *48*
duiker 85, 273, *275*, *300*
   blue *82*, *300*
   red 96
dung beetles *121*, 152, *154*
Dwyka Formation 85, 149,
   170, 207, 265

E

eagle
   booted *271*
   crowned 81
   long-crested *79*
   Verreaux's *129*, *211*
eagle-owl, Cape *224*
earthworms, giant 165, 166
East African Rift valleys 117
Ecca formations 85, 149, 170,
   207, 237
egg-eater *232*, *302*
eland *66*, *216*, 230, *299*
elephant *21*, 27, *52*, 85, *112*,
   113, *146*, 148, *298*
Elliot Mudstone 67, 126
erica *186*
euphorbia, tree, *Euphorbia*
   ingens 175, 179, *313*

F

falcon
   lanner *257*
   red-necked *257*
fever tree
   Vachellia xanthophloea
   103, *116*, 117, *309*
   forest, *Anthocleista*
   grandiflora 312
fig
   broom cluster, *Ficus*
   sur 308
   large-leaved rock, *Ficus*

   abutilifolia 308
   red-leaved rock, *Ficus*
   ingens 109
   sycamore fig, *Ficus*
   sycomorus 308
finfoot, African 90
fireball lily, *Scadoxus*
   multiflorus 307
Fish River Canyon 246
fish traps, ancient 96, 199,
   200, 213
flame goat fish *97*
flame lily, *Gloriosa superba*
   307
flame thorn, *Senegalia*
   ataxacantha 309
flat-crown, *Albizia*
   adianthifolia 309
flycatcher
   African paradise- *143*
   fiscal *203*
fly-fishing 70
Fort Double Drift blockhouse
   175
fort from frontier wars 174
fossils 67, *109*, *207*
   guided walks 209
   human footprints 213
   interpretive trail 205
   mammalian 212
   marine 109
fox
   bat-eared *297*
   Cape *260*, *297*
francolin, grey-winged *197*
frog
   banded rubber *301*
   Cape river *301*
   Drakensberg river *70*
   greater leaf-folding *301*
   marbled rubber *256*
   moss *191*
   Namaqua rain *218*
   Natal tree *301*
   painted reed *144*
   southern foam nest *301*
   strawberry rain *144*
fynbos 184, 191, 199,
   215, 241. *See also* Cape
   heathland
   Agulhas limestone 201
   Bokkeveld sandstone 279
   Elim ferricrete 201
   Overberg sandstone 201

G

galago, southern lesser *43*
galaxias, Cape *204*
game-viewing drives, guided

   20, 30, 36, 55, 60, 87, 106,
   109, 111, 115, 164, 255,
   267
game-viewing hides 32, 55,
   92, 104, 105, 115, 121, 176
   kuBubu and kuMasinga
   104
   Nyamiti Pan 117
   overnight 20
   Thiyeni Hide 90
gannet, Cape *217*
gazania
   Cape, *Gazania rigida 306*
   Gazania krebsiana 306
gecko
   barking *276*
   Bibron's thick-toed *303*
   Moreau's tropical house
   303
   speckled thick-toed *303*
gemsbok. *See also* oryx,
   southern *262*, *270*
genet
   small-spotted *297*
   South African large-
   spotted *297*
George Rex 137
Giant's Castle 64, 66, 67, 68
giraffe *50*, *78*, *93*, *254*, *299*
glasswort samphire 213, *214*
gneissic rocks 253
go-away-bird *23*
Gondwanaland 138, 187
grassbirds, Cape *233*
grasshopper
   bladder *177*
   milkweed *38*
Greater Soutpansberg
   biosphere 40
Greater St Lucia Wetland
   Park 63
grysbok
   Cape *194*, *300*
   Sharpe's 17, *300*
guided
   4x4 trails 20, 261. *See*
   also 4x4 trails
   bike trails 267. *See*
   also mountain bike trails
   bird-watching 58, 104,
   106, 109, 119. *See*
   also birding
   boat cruise 92
   game-viewing, day and
   night 99
game-viewing drives 20, 30,
   36, 55, 60, 87, 106, 109, 111,
   115, 164, 255, 267

   game-viewing walks
   106, 119
   hiking trails 176, 209. *See*
   also hiking trails
   horse trails 267. *See*
   also horse trails
   walks 20, 30, 36, 48, 55,
   60, 68, 78, 87, 92, 99, 106,
   115, 162, 164
   wilderness trails 20
gulls, kelp *202*

H

halfmens, *Pachypodium*
   namaquanum 246, *248*, *308*
hamerkop *23*
hare
   scrub *149*, *296*
   spring- *296*
hartebeest
   Lichtenstein's 17
   red *153*, 162, *165*, *205*,
   243, *300*
hawk, African cuckoo *100*
heather
   Erica hebecalyx 306
   Erica inflata 306
heron
   black-headed *78*
   goliath *46*
   grey *55*, *249*
hiking trails 42, 69, 72, 74, 83,
   99, 155, 170, 187, 196, 202,
   220, 255, 278
   guided 176, 209
   Hoopoe Falls Trail 81
   Otter Trail 141, 142
   overnight 68, 127, 141,
   151, 158, 176, 189, 216,
   223, 229, 249, 281
   Whale Trail 229
hippopotamus 27, 53, *99*, 104,
   117, *174*, *298*
hornbill
   red-billed *6*, *32*
   trumpeter 149
horse trails 127, 151, 271
   guided 267
hyacinth, water 194, *195*
hyaena
   brown *100*, *298*
   spotted *86*, *261*, *297*
hyrax
   rock 85, *143*, 185, *188*,
   252, *298*
   tree *82*

I

ibis, southern bald, nesting
   site 90

318

impala *300*
impala lily, *Adenium multiflorum 306*
inselbergs 57, *59*, 60, 61, 269
intertidal life 139, 185, 227

J
jackal, black-backed *149, 238, 297*
jackalsmouth, *Hoodia bainii 305*

K
kalkoentjie, *Gladiolus alatus 305*
Karoo Supergroup 19, 76, 80, 85, 91, 131, 157, 163, 174, 207, 237
kestrel, rock *271*
keurboom *139*
kingfisher
    malachite *83*
    mangrove *100*
Kirstenbosch National Botanical Garden 185
klipspringer *7*, 206, *249*, 252, *255, 300*
Knersvlakte 277
kokerboom. See quiver tree
korhaan, Barrow's 76
Kosi Bay *95*
kudu *178, 266, 299*

L
lammergeier. See vulture, bearded
lark, Barlow's 246
leadwood, *Combretum imberbe 312*
leopard 17, *42, 110, 170, 298*
    trap, stone *208*
lion 17, *22, 36, 110, 298*
Livingstone, David 58
lizard
    armadillo girdled 220, *225, 281*
    Cape flat *304*
    Cape girdled *304*
    giant plated *32, 304*
    western sandveld *304*
longclaw
    Cape *166*
    rosy-throated *111*
lowveld cluster-leaf, *Terminalia prunioides 312*

M
mahogany, Natal, *Trichilia emetica 312*
malkoha, green *100*
Malmesbury formation 183, 186, 214

mamba
    black *38, 302*
    green *302*
manganese dioxide 126
mangrove *98*
Mapungubwe
    culture 28
    Heritage Site tours 30
March lily, *Brunsvigia sp. 307*
marula, *Sclerocarya birrea 21, 312*
metal-working sites 18, 58, 84, 89, 116
mice, four-striped grass *159*
Middleton (Adelaide) Formation 174
milkbush, yellow, *Euphorbia mauritanica 307*
milkplum, Transvaal *35*
milkwood, white, *Sideroxylon inerme 310*
Mimetes cucullatus (rooistompie) *200*
mining, old gold digs 85
mitre aloe *Aloe mitriformis 306*
Molteno Formation 67
mongoose
    banded *37, 121, 297*
    dwarf *60, 297*
    slender *297*
    small grey *297*
    water 278
    yellow *152, 297*
monitor
    rock *303*
    water *56, 303*
monkey
    Sykes' *40, 81, 82*, 96, *296*
    vervet *30, 296*
mopane, *Colophospermum mopane 312*
mother-in-law's tongue, *Sansevieria aethiopica 305*
moth, mopane *29*
mountain bike trails 68, 127, 141, 170, 189, 196, 202, 223, 229, 244, 249, 255, 267, 271, 275
mousebird
    red-faced *115*
    white-backed *210*
mouse, four-striped grass *296*
Mozaan Group, rocks 85
mudskippers *102*

N
Namaqualand Blomveld 269
Namaqua Metamorphic Province 241

narina trogon *111*
Nature's Valley 139, 141
Ndedema Gorge 65
num-num, Karoo, *Carissa haematocarpa 310*
nyala 90, *106, 115, 299*
nyala tree, *Xanthocercis zambesiaca 312*

O
olive, false, *Buddleja saligna 313*
Operation Phoenix 58
orange
    black monkey, *Strychnos madagascariensis 311*
    green monkey, *Strychnosspinosa 311*
orchid
    golden *7*
    ground 187
    tree, *Cyrtorchis arcuata 305*
oribi 125, *126*
Oribi Gorge *80*
orioles, black-headed *176*
oryx, southern *262, 270, 299*
otter, Cape clawless *141*, 278
owl
    Pel's fishing 117
    southern white-faced *257*
oystercatcher, African (black) 213, *229*
    breeding beaches 199

P
padloper. See also tortoise
    Karoo *303*
    parrot-beaked *303*
palm
    lala, *Hyphaene coriacea 311*
    raffia 96
    wild date, *Phoenix reclinata 311*
Peace Parks Foundation 26
pelican
    great white *217*
    pink-backed *107*
    pink-backed, breeding site 104
penguin, African *190*
    colony at Boulders 185, 190
perlemoen *192*
perskussing, *Lapeirousia oreogena 307*
petroglyphs 246, 264
pictographs 252. See also rock art

pincushion
    creeping *203*
    silky-haired, *Leucospermum vestitum 311*
Plectranthus 41
plough shells *233*
plover
    crowned *160*
    three-banded *281*
Plumbago auriculata 305
polecat, striped *297*
Pongola River gorge *84*
'pop-ups' (geological feature) *253*
porcupine, Cape *296*
porkbush, *Portulacaria afra 254, 310*
Portuguese-man-o-war *145*
praying mantis *177*
predator and prey balance 60
pride-of-De Kaap, *Bauhinia galpinii 307*
Prince Alfred's Pass 138
protea *190*
    Drakensberg *73*
    king protea, *Protea cynaroides 311*
    snow 220, *223*
    wagon tree protea, *Protea nitida 307, 311*
python, southern African *302*

Q
quiver tree, *Aloe dichotoma 244, 247, 248, 269, 313*

R
rabbit, Hewitt's red rock *280*
raptors 23, 36, 65, 74, 79, 143, 158, 210, 244, 256, 262, 271, 276, 280
rat
    acacia *296*
    Brant's whistling 259
    bush Karoo *296*
    dassie *296*
    Littledale's whistling *296*
    Sloggett's (ice) 65, 68, *72*
red-hot poker, *Kniphofia sp. 306*
reedbuck *34*, 76, *99, 131, 300*
    mountain 34, *68*, 125, 162, *299*
renosterbos *279*
renosterveld
    shale 201
rhebok, grey 125, *170*, 194, *222*

319

rhigozum, Karoo, *Rhigozum obovatum 307*
rhinoceros *10*
  hook-lipped *55, 176, 299*
  square-lipped *78, 92, 265, 299*
Robberg Peninsula 138
robin, Kalahari scrub *267*
rock art *27, 28, 40, 65,* 71, 75, 84, 125, 155, 161, 169, 173, *219,* 220, 223, 264, 278
  guided walks 68, 164
rock figs 109
rockjumper
  Cape *224*
  Drakensberg *69*

S

salt works, working inland 40
sand dune system *272,* 273, *274*
sandgrouse *276*
sandstone formations *122*
Sani Pass 68, 69
sausage tree, *Kigelia africana 118, 308*
sawfin *225*
scorpion *239*
seahorse, Knysna *145*
seal, Cape fur *147, 189, 202, 242, 298*
  breeding colony 199
sea-turtle nesting beach 96
sea urchins, Cape *233*
sedimentary formations 66, 67, 72, 174
sengi
  four-toed 109, 113
  round-eared *296*
  western rock *296*
serval *298*
Sesamum alatum 29
shepherd's tree
  Boscia albitrunca 162, 310
  Karoo *150*
  stink *57*
shrikes, red-backed *181*
sickle bush flower,
  Dichrostachys cinerea 105, 308
silver cluster-leaf, *Terminalia sericea 312*
sjambok pod, *Cassia abbreviata 313*
skaapsteker, spotted *302*
skink
  Cape *304*
  eastern striped *304*

red-sided *197*
  western rock *304*
snake
  brown house *302*
  herald *302*
  Karoo whip *302*
  snouted, cobra *6*
  spotted bush *49*
snappers, blue-banded *97*
sorrel, grand duchess, *Oxalis purpurea 305*
sour fig *215*
Soutpansberg Group 40
Spandaukop *155*
sparrow-weaver, white-browed *275*
spider *94, 181*
  golden orb *25*
spoonbill, African *120*
springbok *270, 300*
spring flowers 213, 241, *270, 277, 280*
squirrel
  red bush 96
  southern African ground *248, 296*
  tree *296*
starfish *233*
steenbok *128, 210, 300*
stick insect *154*
stork
  black *172*
  yellow-billed *31*
Storms River suspension bridge *136*
Strandloper fish traps *200*
succulents 278
sugarbush 35
  blue, *Protea neriifolia 307, 311*
  Bredasdorp *230*
  Protea caffra 307
  real, *Protea repens 307, 311*
  smooth-leaf *223*
sunbird
  plain-backed 113
  orange-breasted *190*
suni *110*
suricate *158, 297*
swamphens, purple *47*
sweet thorn, *Vachellia karroo 156, 309*
swift *23*

T

Table Mountain 184
Table Mountain Group 138,

170, 186, 195, 199, 222, 228, 279
Table Mountain sandstone *200, 221*
Tarkastad Formation 67
termite colonies 241
termite mound *57*
terrapin, marsh *303*
Thulamela 18, 20
toad *121*
  flat-backed *301*
  Karoo *7, 166, 301*
  raucous *301*
  red *88, 301*
  western leopard *204*
toad tree, *Tabernaemontana elegans 312*
Tonga-kierie *98*
tortoise. *See also* padloper
  angulate *303*
  Kalahari tent *303*
  Karoo tent *303*
  leopard *44, 107, 154, 172, 303*
  parrot-beaked *191*
  Speke's hinged *24, 303*
tsessebe 34, 46, *48,* 265, *300*
Tshwene 58
turaco
  Knysna *143*
  purple-crested *88*
turtle, loggerhead *101*

U

uKhahlamba 6, 64, 65, 66, 67, 69, 70, 71, 73, 74
umbrella thorn
  Vachellia tortilis 309
  false, *Vachellia luederitzii 309*
Ursinia sp. *306*
  U. cakilefolia 244

V

Valley of Desolation, Camdeboo *134,* 156, 157, 158, 159
Varswater Formation 213
violet, Karoo, *Aptosimum indivisum 208, 307*
viper, Gaboon *101*
volcanic
  rhyolite lavas 104, 117
  rock 19, 108, 125, 186, 247
  tufa *60*
vulture
  bearded *69, 128*
  bearded -, hide 65, 69

breeding colony 36, 40, 227, 232
  Cape 34, *232*
  colony, Cape 41, 43, 232
  white-backed *18*

W

walks. *See* guided walks; hiking trails
War, 2nd Anglo-Boer 18, 147, 156, 264
war graves 174
wars, frontier 179
  fort 174
warthog *180, 299*
Waterberg Biosphere Reserve 33, 38
Waterberg System 46
waterberry tree *90*
waterbuck *31, 299*
waterlily, blue, *Nymphaea nouchali 305*
watsonia 305
wattle, weeping, *Peltophorum africanum 309*
weevil, red-spotted lily *281*
whales 227, 231
  southern right *231*
wheatears, mountain *243*
widowbirds, long-tailed *133*
wildebeest
  black 162, *164, 300*
  blue *54, 61, 300*
wilderness trails. *See* guided wilderness trails
wine cup, *Babiana minuta 305*
Witteberg Group 148, 170, 222
wolftoon *254, 269*
woodpeckers, Bennett's *37*
Woodville Forest 138
World Heritage Site 27, 28, 64, 97, 221

Y

yellowwood, Breede River *195*

Z

zebra
  Cape mountain *159, 161, 298*
  Hartmann's mountain *256*
  mountain 162
  plains *47, 114, 209, 299*

320

Chris & Mathilde Stuart

Stuarts' Field Guide to
**NATIONAL PARKS &
NATURE RESERVES**
of South Africa